James Kent Stone

The Invitation Heeded

Reasons for a Return to Catholic Unity

James Kent Stone

The Invitation Heeded
Reasons for a Return to Catholic Unity

ISBN/EAN: 9783744660792

Printed in Europe, USA, Canada, Australia, Japan

Cover: Foto ©Lupo / pixelio.de

More available books at **www.hansebooks.com**

THE
INVITATION HEEDED:

Reasons

FOR A

RETURN TO CATHOLIC UNITY.

BY

JAMES KENT STONE,

Late President of Kenyon College, Gambier, Ohio; and of Hobart College, Geneva, New York; and S. T. D.

"*Ad unitatem Sedis apostolicæ, divina gratia duce, reversus sum.*"
St. Gregorii M. Opera, tom. ii. p. 1300.

NEW YORK:
THE CATHOLIC PUBLICATION SOCIETY,
9 WARREN STREET.
Boston: Patrick Donahoe.
Baltimore: John Murphy & Co.

—

1870.

Entered, according to Act of Congress, in the year 1870, by
THE CATHOLIC PUBLICATION SOCIETY,
In the Clerk's Office of the District Court of the United States for the Southern District of New York.

THE CALL.

AD OMNES PROTESTANTES, ALIOSQUE ACATHOLICOS.	TO ALL PROTESTANTS AND OTHER NON-CATHOLICS.
Pius PP. IX.	*Pius IX., Pope.*

IAM vos omnes noveritis, Nos licet immerentes ad hanc Petri Cathedram evectos, et iccirco supremo universae catholicae Ecclesiae regimini, et curae ab ipso Christo Domino Nobis divinitus commissae praepositos opportunum existimasse, omnes Venerabiles Fratres totius orbis Episcopos apud Nos vocare, et in Oecumenicum Concilium futuro anno concelebrandum cogere, ut cum eisdem Venerabilibus Fratribus in sollicitudinis Nostrae partem vocatis ea omnia consilia suscipere possimus, quae magis opportuna, ac necessaria sint, tum ad dissipandas tot pestiferorum errorum tenebras, qui cum summo animarum

YOU all know already that We, having been raised, notwithstanding Our unworthiness, to this Chair of Peter, and therefore invested with the supreme government and guardianship of the whole Catholic Church, divinely entrusted to Us by Christ our Lord, have judged it seasonable to call to Us Our Venerable Brethren, the Bishops of the whole earth, and to unite them together, to celebrate, next year, an Œcumenical Council; so that, in concert with these Our Venerable Brethren who are called to share in Our cares, We may take those steps which may be most opportune and necessary, both to disperse the

damno ubique in dies dominantur et debacchantur, tum ad quotidie magis constituendum, et amplificandum in christianis populis vigilantiae Nostrae concreditis verae fidei, iustitiae, veraeque Dei pacis regnum. Ac vehementer confisi arctissimo et amantissimo coniunctionis foedere, quo Nobis, et Apostolicae huic Sedi iidem Venerabiles Fratres mirifice obstricti sunt, qui nunquam intermiserunt omni supremi Nostri Pontificatus tempore splendidissima erga Nos, et eamdem Sedem fidei, amoris, et observantiae testimonia praebere, ea profecto spe nitimur fore ut veluti praeteritis saeculis alia generalia Concilia, ita etiam praesenti saeculo Concilium hoc Oecumenicum a Nobis indictum uberes, laetissimosque, divina adspirante gratia, fructus emittat pro maiore Dei gloria, ac sempiterna hominum salute.

Itaque in hanc spem erecti, ac Domini Nostri Iesu

darkness of the many noxious errors which everywhere increasingly prevail, to the great loss of souls; and also to establish and confirm daily more and more among the Christian people entrusted to Our watchfulness the Kingdom of true Faith, Justice, and the Peace of God. Confidently relying on the close ties and most loving union which in so marked a way unite to Ourselves and to this Holy See these Our Venerable Brethren, who, through all the time of Our Supreme Pontificate, have never failed to give to Ourselves and this Holy See the clearest tokens of their love and veneration; We have the firm hope that this Œcumenical Council, summoned by Us at this time, will produce, by the inspirations of Divine Grace, as other General Councils in past ages have done, abundant fruits of benediction, to the greater glory of God, and the eternal salvation of men.

Sustained by this hope, and roused and urged by

Christi, qui pro universi humani generis salute tradidit animam suam, caritate excitati, et compulsi, haud possumus, quin futuri Concilii occasione eos omnes Apostolicis, ac paternis Nostris verbis alloquamur, qui etiamsi eumdem Christum Iesum veluti Redemptorem agnoscant, et in christiano nomine glorientur, tamen veram Christi fidem haud profitentur, neque catholicae Ecclesiae communionem sequuntur. Atque id agimus, ut omni studio et caritate eos vel maxime moneamus, exhortemur, et obsecremus, ut serio considerare et animadvertere velint, num ipsi viam ab eodem Christo Domino praescriptam sectentur, quae ad aeternam perducit salutem. Et quidem nemo inficiari, ac dubitare potest, ipsum Christum Iesum, ut humanis omnibus generationibus redemptionis suae fructus applicaret, suam hic in terris supra Petrum unicam aedificasse Ecclesiam, idest unam, sanctam, catholicam, apostolicam, eique necessariam

the love of our Lord Jesus Christ, who gave his life for the whole human race, We cannot refrain Ourselves, on the occasion of the future Council, from addressing Our Apostolic and paternal words to all those who, whilst they acknowledge the same Jesus Christ as the Redeemer, and glory in the name of Christian, yet do not profess the true faith of Christ, nor hold to and follow the Communion of the Catholic Church. And We do this to warn, and conjure, and beseech them with all the warmth of Our zeal, and in all charity, to consider and seriously examine whether they follow the path marked out for them by Jesus Christ our Lord, and which leads to Eternal Salvation. No one can deny or doubt that Jesus Christ himself, in order to apply the fruits of his redemption to all generations of men, built his only Church in this world on Peter; that is to say, the Church, One, Holy, Catholic, and Apostolic;

8 The Call.

omnem contulisse potestatem, ut integrum inviolatumque custodiretur fidei depositum, ac eadem fides omnibus populis, gentibus, nationibus traderetur, ut per baptisma omnes in mysticum suum corpus cooptarentur homines, et in ipsis semper servaretur, ac perficeretur illa nova vita gratiae, sine qua nemo potest unquam aeternam mereri et assequi vitam, utque eadem Ecclesia, quae mysticum suum constituit corpus, in sua propria natura semper stabilis et immota usque ad consummationem saeculi permaneret, vigeret, et omnibus filiis suis omnia salutis praesidia suppeditaret. Nunc vero qui accurate consideret, ac meditetur conditionem, in qua versantur variae, et inter se discrepantes religiosae societates seiunctae a catholica Ecclesia, quae a Christo Domino, eiusque Apostolis sine intermissione per legitimos sacros suos Pastores semper exercuit, et in praesentia etiam exercet divinam potestatem sibi ab ipso Domino traditam,	and that he gave to it all necessary power, that the deposit of Faith might be preserved whole and inviolable, and that the same Faith might be taught to all peoples, kindreds, and nations, that through baptism all men might become members of his mystical body, and that the new life of grace, without which no one can ever merit and attain to life eternal, might always be preserved and perfected in them; and that this same Church, which is his mystical body, might always remain in its own nature firm and immovable to the end of time, that it might flourish, and supply to all its children all the means of Salvation. Now, whoever will carefully examine and reflect upon the condition of the various religious societies, divided among themselves, and separated from the Catholic Church, which, from the days of our Lord Jesus Christ and his Apostles has never ceased to exercise, by its lawful pastors, and still con-

vel facile sibi persuadere debebit, neque aliquam peculiarem, neque omnes simul coniunctas ex eisdem societatibus ullo modo constituere, et esse illam unam et catholicam Ecclesiam, quam Christus Dominus aedificavit, constituit, et esse voluit, neque membrum, aut partem eiusdem Ecclesiae ullo modo dici posse, quandoquidem sunt a catholica unitate visibiliter divisae. Cum enim eiusmodi societates careant viva illa, et a Deo constituta auctoritate, quae homines res fidei, morumque disciplinam praesertim docet, eosque dirigit, ac moderatur in iis omnibus, quae ad aeternam salutem pertinent, tum societates ipsae in suis doctrinis continenter variarunt, et haec mobilitas, ac instabilitas apud easdem societates nunquam cessat. Quisque vel facile intelligit, et clare aperteque noscit, id vel maxime adversari Ecclesiae Christo Domino institutae, in qua veritas semper stabilis, nullique unquam immutationi obnoxia persistere tinues to exercise, the divine power committed to it by this same Lord; cannot fail to satisfy himself that neither any one of these societies by itself, nor all of them together, can in any manner constitute and be that One Catholic Church which Christ our Lord built, and established, and willed should continue; and that they cannot in any way be said to be branches or parts of that Church, since they are visibly cut off from Catholic unity. For, whereas such societies are destitute of that living authority established by God, which especially teaches men what is of Faith, and what the rule of morals, and directs and guides them in all those things which pertain to eternal salvation, so they have continually varied in their doctrines, and this change and variation is ceaselessly going on among them. Every one must perfectly understand, and clearly and evidently see, that such a state of things is directly opposed to the nature

debet, veluti depositum eidem Ecclesiae traditum integerrime custodiendum, pro cuius custodia Spiritus Sancti praesentia, auxiliumque ipsi Ecclesiae fuit perpetuo promissum. Nemo autem ignorat, ex hisce doctrinarum, et opinionum dissidiis socialia quoque oriri schismata, atque ex his originem habere innumerabiles communiones, et sectas, quae cum summo christianae, civilisque reipublicae damno magis in dies propagantur.

of the Church instituted by our Lord Jesus Christ; for in that Church truth must always continue firm and ever inaccessible to all change, as a deposit given to that Church to be guarded in its integrity, for the guardianship of which the presence and aid of the Holy Ghost have been promised to the Church for ever. No one, moreover, can be ignorant that from these discordant doctrines and opinions social schisms have arisen, and that these again have given birth to sects and communions without number, which spread themselves continually, to the increasing injury of Christian and civil society.

Enimvero quicumque religionem veluti humanae societatis fundamentum cognoscit, non poterit non agnoscere, et fateri quantam in civilem societatem vim eiusmodi principiorum, ac religiosarum societatum inter se pugnantium divisio, ac discrepantia exercuerit, et quam vehementer negatio auctoritatis a Deo consti-

Indeed, whoever recognizes religion as the foundation of human society cannot but perceive and acknowledge what disastrous effect this division of principles, this opposition, this strife of religious sects among themselves, has had upon civil society, and how powerfully this denial of the authority established by God,

tutae ad humani intellectus persuasiones regendas, atque ad hominum tum in privata, tum in sociali vita actiones dirigendas excitaverit, promoverit, et aluerit hos infelicissimos rerum, ac temporum motus, et perturbationes, quibus omnes fere populi miserandum in modum agitantur et affliguntur.

Quamobrem ii omnes, *qui Ecclesiae catholicae unitatem et veritatem* non tenent,* occasionem amplectantur huius Concilii, quo Ecclesia Catholica, cui eorum Maiores adscripti erant, novum intimae unitatis, et inexpugnabilis vitalis sui roboris exhibet argumentum, ac indigentiis eorum cordis respondentes ab eo statu se eripere studeant, in quo de sua propria salute securi esse non possunt. Nec desinant ferventissimas miserationum Domino offerre preces, ut divisionis murum disiiciat, errorum caliginem depellat, eosque ad sinum sanctae Matris Ecclesiae reducat, in qua eorum Maiores

* S. August. ep. lxi., al. ccxxiii.

to determine the belief of the human mind, and to direct the actions of men as well in private as in social life, has excited, spread, and fostered those deplorable upheavals, those commotions by which almost all peoples are grievously disturbed and afflicted.

Wherefore, let all those who do not hold to the unity and truth of the Catholic Church avail themselves of the opportunity of this Council, whereby the Catholic Church, of which their forefathers were members, displays a fresh proof of her perfect unity and her unconquerable vitality; and let them, in obedience to the longings of their own hearts, be in haste to rescue themselves from a state in which they cannot be assured of their own salvation. And let them not cease to offer most fervent prayers to the God of Mercy, that he may break down the wall of separation, that he may scatter the mists of error, and that he may lead

salutaria vitae pascua habuere, et in qua solum integra Christi Iesu doctrina servatur, traditur, et caelestis gratiae dispensantur mysteria.

Nos quidem cum ex supremi Apostolici Nostri ministerii officio Nobis ab ipso Christo Domino commisso omnes boni pastoris partes studiosissime explere, et omnes universi terrarum orbis homines paterna caritate prosequi, et amplecti debeamus, tum has Nostras ad omnes christianos a Nobis sciunctos Litteras damus, quibus eos etiam, atque etiam hortamur et obsecramus, ut ad unicum Christi ovile redire festinent; quandoquidem eorum in Christo Iesu salutem ex animo sumopere optamus, ac timemus ne eidem Nostro Iudici ratio a Nobis aliquando sit reddenda, nisi, quantum in Nobis est, ipsis ostendamus, et muniamus viam ad eamdem aeternam assequendam sa-

them back to the bosom of Holy Mother Church, where their fathers found the wholesome pastures of life, and in which alone the doctrine of Jesus Christ is preserved and handed down entire, and the mysteries of heavenly grace dispensed.

As for Us, seeing that We ought, in accordance with the duty of Our supreme Apostolic Ministry intrusted to Us by our Lord Jesus Christ himself, to fulfil with most fervent zeal all the offices of a good Shepherd, and with paternal love to follow and embrace all men throughout all the world— We therefore address this Our Letter to all Christians separated from Us, wherein We exhort and entreat them, again and again, to hasten their return to the One Fold of Christ; for with Our whole soul We ardently desire their salvation in Jesus Christ, and We fear lest We may one day have to render an account to the same Lord, who is Our Judge, if We do not, so far as is in Our pow-

lutem. In omni certe oratione, et obsecratione, cum gratiarum actione nunquam desistimus dies noctesque pro ipsis caelestium luminum, et gratiarum abundantiam ab aeterno animarum Pastore humiliter, enixeque exposcere. Et quoniam vicariam Eius hic in terris licet immerito gerimus operam, iccirco errantium filiorum ad catholicae Ecclesiae reversionem expansis manibus ardentissime expectamus, ut eos in caelestis Patris domum amantissime excipere, et inexhaustis eius thesauris ditare possimus. Etenim ex hoc optatissimo ad veritatis, et communionis cum catholica Ecclesia reditu non solum singulorum, sed totius etiam christianae societatis salus maxime pendet, et universus mundus vera pace perfrui non potest, nisi fiat unum ovile, et unus pastor.

er, show them, and prepare for them the way to attain to this eternal salvation. Truly, in every prayer of Ours, beseeching and giving thanks, We cease not, day and night, to entreat humbly and earnestly for them, from the Eternal Pastor of souls, the abundance of light and heavenly grace. And since, notwithstanding Our unworthiness, We are his Vicar here upon earth, We therefore wait, with outstretched hands, and with most ardent desire, the return of Our wandering children to the Catholic Church, that We may most lovingly welcome them to the home of their Heavenly Father, and enrich them with his exhaustless treasures. Upon this longed-for return to the truth and unity of the Catholic Church depends the salvation not only of individuals, but also of all Christian society; and never can the whole world enjoy true peace, unless there shall be one Fold and one Shepherd.

Datum Romae apud S. Petrum die 13 Septembris 1868. Pontificatus Nostri Anno Vicesimotertio.	Given at Rome, in St. Peter's, on the 13th day of September, 1868, and in the year of Our Pontificate the twenty-third.

THE ANSWER.

A PRAYER FOR GRACE IN ORDER TO MAKE A GOOD CONFESSION.

"O Almighty and most merciful God, who hast made me out of nothing, and redeemed me by the precious blood of thy only Son; who hast, with so much patience, borne with me to this day, notwithstanding all my sins and ingratitude; ever calling after me to return to thee from the ways of vanity and iniquity, in which I have been quite wearied out in the pursuit of empty toys and mere shadows; seeking in vain to satisfy my thirst with muddy waters, and my hunger with husks of swine; behold, O most gracious Lord, I now sincerely desire to leave all these my evil ways, to forsake the region of death, where I have so long lost myself, and to return to thee, the Fountain of life. I desire, like the prodigal child, to enter seriously into myself, and, with the like resolution, to arise, without delay, and to go home to my Father, though I am infinitely unworthy to be called his child, in hopes of meeting with the like reception from his most tender mercy. But, O my God! though I can go astray from thee of myself, yet I cannot make one step towards returning to thee, unless thy divine grace stir me up and assist me. This grace, then, I most humbly implore, prostrate in spirit before the throne of thy mercy. I beg it for the sake of Jesus Christ, thy Son, who died upon the cross for my sins; I know thou desirest not the death of a sinner, but that he be converted and live; I know thy mercies are above all thy works; and I most confidently hope, that as in thy mercy thou hast spared me so long, and hast now given me this desire of returning to thee; so thou wilt finish the work that thou hast begun, and bring me to a perfect reconciliation with thee.

"I desire now to comply with thy holy institution of the sacrament of penance; I desire to confess my sins with all sincerity to thee, and to thy minister; and, therefore, I desire to know myself, and to call myself to an account by a diligent examination of my conscience. But, O my God! how miserably shall I deceive myself, if thou assist me not in this great work by thy heavenly light. Oh! remove, then, every veil that hides any of my sins from me, that I may see them all in their true colors, and may sincerely detest them. Oh! let me not any longer be imposed upon by the enemy, or by my own self-love, so as to mistake vice for virtue, to hide myself from myself, or any way to flatter myself in my sins.

"But, O my good God! what will it avail me to know my sins, if thou dost not also give me a hearty sorrow and repentance for them? Without this, my sins will be all upon me still, and I shall be still thy enemy and a child of hell. Thou insistest upon a change of heart, without which there can be no reconciliation with thee; and this change of heart none but thou canst give. Oh! give it me, then, dear Lord, at this time. Give me a lively faith and a firm hope in the passion of my Redeemer. Teach me to fear thee and to love thee. Give me, for thy mercy's sake, a hearty sorrow for having offended so good a God. Teach me to detest my evil ways; to abhor all my past ingratitudes; to hate myself now with a perfect hatred for my many treasons against thee. Oh! give me a full and a firm resolution of a new life for the future, and unite me to thee with an eternal band of love, which nothing in life or death may ever break.

"Grant me also the grace to make an entire and sincere confession of my sins, and to accept of the confusion of it, as a penance justly due to my transgressions. Let not the enemy prevail upon me to pass over anything through fear or shame; rather let me die than consent to so great an evil. Let no self-love deceive me, as I fear it has done too often. Oh! grant that this confession may be good; and for the sake of Jesus Christ, thy Son, who died for me, and for all sinners, assist me in every part of my preparation for it, that I may go through it with the same care and diligence as I should be glad to do at the hour of my death; that, so being perfectly reconciled to thee, I may never offend thee more.

"O Blessed Virgin! Mother of my Redeemer, mirror of innocence and sanctity, and refuge of penitent sinners, intercede for me through the passion of thy Son, that I may have the grace to make a good confession. All ye blessed angels and saints of God, pray for me, a poor miserable sinner, that I may now, for good and all, turn from my evil ways, that so, henceforward, my heart may for ever be united with yours in eternal love, and never more go astray from the Sovereign Good. Amen."

Dec. 8, 1869.
In Festo Imm. Concept. B. M. V.

CONTENTS.

	PAGE.
Prefatory Chapter,	21

PART I.

THE CHURCH CONSIDERED IN CERTAIN HISTORICAL ASPECTS.

	PAGE
Chapter I. The Attitude of the World towards the Church,	37
Chapter II. The Perpetuity of the Church,	44
Chapter III. The Church the Guardian of Morals,	54
Chapter IV. The Failure of Protestantism,	63
Chapter V. The Church and Civilization,	80
Chapter VI. The Charge of Persecution,	95

PART II.

THE CHURCH CONSIDERED AS A DIVINE CREATION.

Chapter I. The Incarnation and the Mission of the Holy Ghost,	109
Chapter II. Infallibility,	120
Chapter III. The Appeal to Scripture,	139
Chapter IV. The Appeal to Antiquity,	154
Chapter V. The Notes of the Church,	180

PART III.

THE CHURCH CONSIDERED AS AN ORGANIZATION.

	PAGE.
Chapter I. The Primacy and Christianity,	207
Chapter II. The Primacy and Prophecy,	223
Chapter III. The Primacy and Antiquity,	248
Chapter IV. The Primacy and Unity,	276
Chapter V. The Primacy and Authority,	285
Chapter VI. The Primacy and Infallibility,	314

PREFATORY CHAPTER.

MAY God pardon my hasty pride, but I used to fancy myself quite free from prejudice, and boasted in my heart of a readiness to welcome truth wherever found, and to follow it in whatever hard path it might lead. I remember long ago copying a golden sentence from one who has done me more service than all other Anglican teachers combined—my beloved Richard Hooker—and how, in a figure, I hung the words as a memorial before my eyes: "If truth do anywhere manifest itself, seek not to smother it with glossing delusions; acknowledge the greatness thereof; and think it your best victory when the same doth prevail over you."* If I may confess a thing so sacred, the prayers which for years were oftenest on my lips were those beautiful Collects, which I had learned through the English Prayer-Book—petitions for the light of the Holy Spirit, that I might have a right judgment in all things; and that I might not only know what things I ought to do, but also have power faithfully to fulfil the same.† The prayers were, indeed, graciously answered; but

---

* *Ecclesiastical Polity*, Pref. ch. ix.

† Deus, qui corda fidelium Sancti Spiritus illustratione docuisti: da nobis in eodem Spiritu recta sapere, et de ejus semper consolatione gaudere. Per Dominum, in unitate ejusdem.—*In Dom. Pent. et in Missa Vot. de S. S.*

Vota, quæsumus Domine, supplicantis populi cœlesti pietate

not according to the imperfect intention of him who uttered them.

When the Letter Apostolic of Pius IX., 'To all Protestants and other Non-Catholics,' first came under my notice, I read it with interest, indeed, but, incredible though it now seems, with little other emotion than one of rather contemptuous pity for the august Writer. I supposed that I had mastered the Roman question, which I always thought the greatest of all questions in theology or history; and imagined myself familiar with the strong ground upon which every true Catholic ought to stand. For I looked upon myself as a genuine Catholic—an Israelite indeed. I do not mean that I ever had any sympathy with the Ritualistic movement. I never could regard the leaders of that movement with any other feeling than one, I fear, of impatience. I considered them, I regret to say, the most illogical of all thinkers. If the Ritualists were right, the Reformers were wrong. The great sin of schism could never have been justified by any such paltry differences as separate our 'advanced' friends from the great Roman Communion. The only consistent course for men to take who believed in the Sacrifice of the Altar and in the Invocation of Saints was to go back, promptly and penitently, to the ancient Church which had proved its infallibility by being in the right after all.

No; I defended the Anglican Reformation with all my soul. I did so upon what I called high ground, in company with such sturdy Catholics (so I termed them) as Andrewes, and Bull, and Hammond. I threw myself back

prosequere: ut et quæ agenda sunt, videant; et ad implenda quæ viderint, convalescant. Per Dominum nostrum.—*Dom. inf. Oct. Epiph.*

upon 'the primitive Church,' and upheld the doctrinal standards of the Anglican Communion as faithfully reproducing the uncorrupted model. I loved this reformed Church, supposing her to be indeed Apostolic, both in succession and in creed, and not knowing an Older and a Better; I gave her all my devotion (my eyes being blinded), as the Mother and Mistress of my soul; and I hoped to die, as Bishop Ken declared that he died, " in the Holy, Catholic, and Apostolical Faith, professed by the whole Church before the disunion of East and West—more particularly in the communion of the Church of England, as it stands distinguished from all Papal and Puritan innovation, and as it adheres to the doctrine of the Cross."

The *Responsio Anglicana* of Canon (now Bishop) Wordsworth did not satisfy me. The writer, I thought, wasted his strength on minor points. It was not such an answer as I conceived Bishop Bull would have given; who, by one short move, would have carried the war into Africa, and would have put the Bishop of Rome immediately on the defensive, by denouncing *him* as the innovator, the wanderer, the schismatic, and by calling upon *him* to return to that Catholic Unity which the arrogance of his predecessors had first broken.

Well, time went on; and I was not conscious of the smallest change in my theological opinions and sympathies; when all at once the ground upon which I had stood, with such careless confidence, gave way. Like a treacherous island, it sank without warning from beneath my feet, and left me struggling in the wide waters. Thanks be to God that I was not left to perish in that cold and bitter flood, and that my feet so soon rested for ever on the eternal Rock! How it came about—by what intellectual process my position had been undermined—by what unconscious steps my feet had been led to an unseen brink, I did not know. I was only aware of the sudden terror with which I found myself slipping and going, and the darkness which succeeded the swift plunge.

So far as I can recall the order of impressions, the first intimation which I received of my insecurity was the return to my mind, unbidden, of some of the words of the Holy Father; they would not be dismissed; they haunted me, uncomfortably: " Domini Nostri Jesu Christi, qui pro universi humani generis salute tradidit animam suam, caritate excitati et compulsi;" "id agimus, ut omni studio et caritate eos vel maxime moneamus, exhortemur, et obsecremus, ut serio considerare et animadvertere velint, num ipsi viam ab eodem Christo Domino præscriptam sectentur, quæ ad æternam perducit salutem." There was something in the tone of this appeal which compelled me to listen. The image of the apostolic Pleader came up before me; I saw the beautiful, benignant face again, which I saw as a boy in Rome; I beheld the outstretched hand, extended then in blessing, now in gracious invitation and entreaty: " Errantium filiorum ad catholicæ Ecclesiæ reversionem expansis manibus ardentissime expectamus, ut eos in cœlestis Patris domum amantissime excipere, et inexhaustis ejus thesauris ditare possimus."

At the same time (strange that passages from such remote sources should appear in conjunction) a detached sentence from that extraordinary book, *Ecce Homo*, came floating into consciousness on some breeze of memory, and caught, and would not be brushed away: " Habit dulls the senses and puts the critical faculty to sleep." It suggested to me —whether legitimately or not, I am not sure; for I do not remember the context—the possibility that my familiarity with my position was no real assurance of its impregnability, and that the very frequency with which I had gone over its defences had rendered me incapable of detecting the weak points. There was a quick misgiving; I feared blankly that there were realities which others were able to see clearly, but from which my eyes were holden; that there might be some deep undertone of truth which I had never been able to catch, like the cosmic harmony of the ancients, which to gross mortal ears, alive to lesser but sharper sounds, was inaudible.* I found myself reflecting upon the immeasurable influence of education, and how incalculable must be the power over a mind of opinions imbibed from infancy through every pore and never counteracted. If these opinions were prejudices, how almost impossible would it be for truth to penetrate them! I thought of the English Language, in which I had learned to think and to express my thoughts; and I remembered how for three hundred years that tongue had been one vast engine of ceaseless attack upon the Roman Catholic Church; how its literature was saturated with a spirit of the most deadly antagonism to that Church, not in the department of theology only, but of history, and poetry, and travels, and fiction, aye! and the very primers in the hands of the little children. If such a fountain should prove to be poisoned, what effect might not be anticipated in those who all their lives long had drunk of its streams! All this passed through my mind more rapidly than I have been able to record it; and I felt my heart growing faint at a whisper—to which

* Hoc sonitu oppletæ aures hominum obsurduerunt.—*Som. Scip.*

nevertheless I listened intently—that perhaps I had prejudged the case after all.

The effect of this impression was soon after indefinitely increased by a passage of Moehler, which forcibly arrested my attention. Speaking of the delusions of the early heretics, the learned writer says: "There are certainly few who have studied the Gnostic errors, that are not seized with the deepest astonishment, how their partisans could possibly deem their whimsical opinions, the fantastic forms of their demonology, and the rest, to be *Christian apostolic* doctrines; and many a man among us perhaps believes, that he could in a single hour confute thousands of them by the Bible, and bring them back to pure Christianity; so much so indeed, that he is even disposed to accuse their then opponents of a want of dexterity, because they did not succeed.* But, when once a peculiar system of moral life hath been called into existence, should it even be composed of the most corrupt elements, no ordinary force of external proofs, no conclusions of ratiocination, no eloquence, are able to destroy it: its roots lie mostly too deep to be pervious to mortal eye: it can only perish of itself, become gradually exhausted, spend its rage, and disappear. But, as long as it flourishes, all around is converted into a demonstration in its favor: the earth speaks for it, and the heavens are its warranty. Meanwhile, a new age, with another spirit and other elements of life, springs up: this, without any points of internal contact with the past, is often at a loss to comprehend it, and demands with astonishment how its existence had been possible. But, should Divine Grace, which can alone kindle the opposite *true life*, suc-

---

* Mr. Robertson's translation of this sentence is so imperfect that I have ventured to alter it.

ceed in delivering one individual from such errors, then he expresses the incomprehensible and inconceivable nature of his former state, by saying that he had been, as it were, enchanted, and that something, like scales, has fallen from his eyes."*

I remembered how St. Augustine, "one of the profoundest thinkers of antiquity,"† even for four years after he had become a catechumen under St. Ambrose, was entangled in the meshes of his Manichæan heresy. I admitted instantly that I, too, *might be* under a spell; that my case might be—I do not dare to say like that of the great Saint and Father, but that of the Donatists or the Gnostics; since I was certainly not more positive in my convictions than they, neither could I furnish myself with any satisfactory reason for believing that I was blessed with greater light. And then the Hand of God drew back the veil of my heart; and I saw for the first time, and all at once, how utterly steeped I had been in prejudice, how from the beginning I had, without a question or suspicion, assumed the very point about which I ought reverently to have enquired with an impartial and a docile mind. I had studied the Roman controversy; so I thought—if in my short life I could fairly be said to have studied anything; but *how* had I studied it? Had there ever been a time when it was an *open question* in my mind whether the claims of the Roman Church were valid? Had I begun by admitting that the Pope might be right? Had it ever crossed my thoughts that the Church in communion with the See of Peter might be indeed the one only Catholic Church of our Lord Jesus

---

* *Symbolism*, part i. ch. v. § xxxix.
† Sir William Hamilton.

Christ? And had I ever resolved, with all my soul, as one standing on the threshold and in the awful light of eternity, to begin by tearing down every assumption and divesting myself of every prejudice, and *then*, wherever truth should lead the way, to follow—"leave all and follow"? Alas! never. I had studied simply to combat and refute. The suggestion that 'Romanism' might after all be identical with Christianity was preposterous. The Papacy was the great Apostasy, the mystery of iniquity; it was the masterpiece of Satan, who had made his most successful attack upon the Church of God by entering and corrupting it. The rise of the Papal pretensions was matter of the plainest history; and every well-instructed child could point out how one fiction after another had been grafted into the creed of that apostate Church, until now the simple faith of early days was scarce recognizable under the accumulated error of centuries. 'History'—who *wrote* that history? 'Well-instructed child'—why, that was the very point at issue!

Of course I had not yet begun to examine and appreciate the Catholic argument (I may as well use the word at once as synonymous with Roman Catholic); I merely saw that there had been an appeal, and that the case which I had supposed settled had been carried into a higher court. The decision of the past had not been reversed; but it *might be* reversed. I discovered that I had been laboriously building without thoroughly inspecting my foundation, and that I would have to do my work all over again. I saw that I had committed "the very illogical mistake" against which I had often warned young men under my instruction, the error of those who first canvass "all the objections against any particular system whose pretensions to truth they would examine, before they consider the direct arguments in its favor."* I saw that I had been guilty of what Bossuet calls "a calumny," and what I now acknowledged to be an act of injustice, namely, of charging upon Catholics *inferences* which I had myself drawn from their doctrines, but against which Catholics indignantly protest.† I could not say with St. Augustine that "I blushed with joy," but with shame I blushed, "at having so many years barked not against the Catholic faith, but against the fictions of carnal imaginations. For so rash and impious had I been, that what I ought by enquiring to have learned, I had pronounced on, condemning. . . . I should have knocked and proposed the doubt, how it was to be believed, not insultingly opposed it as if believed."‡

This is the 'plunge' I spoke of. I used the word because it expressed, as well perhaps as any other, the terrifying rapidity which marked the steps of my intellectual crisis. Upon some men the discovery of a life-long error may break gradually; truth may be said to have its dawning; but to me it came with a shock. The rain descended and the floods came; my house fell; and great was the fall of it.

Then followed a sense of blank desolateness. I was groping among ruins; and wherewith should I go to work to build again? I do not mean that I faltered. Thank God that he kept me true, and suffered me not to shrink from the sharp agony which I perceived was *possibly* in store for me. To borrow words of the great Father from whose experience I have already drawn, "God gave me

---

* Dr. Hawkins, *Essay on Tradition*, p. 82.
† *Exposition*, ch. ii.
‡ *Confessions*, lib. vi. c. 4, 5.

that mind, that I should prefer nothing to the discovery of truth, wish, think of, love naught besides." But the task of reconstruction seemed almost hopeless.

I began by taking note of, and ruling out, all considerations which could conceivably stand in the way of an impartial investigation. I challenged the witnesses. On the one hand, I put aside such as these : cherished opinions; hallowed associations; the intellectual and social accumulations of my life thus far; a useful and honorable position; fair hopes, and plans long pondered; the grief of hearts more dear than hopes, or plans, or life itself. On the other side, I had to be on my guard against—*what?* Aye, what! Ah, dear souls! who can talk so bravely about the fascinations of Romanism and the duty of resisting its seductive charms, what do *you* know of the anguish of a heart that is called to give up all for truth, and is ready, if need be, to make the sacrifice? No; on the side of the Church of Rome there was *absolutely nothing*—unless, indeed, it might be some attraction lurking in the very completeness of the immolation. Well, there might be something in this; so I marked it down as a danger to be carefully watched against.

And so I set my face forward with desperate earnestness; and in due time—it may seem, a very short time—I had not a trace of doubt left that I had all along been a vain enemy of the One, Catholic, and Apostolic Church. Why *not* in a short time? Why not in a month, or a week, or a day? Is it any reflection upon Truth that she surrenders herself quickly to a soul whose every nerve is strained in her pursuit? Is it any argument against the Church of God that it is easily identified? Surely, if there be a Kingdom of Heaven upon earth, it must be known by marks which cannot be mistaken. Yes! I knew it when I had found it. And I found it as in the parable, like a treasure hidden in a field—in the self-same field up and down which I had wandered for years, and where I had often trampled it under my feet. And when I had found it, I hid it, scarce daring to gaze at its splendor, and crying, as St. Augustine cried, "Too late, alas! have I known thee, O ancient and eternal Truth!" And then, for joy thereof, I went and sold all that I had, and bought that field.

What were the signs by which I recognized this divine Church, I shall endeavor to state in the following pages. I shall not attempt to suppress or disguise the earnestness of an advocate. For let me say at once, that I do not write in the forlorn hope of winning a brief and profitless notoriety; nor yet in needless vindication of the step I have taken; but with the sole desire, in God's sight, of doing possible good to the few whose attention may have been momentarily arrested by what they deem my perversion. I must improve an opportunity which will never recur. I know well that the same things, and better things than I can ever hope to say, have been said already by those who have travelled the same path before me; but then—*utile est plures a pluribus fieri libros, diverso stylo non diversa fide, ut ad plurimos res ipsa perveniat, ad alios sic, ad alios autem sic.** Need I confess also that these pages are written with many prayers, and by a hand which trembles lest through its unskilfulness it should distort the fair features of the truth it would portray?

Yes, this is my only apology for writing. I was once deceived by the unreal charms of a false prophetess; but now the thin mask has been torn away. I once had only bitter

---

* St. Augustine, *De Trinitate*, lib. i. c. 5.

thoughts and scornful words for her whose glories I had never seen, and to whom I did not know that my soul owed high allegiance; but now divine compassion has led me to the feet of my true Mother, who through all my railing stood patiently and with tearful love awaiting my return. And in the joy of the present I cannot forget what now seems the gloom of the past. I have been brought into the fragrant garden; and I think of the weary wilderness. I have drunk of the flowing fountain; and I remember the broken cisterns over which I once labored—

> "The toil
> Of dropping buckets into empty wells,
> And growing old in drawing nothing up."

Therefore I am fain to look back, and call to those whom I have left behind.

O my brother! am I taking too much upon myself, shall I say what becomes me not to say, when I ask you to look anxiously at the grounds of your faith, and to do so in a spirit of unflinching truthfulness, with a candor which you are sure is not tarnished by a reservation? Fear not the frown, or the scorn, of those who would stigmatize your honest enquiry as vacillation and weakness. " Let those treat you harshly who are not acquainted with the difficulty of attaining truth and avoiding error;"—it is St. Augustine who addresses you— " let those treat you harshly who know not how hard it is to get rid of old prejudices; let those treat you harshly who have not learned how very hard it is to purify the interior eye, and render it capable of contemplating the sun of the soul, truth." And do not forget to begin and to continue your work of examination with importunate prayer for that assistance without which we cannot hope to be guided aright. I do not ask you to pray that you may become a Roman Catholic; that would be most irrational. But pray earnestly that, *if* the Roman Catholic Church *be* Christ's true Church, your eyes may be opened to see the truth and your heart fortified to embrace it. Surely, if you are, I do not say a brave man, but a sincere man, living for God alone and for eternity, you cannot hesitate to do this—even though you know I believe from the bottom of my heart that God will answer your petition as, in his mercy, he answered mine. You are not willing—you do not dare—to offer such a prayer? Ah! there is only one thing that ever can, and that ever will, enable you with all your soul to make it—and that is, the grace of God.

PART I.

THE CHURCH CONSIDERED IN CERTAIN HISTORICAL ASPECTS.

CHAPTER I.

THE ATTITUDE OF THE WORLD TOWARDS THE CHURCH.

THE Catholic Church is the great incubus which is perpetually haunting and troubling the dreams of the world. Men try to ignore it; but it obtrudes itself upon their unwilling notice. They would fain remand it to a place among the effete superstitions of the past; but when they think the spectre is laid, it returns unbidden, and casts its vast shadow over the present. In that shadow the world lies uneasily; and, consciously or unconsciously, it betrays its dissatisfaction. In every great political and social movement, in the literature of the day, nay, in every magazine and newspaper which drops from the teeming press, the influence may be more or less distinctly discerned of the mysterious presence of this great spiritual organization. The world has always been puzzled to account for this influence. Protestantism it can understand perfectly— there is nothing unearthly or mysterious about *that;* but in the life and progress of the Catholic Church there is something which defies every attempt at rational and systematic explanation.

To be sure, men have their theories; but, if the truth be told, they are by no means so satisfactory as might be wished. Such expressions as 'the consummate policy of Rome,' and 'the marvellous machinery of the Catholic Church,' are after all but stock phrases, with which men dispose of phenomena which must have at least a nominal resolution. What is there behind the policy? What puts *life* into the machinery, and guides the great engine in its noiseless, frictionless activity? Will 'discipline' explain the devotion of the Catholic Priesthood? Men do not turn hypocrites in order to spend their years in prayer and fasting; neither do they voluntarily elect to become the passive tools of a sordid despotism, to be rewarded only by a life of sacrifice and toil. Indeed, the world does not believe its own slanders. And now and then, when some periodic gust of persecution assails the Church, and not a martyr flinches; or when pestilence goes through the land, and faithful seekers of souls follow quickly in the trail of the destroyer, and the places of those who fall are instantly and noiselessly filled; or when tidings come that a score or so of missionaries and a few thousand converts have been massacred in some hitherto unheard-of province of China; the world, conscience-smitten, holds its peace, and pays to the Kingdom which is 'not of this world' the tribute of a sullen, if not a respectful silence.

One of the best things ever said by that acute thinker, the Count de Maistre, was that "no test is so infallible as the instinct of infidelity."* Certainly in examining the claims of rival Christian bodies it will be the part of prudence to watch narrowly the tactics of the opponents of all Christianity. And here at once we come upon something definite; for the application of this criterion gives us results which no sincere lover of truth can disregard. Infidelity does not stop to make war upon Protestantism; it is too cunning by far to quarrel with those who are ignorantly doing its own work; it greets them with a covert sneer, or an insolent nod of recognition, and goes on to do battle with its ancient and

---

* *Du Pape*, liv. iv. ch. xi. § 14.

inveterate foe. Look at the character of the unbelief of Catholic and of Protestant countries. Doubtless some of my readers are amazed at this challenge. They have been accustomed to regard the religious condition of Catholic nations as one of the strongest arguments against the Catholic Church; nowhere, say they, is infidelity so thoroughgoing and so bold; and in no way can this virulent scepticism be explained but as the inevitable reaction from the degrading superstition in which the people have for centuries been held. Surely observation was never more hasty nor inference more illogical. There is less of real irreligion in Catholic than in Protestant countries. What there is, is indeed rampant. And why? Not as a necessary recoil from a religion which degrades rather than enlightens. I am convinced, from my own experience in Catholic countries, that this supposed religious degeneracy is a huge bugbear. The explanation is far more simple. The Catholic Church makes no truce, holds no parley, with the world, the flesh, nor the devil. Her enemies can neither frighten her into silence nor cajole her into compromise. At every point they find her guarded, vigilant, and unrelenting; and, driven from her citadel, they are forced to stand forth in open warfare and rail at her in furious defiance. In France and Spain and Italy a man is either a Catholic or an infidel. But in Protestant countries unbelief salutes Christianity; it puts on the livery of the saints, and builds its chapels, and pays its preachers; and in the course of a generation or two it has made Protestantism as godless as itself.

Read the history of Europe for the last two centuries. It is that of one long, desperate struggle, waged by all the anarchic powers of human nature, and with all the weapons which craft and hatred could furnish—against what? Not against Protestantism, but against the Catholic Church. Deists, Encyclopædists, Republicans, Jacobins, Rationalists, Free-thinkers—they are good Protestants all; they laud the Reformation; they boast that they carry out its principles; and with one consent, though by divers arts—by argument, by satire, by blasphemy, and by the guillotine—they assail Her within whom dwells the everlasting Presence, before which the devils of old cried out, saying, 'Let us alone; what have we to do with thee, Jesus of Nazareth? Art thou come to destroy us? I know thee who thou art, the Holy One of God.'

If all the cruel things which in a single day are written and spoken throughout the world against the Roman Catholic Church could be brought together, they would make a volume which few would have the stomach to read. Every hour calumnies are uttered against that Church which in their essence are but repetitions of the dreary tales refuted by Tertullian and St. Justin seventeen centuries ago. Surely this undying hate of the world is a sign which cannot be misunderstood. To be hated of the world is a note of the Church. "If the world hate you; know ye that it hated me before you. If you had been of the world, the world would love its own: but because you are not of the world, but I have chosen you out of the world, therefore the world hateth you. Remember my word that I said to you: The servant is not greater than his lord. If they have persecuted me, they will also persecute you: if they have kept my word, they will keep yours also. But all these things they will do to you for my name's sake, because they know not him that sent me."

Enough on this point for the present. We shall have

occasion to recur to it hereafter, when we shall have gotten well into our subject. Meanwhile, in concluding this chapter, let us bring out some testimony of a somewhat different sort, and less painful to contemplate. There are here and there men of high intellectual powers, who, while they do not believe in the divine origin of Christianity, and even acknowledge themselves its adversaries, have yet the chivalry to treat Christianity with respect, or, at least, without passion. The opinion of such thinkers is invaluable. The issue between Protestantism and Catholicity is one in which they have no personal interest. They look at the whole matter from a distance, and from what they consider a higher plane. Now, these men, with their clear, cool heads, see well enough that Christianity and Catholicism are one and the same thing, and that Protestantism of all degrees is only a recent and very poor imitation of the old religion— that the sects of the day are but the stragglers which hang on the skirts of the great army of the Church.

Professor Huxley, in the course of some remarks on 'Scientific Education,' delivered not long ago, after alluding to the feeble *guerilla* by which the English clergy (notoriously the best educated Protestants in the world) attempt to withstand the advance of modern 'science,' went on to say: "Our great antagonist—I speak as a man of science— the Roman Catholic Church, the one great spiritual organization which is able to resist, and must, as a matter of life and death, resist, the progress of science and modern civilization, manages her affairs much better. It was my fortune, some time ago, to pay a visit to one of the most important of the institutions in which the clergy of the Roman Catholic Church in these islands are trained; and it seemed to me that the difference between these men and the comfortable champions of Anglicanism and of Dissent was comparable to the difference between our gallant volunteers and the trained veterans of Napoleon's Old Guard. The Catholic priest is trained to know his business and do it effectually. The professors of the college in question—learned, zealous, and determined men—permitted me to speak frankly with them. We talked like outposts of opposed armies during a truce—as friendly enemies; and when I ventured to point out the difficulties their students would have to encounter from scientific thought, they replied: 'Our Church has lasted many ages, and passed safely through many storms. The present is but a new gust of the old tempest, and we do not turn out our young men less fitted to weather it than they have been, in former ages, to cope with the difficulties of those times. The heresies of the day are explained to them by their professors of philosophy and science, and they are taught how these heresies are to be met.' I heartily respect an organization which faces its enemy in this way; and I wish that all ecclesiastical organizations were in as effective a condition. I think it would be better, not only for them, but for us. The army of liberal thought is at present in very loose order; and many a spirited free-thinker makes use of his freedom mainly to vent nonsense. We should be the better for a vigorous and watchful enemy to hammer us into cohesion and discipline."

Our other witness shall be Auguste Comte—a savant, by the way, with whom Professor Huxley would perhaps not thank us for associating him, but in whose company, nevertheless, we consider it a very high honor to have placed our gallant physicist. The father of modern Positivism, in his scientific classification of the religions of humanity, absolutely ignores

Protestantism, as a shapeless, incoherent system, from which he hopes to be "preserved." Not only this; he speaks of *Christianity* always under the name of *Catholicism;* he deliberately rejects the former title, and uses only the latter. And this is his reason for doing so: "Everybody," says he, "knows well enough what a Catholic is; whereas no man of intelligence can flatter himself nowadays that he understands what a Christian is." *

Surely, M. Comte is not far from right. For a Christian may be one who can 'swallow everything except the Supremacy,' or he may be one who reverences Christ as, on the whole, a nobler character than Socrates. You would insult either if you denied him the title; but, if you want to know what a Catholic is, go out and ask the first man who meets you in the street.

* "Chacun sait certainement encore ce que c'est qu'un catholique, tandis qu'aucun bon esprit ne saurait aujourd'hui se flatter de comprendre ce que c'est qu'un chrétien."—*Philosophie Positive*, v. 212, n₁ (Paris, 1864.) Comp. *Phil. Pos.* v. 241 ; *Pol. Pos.* iii. 556.

CHAPTER II.

THE PERPETUITY OF THE CHURCH.

WHAT Protestant has not heard it said, perhaps by some popular preacher of the day, that "though the body of the Papacy exists still, the spirit and life have forsaken it, so as to leave nothing but a dead carcass?" Do Protestants know who first hazarded that remarkable sentiment? It was John Calvin, in his 'Gratulations' to a 'Venerable Presbytery,' three hundred years ago.* Men talk of the 'ages of faith' as though they had long passed by; but, verily, when I look abroad over this new American Continent, and observe the work which is noiselessly but ceaselessly going on here, and then think of the blindness which can still repeat that hackneyed flourish of Calvin's, another quotation comes into my mind, which was made once at Antioch in Pisidia: "Behold, ye despisers, and wonder, and perish; for I work a work *in your days*, a work which *you will not believe, if any man shall tell it you.*"

And now let us face a problem which cannot fail to interest any intellectual man, whatever be his religious faith. Why is it that the Roman Catholic Church is so perpetually disappointing the prophecies of mankind? The standing prediction of its approaching dissolution is good evidence that the Papacy does not contain *in itself* any apparent principle of life and growth, and yet it continues to put forth the signs of immortal youth after empires have fallen and passed away.

---

* Luther, too, wrote this modest epitaph for himself: "Pestis eram vivens, moriens ero mors tua, papa."

It would be entertaining, if we had the time, to get together some of the theories which have been proposed for the solution of this enigma, and to test their satisfactoriness. There is Hobbes's famous saying, for instance, that the Papacy is "the ghost of the deceased Roman Empire, sitting crowned upon the grave thereof." It is very witty, one of the most brilliant *jeux d'esprit* I know of, but nothing more. I am going to confine myself, however, to a single attempt at an explanation, and that by a man who certainly attacked the difficult questions of history with a gallantry seldom surpassed.

Lord Macaulay's review of Ranke's *History of the Popes* is one of the most remarkable bits of literature with which we are acquainted. All things considered, it is perhaps as significant a tribute to the supernatural genius of the Catholic Church as was ever paid by one who professed to criticise it as the work of man. He opens with the familiar and superb exordium:

"There is not, and there never was on this earth, a work of human policy so well deserving of examination as the Roman Catholic Church. The history of that Church joins together the two great ages of human civilization. No other institution is left standing which carries the mind back to the times when the smoke of sacrifice rose from the Pantheon, and when camelopards and tigers bounded in the Flavian amphitheatre. The proudest royal houses are but of yesterday, when compared with the line of the Supreme Pontiffs.* That line we trace back in an unbroken series from the Pope

---

* "Before Hapsburg, or Bourbon, or Romanoff, or Brunswick, or Hohenzollern,—before Bonaparte or Carignan, I was old; for I have seen the Cæsars and the Antonines die; to-morrow I will be; for I am ever the same."—Mgr. Dupanloup.

who crowned Napoleon in the nineteenth century to the Pope who crowned Pepin in the eighth; and far beyond the time of Pepin the august dynasty extends, till it is lost in the twilight of fable. The republic of Venice came next in antiquity. But the republic of Venice was modern when compared with the Papacy; and the republic of Venice is gone, and the Papacy remains. The Papacy remains, not in decay, not a mere antique, but full of life and useful vigor. The Catholic Church is still sending forth to the farthest ends of the world missionaries as zealous as those who landed in Kent with Augustine, and still confronting hostile kings with the same spirit with which she confronted Attila. The number of her children is greater than in any former age. Her acquisitions in the New World have more than compensated for what she has lost in the Old. Her spiritual ascendency extends over the vast countries which lie between the plains of the Missouri and Cape Horn, countries which, a century hence, may not improbably contain a population as large as that which now inhabits Europe. The members of her communion are certainly not fewer than a hundred and fifty millions; and it will be difficult to show that all other Christian sects united amount to a hundred and twenty millions. Nor do we see any sign which indicates that the term of her long dominion is approaching. She saw the commencement of all the governments and of all the ecclesiastical establishments that now exist in the world; and we feel no assurance that she is not destined to see the end of them all. She was great and respected before the Saxon had set foot on Britain, before the Frank had passed the Rhine, when Grecian eloquence still flourished in Antioch, when idols were still worshipped in the temple of Mecca. And she may still exist in undiminished vigor when some traveller from New Zealand shall, in the midst of a vast solitude, take his stand on a broken arch of London Bridge to sketch the ruins of St. Paul's."

Now, if we went no further, we might content ourselves with saying that this passage is itself a sufficient refutation of the <u>assumption</u> (for it is a pure assumption) with which it begins. An institution which has thus vindicated its immortality cannot be coolly put down as a mere master-piece of human policy. The fact is, the mystery which the writer set out to solve was a noble theme for the eloquence of which he was so ready a master, and tempted him to state the case against himself so strongly, and let us say at once so truthfully, that all his subsequent efforts will not avail to save his cause. The reader finishes the essay with the impression that the author has said a great many brilliant things; but, if he is cool enough to see through the glitter of the periods, he is aware that nothing has been furnished by way of explanation at all adequate to the topics discussed. We will attempt a brief synopsis:

The Church of Rome is a very wonderful phenomenon, and no work of human policy is so well deserving of examination; let us see how she has maintained her strange ascendency. Four times has the human intellect risen in rebellion against her.

1. There was the Albigensian heresy. But this was stamped out (as Americans say) by a vigorous crusade.

2. Then came the struggle with the secular power and Philip the Fair, and the troubles which ended with the schism of the fourteenth century. But *somehow* (heaven alone knows how) this peril also passed, and the Church was found in her old place.

3. Next was the memorable uprising of the sixteenth century.

Here, of course, our critic bestirs himself most energetically. And what is his interpretation of the fact that 'Catholicism' not only stood firm, but in a very short time had driven Protestantism to bay on the shores of the Baltic? Why, merely that the Church understands how to deal with enthusiasts. "We have dwelt long on this subject," he writes, "because we believe that, of the many causes to which the Church of Rome owed her safety and her triumph at the close of the sixteenth century, the chief was the profound policy with which she used the fanaticism of such persons as St. Ignatius and St. Theresa." This is very ingenious and very suggestive, but quite insufficient to solve the difficulty. Besides, who clothed the Church with the subtile grace which can elicit the passion of the soul as nothing human ever did before; and then taught her how to guide and use aright such high and delicate devotion?*

4. Finally, we come to the persecution of the last century (which De Maistre says "infinitely surpasses all the rest"), culminating in the French Revolution.

And now, what causes are mentioned which may account for the ignominious failure of this last and deadliest assault? Positively, none at all. We may be pardoned a smile if we fancy we detect the uneasiness with which the learned writer finds himself approaching the end of his disquisition. He has gotten himself into a difficulty from which he can

---

* Hallam, after enumerating all the apparent causes which might account for the fact that the Church of Rome survived the sixteenth century, admits their insufficiency, and says: "It must be acknowledged that there was a principle of vitality in that religion, independent of its external strength."—*Literature of Europe*, part ii. c. ii. § 15. This "principle of vitality" he afterwards calls "an intense flame of zeal and devotion." But the difficulty remains. What was it which could kindle and sustain so holy a fire?

escape only by a resort to literary legerdemain. His last historical paradox is one of which no mortal ingenuity can render even a plausible account. So he dashes boldly into a peroration, makes a magnificent bow, and is gone. Like the pearl-diver of the Indies who sees his enemy approaching, he betakes himself to a desperate scratching in the sand, and nimbly slips away under cover of the cloud he has excited. Here is how he does it:

"It is not strange that, in the year 1799, even sagacious observers should have thought that, at length, the hour of the Church of Rome was come.* An infidel power ascendant, the Pope dying in captivity, the most illustrious prelates of France living in a foreign country on Protestant alms, the noblest edifices which the munificence of former ages had consecrated to the worship of God turned into temples of Victory, or into banqueting-houses for political societies, or into Theophilanthropic chapels, such signs might well be supposed to indicate the approaching end of that long domination. But the end was not yet. Again doomed to death, the milk-white hind was still fated not to die. Even before the funeral rites had been performed over the ashes of Pius the Sixth, a great reaction had commenced, which, after the lapse of more than forty years, appears to be still in progress. Anarchy had had its day. A new order of things rose out of the confusion, new dynasties, new laws, new titles; and amidst them emerged the ancient religion.

* Compare Hallam: "In the year 1560, every Protestant in Europe doubtless anticipated the overthrow of Popery; the Catholics could have found little else to warrant hope than their trust in heaven."—*Ibid.* Well might the same historian observe: "This great revival of the Papal religion, after the shock it had sustained in the first part of the sixteenth century, ought for ever to restrain that temerity of prediction so frequent in our ears."

The Arabs have a fable that the Great Pyramid was built by antediluvian kings, and alone, of all the works of men, bore the weight of the flood. Such as this was the fate of the Papacy. It had been buried under the great inundation; but its deep foundations had remained unshaken; and, when the waters abated, it appeared alone amidst the ruins of a world which had passed away. The republic of Holland was gone, and the empire of Germany, and the great Council of Venice, and the old Helvetian League, and the House of Bourbon, and the parliaments and aristocracy of France. Europe was full of young creations, a French Empire, a Kingdom of Italy, a Confederation of the Rhine. Nor had the late events affected only territorial limits and political institutions. The distribution of property, the composition and spirit of society, had, through great part of Catholic Europe, undergone a complete change. But the unchangeable Church was still there.

"Some future historian, as able and temperate as Professor Ranke, will, we hope, trace the progress of the Catholic revival of the nineteenth century. We feel that we are drawing too near our own time, and that, if we go on, we shall be in danger of saying much which may be supposed to indicate, and which will certainly excite, angry feelings."

We will not do Lord Macaulay the injustice of supposing that he was incapable of appreciating the grand simplicity of the only obvious answer to the questions at which he labored with such erudite earnestness. Indeed, it affords us more than ordinary pleasure to be able to give that answer in his own eloquent words. The review of Von Ranke was written in 1840. In 1845, he delivered a speech on the Maynooth College Bill, the same, if we mistake not, which cost him, two years later, his seat as member from Edinburgh. There is a passage of this speech which, by its repetition of a striking phrase, recalls the essay on the *History of the Popes*, and leads us to believe that the problem of the perpetuity of the Catholic Church was one which he had long been revolving. Speaking of the Irish Establishment, he said:

"Two hundred and eighty-five years has this Church been at work. What could have been done for it in the way of authority, privileges, endowments, which has not been done? . . . And what have we to show for all this lavish expenditure? What, but the most zealous Roman Catholic population on the face of the earth? On the great solid mass of the Roman Catholic population you have made no impression whatever. There they are, as they were ages ago, ten to one against the members of your Established Church.* Explain this to me. I speak to you, the zealous Protestants on the other side of the House. Explain this to me on Protestant principles. If I were a Roman Catholic, I could easily account for the phenomenon. If I were a Roman Catholic, I should content myself with saying that the mighty Hand and the outstretched Arm had been put forth according to the promise, in defence of the unchangeable Church; that he who, in

---

* "That very acute observer, Arthur Young, declared, at the close of the penal laws, that the relative proportion of Catholics to Protestants had not been at all reduced—if anything, rather the reverse; and that those who denied this admitted that, at the past rate of conversions, 4,000 years would be required to make Ireland Protestant. In the Irish Parliament it was stated that 71 years of the penal system had only produced 4,055 converts."—Lecky, *Rationalism in Europe*, ii. 15.

the old time, turned into blessings the curses of Balaam, and smote the host of Sennacherib, had signally confounded the arts and the power of heretic statesmen."

All we have to say is, why is not the Roman Catholic explanation as simple, and, on the whole, as *rational* as any other that has ever been proposed?

And now I have played at *sartor resartus* long enough. I find I have copied a good deal of choice English into these pages; but I am not going to apologize for it, for my object—at least in this stage of my undertaking—is to lay hold of all the testimony I can. And I shall be happy to speak, whenever I can do so effectively, by the mouth of those whose words will be worth far more than my own. Let me close this topic, then, by way of contrast to what has already been given, with a passage from one who *did* believe, with all his soul, in the Roman Catholic explanation. It is from a sermon preached in Notre Dame by the great Dominican, le Père Lacordaire:

"Assuredly the desire has not been wanting to lay hold of us, or put us to fault against immutability; for what a weighty privilege to all those who do not possess it; a doctrine immutable when everything upon earth changes! a doctrine which men hold in their hands, which poor old men in a place called the Vatican guard under the key of this cabinet, and which without any other defence resists the course of time, the dreams of sages, the designs of kings, the fall of empires—always one, constant, identical with itself! What a prodigy to deny! What an accusation to silence! Therefore, all ages, jealous of a glory which disdained their own, have tried their strength against it. They have come, one after the other, to the doors of the Vatican; they have knocked there with buskin and boot, and the doctrine has appeared under the frail and wasted form of some old man of threescore years and ten. It has said:

"'What do you desire of me?'

"'Change.'

"'I never change.'

"'But everything is changed in this world. Astronomy has changed, chemistry has changed, philosophy has changed, the empire has changed. Why are you always the same?'

"'Because I come from God, and because God is always the same.'

"'But know that we are the masters; we have a million of men under arms; we shall draw the sword; the sword which breaks down thrones is well able to cut off the head of an old man and tear up the leaves of a book.'

"'Do so; blood is the aroma in which I recover my youthful vigor.'

"'Well, then, here is half my sceptre; make a sacrifice to peace, and let us share it together.'

"'Keep thy purple, O Cæsar! to-morrow they will bury thee in it; and we will chant over thee the *Alleluia* and the *De Profundis*, which never change.'"

CHAPTER III.

THE CHURCH THE GUARDIAN OF MORALS.

NO Catholic ever turned Protestant in order to reform his morals and lead a better life. So undeniable is this fact that the Duke of Brunswick and Lunenburg numbered it among the *Fifty Reasons* which induced him to abjure Lutheranism and return to the Church of his forefathers. Let us put the matter in such a shape that no one will have the hardihood to demur. No Protestant ever became a Catholic in order to throw off restriction and indulge his passions. The system of the Catholic Church is a system of restraints; the sinner is hedged about by her on every side, and, if his heart be not right, her yoke is galling.* I have been asking for an explanation of the

---

* Erasmus wrote, while the Reformation was yet in progress: "It seems as if the Reformation aimed at nothing more than to strip a few monks of their habits, and to marry a parcel of priests; and this great tragedy terminates at last in a conclusion that is entirely comical, since, just like comedies, all ends in marriage." "What an evangelical generation this is!" "Nothing was ever seen more licentious, and, withal, more seditious; nothing, in a word, less evangelical than these pretended evangelists." "They set fire to the house in order to cleanse it. Morals are neglected; luxury, debauchery, adulteries, increase more than ever; there is no order, no discipline among them. The people indocile, after having shaken off the yoke of their superiors, will believe no person; and in so disordered a licentiousness, Luther will soon have reason to regret what he calls the tyranny of bishops." "I find more piety in one good Catholic bishop than in all these new evangelists."—*Epist.* lib. xix., xxxi., *apud* Bossuet.

Bossuet says himself: "Those who exclaimed against abuses in

fact that the Church has so long withstood the assaults upon her; if I am requested in turn to furnish an intelligible reason why mankind should cherish against her such undying animosity, here is a sufficient answer: the Catholic Church wages ceaseless warfare against the lusts of the flesh.

I have not the leisure, nor indeed the attainments, to say what might be said with profit, even in such a desultory work as this, on the subject of moral theology. It is a department of sacred science which in Protestant systems has no existence;* but in the Catholic Church it takes its place side by side with that of dogmatics. The works on moral theology written by the saints and doctors of that Church (and they are "a library by themselves") are a perpetual memorial with what devotedness and practical efficiency she has applied herself to the great work which she was sent to do, of seeking out and healing diseased and dying souls. I know well what hard things have been said on this matter by some Protestant divines. I have uttered such libels myself, and their memory now fills me with shame and

order to render the Church odious, themselves commit much stronger and more numerous ones at the very beginning of their Reformation than they could either rake up or invent during the course of so many ages that they upbraid the Church with her corruption."—*Var.* lib. vi. § 6.

Any one at all acquainted with the real history of the sixteenth century, knows the sober truth of these words.

* Archbishop Manning notices the fact that Andrewes' *Exposition of the Ten Commandments*, Taylor's *Ductor Dubitantium*, and Sanderson's *Cases of Conscience*, are the only attempts which the Anglican Church has made to supply this void in her 'theology,' and that no three works have been more completely forgotten.

sorrow.* The Protestant minister, in general, vibrates between his study and his pulpit. He lives in his books. He preaches to an ideal congregation, and knows the members of his flock only as friends and admirers, or as well-bred acquaintances. Moral questions he looks at only in the abstract. He knows almost nothing of the wants and weaknesses of individual souls; and the deep festering corruption of human nature is something which he would gladly cover up and forget. Perhaps his only acquaintance with the great moral theologians is through the unclean medium of such works as *Le Confesseur.* Or, if he has read for himself, he has done so, not only with prejudice, but without appreciating the design of his authors, and therefore without the key to their meaning. He is perplexed by the minuteness of detail which he is compelled to follow; and he is almost angry at finding the wounds of the soul laid bare as by some keen scalpel. He forgets that these works were written, "not for the Preacher, but for the Confessor;" he forgets that "sin consists in the thoughts of the heart;" it never occurs to him that the true physician, if he would prescribe for his patients, must both know them and understand their maladies; and he comes to the hasty and unjust conclusion that Catholic priests must be men of subtle and even prurient minds. O holy and most tender Mother! alas! that men should so mistake and malign thee. With what care, with what faithful love, dost thou keep watch over thy poor wandering children! Intent alone upon their salvation, thou dost follow them, even into the mire and the

---

* A gratuitous insult to that great and holy man, St. Alphonso de Liguori, occurred in an inaugural address, delivered as President of Hobart College, and afterwards appeared in print. As the slander was publicly made, it is publicly retracted.

thorns; and men, beholding thee thus solicitous, have dared cruelly to insult thee!

I wish to say a few words, however, upon the general subject of this chapter, which, I trust, may prove not unworthy the attention of such as have given serious thought to the state of morals in our own country. It will hardly be denied that the tone of public morality is very low, and that there is even cause for grave apprehension in the lawlessness and fierce incontinence which abound on every hand. For myself, I sometimes shudder lest sins which rival those of Sodom should call down upon our nation some stroke of divine vengeance. If, then, we were asked to name those evils which have made the most fearful inroads among us, so as already to have extorted a warning cry, we should probably mention these two: the contempt of the marriage tie, and that other crime which might well be called (perhaps has already been called) the murder of the innocents. Now, I have no hesitation in expressing my belief that the prevalence of these great sins is directly traceable to the fact that Protestantism has abolished and trampled upon two of the Sacraments of Christ's holy Church—the sacrament of Matrimony and the sacrament of Penance.

The occasion of the English Reformation was the refusal of a Pope to put asunder those whom God had joined together.* The decision of Clement VII. will yet be

---

* If any one wishes to learn how the Continental Reformers regarded the Sacrament of Matrimony, let him read Luther's sermon on Marriage (if he can do so without a blush); or, better still, the dogmatical judgment of Luther, Melancthon, Bucer, and the rest, giving permission (!) to the incontinent Landgrave of Hesse to commit bigamy, pure and simple. This precious document is given in full by Bossuet, in the sixth book of the *Variations*.

acknowledged to be, not only, as Bossuet calls it, "a testimony," but the grandest of all testimonies, that "the Church knows not how to flatter the passions of princes nor approve their scandalous proceedings." When the world has grown older, and men have grown calmer, they will agree to bring their tribute of homage to the memory of the faithful Pontiff who, in days of darkness and anguish, though he had already seen the sacred City stormed and sacked, though he had himself been a captive, and had endured the ignominy of flight and concealment, when kingdom after kingdom had abjured its allegiance, and though he knew that his sentence would cost him another, and the fairest, of his spiritual provinces, yet dared to brook the passion of that truculent King, that roaring Prince, who "never spared woman in his lust nor man in his anger,"* and to maintain, at any hazard, as his predecessors had done before him, and as the Church of God commanded him to maintain, the Inviolability of Marriage. All hail! true soldier and servant of Christ! Euge, serve bone et fidelis!

I say, as his predecessors had done before him. The maintenance by the Popes of the sacredness of marriage is the key to half the struggles of the Middle Ages. The contest between Clement and Henry Tudor, in the sixteenth century, was but a repetition of that very assertion of the supremacy of divine law over the turbulence of man which had been made by Nicholas I. and Adrian II. against Lothaire, in the ninth; by Urban II. and Pascal II. against Philip of France, in the eleventh; by Celestine III. and Innocent III. against Philip Augustus, and by Clement IV. against James of Aragon, in the thirteenth. And if you

---

* Heylin (*Hist. of Reform.* p. 15).

would know whether 'the unchangeable Church' still upholds her ancient doctrine, remember how not even the fear of the great Napoleon could induce Pius VII. to annul the marriage of Jerome Bonaparte with an American Protestant; remember the much-maligned 'Syllabus' of 1864.*

Barrow, whom I always thought to be one of the most insolent of writers, cries out: " What can be more ridiculous than to say that marriage was instituted by Christ, or that it doth confer grace!"† What the Church says (and Barrow knew it only too well) is that the *Sacrament* of marriage was instituted by Christ, and that it doth confer grace. The best answer to such a sneer as this will be to quote the Preface with which the Council of Trent introduces the Canons of its Twenty-fourth Session—words which are as fraught with meaning for the men of this generation as they were for those of the age of which it speaks: "The first parent of the human race, under the influence of the Divine Spirit, pronounced the bond of matrimony perpetual and indissoluble, when he said: *This now is bone of my bones, and flesh of my flesh. Wherefore a man shall leave father and mother, and shall cleave to his wife, and they shall be two in one flesh.*‡ But, that by this bond two only are united and joined together, our Lord taught more plainly, when, rehearsing those last words as having been uttered by God, he said, *Therefore now they are not two, but one flesh;* and straightway confirmed the firmness of that tie, proclaimed so long before by Adam, by these words: *What therefore God hath joined together, let no man put asunder.*§ But the

---

* § viii. *Errores de Matrimonio Christiano*, lxv.-lxxiv.
† *Supremacy*, p. 468. London, 1851.
‡ Gen. ii. 23, 24.
§ St. Matt. xix. 6.

grace which might perfect that natural love, and confirm that indissoluble union, and sanctify the married, Christ himself, the institutor and perfecter of the venerable sacraments, merited for us by his passion; as the Apostle Paul intimates, saying: *Husbands, love your wives, as Christ also loved the Church, and delivered himself up for it;* adding shortly after, *This is a great sacrament, but I speak in Christ, and in the Church.** Whereas, therefore, matrimony, in the evangelical law, excels in grace, through Christ, the ancient marriages; with reason have our holy Fathers, the Councils, and the tradition of the universal Church, always taught, that it is to be numbered amongst the sacraments of the new law; against which, impious men of this age raging, have not only had false notions touching this venerable sacrament, but, introducing according to their wont, under the pretext of the Gospel, a carnal liberty, they have by word and writing asserted, not without great injury to the faithful o Christ, many things alien from the sentiment of the Catholic Church, and from the usage approved of since the times of the apostles; the holy and universal Synod, wishing to meet the rashness of these men, has thought it proper, lest their pernicious contagion may draw more after it, that the more remarkable heresies and errors of the above-named schismatics be exterminated, by decreeing against the said heretics and their errors the following anathemas."

As to that other sin, the very name of which is written with a shudder, little, fortunately, need be said; for everybody knows, who knows anything about the subject, that among our Roman Catholic population the crime of fœticide

---

* Eph. v. 25, 32.

is unknown. A few extracts from the work of a distinguished Protestant physician will suffice. Dr. Storer says: "We are compelled to admit that Christianity itself, or, at least, Protestantism, has failed to check the increase of criminal abortion."* "There can be no doubt that the Romish ordinance, flanked on the one hand by the confessional, and by denouncement and excommunications on the other, has saved to the world thousands of infant lives."† "During the ten years which have passed since the preceding sentence was written, we have had ample verification of its truth. Several hundreds of Protestant women have personally acknowledged to us their guilt, against whom only seven Catholics, and of these we found, upon further enquiry, that all but two were only nominally so, not going to the confession."‡ Dr. Storer quotes the following testimony of the late Bishop Fitzpatrick: "The doctrine of the Catholic Church, her canons, her pontifical constitutions, her theologians, without exception teach, and constantly have taught, that the destruction of the human fœtus in the womb of the mother, at any period from the first instant of conception, is a heinous crime, equal at least in guilt to that of murder."§

And, now, go back to the very beginning, to the second and third centuries—you will find, even in the scanty Christian literature of that early age, evidence of the persevering and successful struggle of the Church to suppress this very practice, which, among the polite heathens of the Empire, was scarcely regarded as criminal.‖ Look well upon this picture and upon that—on the Christianity of the

---

* *Criminal Abortion*, p. 55.   ‡ *Ibid.*
† *Ibid.* p. 74.   § *Ibid.* p. 72.
‖ *Vide* Tertullian, *Apol.* c. 9; also the Epistle ascribed to St. Barnabas.

days of Tertullian, and the 'Christianity' which, according to Dr. Storer, has failed to check the progress of unnatural crime in this nineteenth century.*

* In what has been briefly written under the heading of this chapter, I have studiously taken no notice of the popular calumnies against Roman Catholics which are so lightly made and so cheerfully received by many Protestants. I have so abstained on my own account, lest I should lose my temper, as I did when I first comprehended the character of this dastardly defamation. Thank God that I never helped along such tales myself!

CHAPTER IV.

THE FAILURE OF PROTESTANTISM.

THE Founder of Christianity declared, concerning the unbelief of his contemporaries: 'If I had not done *among them* the works that no other man hath done, they would not have sin.' If Protestantism be identical with Christianity, then thinking men to-day are not without excuse for their incredulity. Where are the supernatural credentials of this modern Christianity? Where is the shining of the divine Presence in the midst of it? Where is the seal of God upon its brow? The world is terribly in earnest in these latter days; everything is to be tested now in the crucible of a remorseless rationalism, and no belief is going to be spared merely because it is cherished or time-honored. Is it to be wondered at that men, beholding the contradictions, the shiftings, the animosities, the countless extravagances of modern sectarianism, should say: 'If this be the Kingdom of God upon earth, established and perpetually governed by the Almighty himself,—then it is high time the monstrous delusion were exposed; let it obstruct the march of the human mind no longer; away with such a fiction from the face of the earth'? If this *be* the Kingdom of God upon earth, then its doom has been foretold by its very Founder; for a kingdom divided against itself '*shall not stand.*' And yet that Founder declared, concerning his Church, that he would build it upon a Rock, and that the gates of hell should not prevail against it. If Protestantism be that Church, how shall these two sayings hold together? Christ prayed for his disciples that they all might be one, that the world might believe that the Father had sent him. He made the conversion of the world contingent upon the unity of his followers. Christendom is divided; the world is not converted. How sharply does this single fact cut through the web of Protestant delusion! In how clear a light, as though the prayer had been a prophecy, does it set the mistakes and wanderings of the past three hundred years!

Thus much I could have said, and actually did say, while yet ignorantly remaining a veritable and unmitigated Protestant.* That I should have so continued, is to me now (the 'scales' having fallen from my eyes) simply amazing. The hallucination by which a Protestant Episcopalian believes that Anglicanism is something different in its essence from Protestantism, and that *it* has nothing to do with the 'contradictions and wanderings of the past three hundred years,' is a psychological phenomenon which would be amusing, did I not know, alas! too well, the disastrous fascination of the illusion. Such a man is, as Moehler says, 'enchanted.' He lives in a dream. *Animum pictura pascit inani.*

But without stopping to fight that phantom here, let us pass on to a more systematic treatment of the subject which as a Protestant I have introduced. And let it be kept in mind that we are not now attempting to find reasons for the failure of Protestantism, but merely to evidence the fact of that failure.

First, then, Protestantism has made no conquests since

---

* It may be prudent to note that as a Catholic—a real Catholic—I should change some of my expressions.

the sixteenth century. It was a sudden and violent movement, which spent itself within fifty years from its first outbreak, and whose subsequent history is a demonstration that as a system it has no aggressive power which may entitle it to rank among the forces which are struggling for the dominion of the world. And having taken position, let me at once bring up my artillery—my big guns; let me plant them where they will make sad havoc of any who may be doughty enough to attack such an intrenchment; and then move on. Hallam says: "The prodigious increase of the Protestant party in Europe, after the middle of the [sixteenth] century, did not continue more than a few years. It was checked and fell back, not quite so rapidly or completely as it came on, but so as to leave the antagonist church in perfect security."* Macaulay says: "We think it a most remarkable fact, that no Christian nation, which did not adopt the principles of the Reformation before the end of the sixteenth century, should ever have adopted them. Catholic communities have, since that time, become infidel and become Catholic again; but none has become Protestant."† Mr. Lecky says: "In the sixteenth and to a certain degree in the seventeenth century, Protestantism exercised a commanding and controlling influence over the affairs of Europe. . . . During the last century all this has changed. Of the many hundreds of great thinkers and writers, in every department, who have separated from the teachings and practices of Catholicism, it would be difficult to name three men of real eminence and unquestionable sincerity who have attached themselves permanently to any

---

* *Lit. of Europe*, part ii. ch. ii. §§ 14, 15.
† *Essays*, vol. iv. pp. 348, 349.

of the more conservative forms of Protestantism. Amid all those great semi-religious revolutions which have unhinged the faith of thousands, and have so profoundly altered the relations of Catholicism and society, Protestant Churches have made no advance and have exercised no perceptible influence." "Of all the innumerable forms into which the spirit of dogmatism crystallized after the Reformation, not one seems to have retained the power of attracting those beyond its border. Whatever is lost by Catholicism is gained by Rationalism; wherever the spirit of Rationalism recedes, the spirit of Catholicism advances."*

But Protestantism is not only not aggressive, it is utterly without conservative vitality; its only forces are centrifugal and self-destructive. Reason and logic may convince us, *a priori*, that this must be so; what we now say is that observation affirms that it is so. If we would only abstract the local and the present, if we would stand off, as it were, so as to look at time by centuries and space by continents, a single glance would show that as an organization 're-formed' Christianity is an irretrievable failure. We behold a seceding host which, at the very moment of schism, broke into innumerable divisions; we see these sects multiplying ever since with astonishing rapidity; we behold them without one faith, without common authority, without concerted action, dissentient, antagonistic, swayed by change of time and circumstance, driven forward and modified as if by the same forces which control, in a manner yet unknown to us, the movements of the social and political worlds. So far as such a body has any cohesion, it is that of a mere congeries, like the *concursus atomorum* of the old philosophers; it is an

---

* *Hist. of Rat.* vol. i. pp. 185, 186.

amorphous conglomerate, which needs but the hammer of some great crisis to shatter it into individual particles.

The Church of England forms no exception to this judgment. No country in the world is to-day so full of multifarious Dissent. And any one but a High Churchman (I do not mean to be discourteous) can see that it is only the accidental pressure of the Establishment which gives to that motley Church even the semblance of uniformity. " The religion of the Church of England," writes Macaulay, " is so far from exhibiting that unity of doctrine which Mr. Gladstone represents as her distinguishing glory, that it is, in fact, a bundle of religious systems without number. . . . Is it not mere mockery to attach so much importance to unity in form and name, where there is so little in substance, to shudder at the thought of two churches in aliance with one State, and to endure with patience the spectacle of a hundred sects battling within one church?"*

If, instead of looking at the matter in this objective way, we appeal at once to consciousness and individual experience, I am sure we shall come to a similar conclusion. What Protestant—if he be a sincere and earnest man, laboring and praying night and day for the advancement of his Master's Kingdom—what Protestant, I say, does not know all too well the vague feeling of oppression, the burden scarcely ever lifted, the sinking of the heart which follows the oft-recurring sense of isolation and desertion? Has he not sometimes leaned his head upon his hands, and cried : ' Why standest

---

* *Review of Gladstone on Church and State.* If Macaulay were now living, he would perhaps find Mr. Gladstone not so unreasonable on this subject.

thou so far off? Return, O Lord,—how long?"* And is not this a confession, though unacknowledged to himself, that what both reason and faith tell him must not and cannot fail has yet failed—or seemed to fail—in *fact?* Protestants have no faith in their own religion, as a system, as an organization apart from themselves. This is true even of those who have in some measure approached the Catholic conception of the Church. They have only succeeded in creating a Church for themselves by a violent effort of their imagination; and they are troubled when they find that other men behold in what they thought so fair an *ideal* only an evil delusion. How familiar we all are with the lamentations over the individualism and self-will of these latter days! How weary of the sighs for peace, and the longings for the return of a unity which seems farther and farther away! How long, brethren—let me speak as a Protestant—are we to go on thus complaining? Is it likely that anything will ever be written more persuasive than those grandly mournful passages of Hooker, in which he bewails the insubordination which had already followed the Reformation? Or more pathetic than the letters of Melancthon, whose tears " for thirty years ceased not to flow," and to whom " the Elbe, with all its streams, would not have furnished water sufficient to weep for the sorrows of the divided Reformation?"† How foolish to think that we are any nearer to peace and harmony than were Melancthon and Hooker! We say (which of us has not said?) that we are passing through a crisis, that we are living in times of transition, that the future at least is full

---

* " O, *quam honesta voluntate* miseri errant!"—Lactantius, *De Justitia.*

† *Opera,* lib. ii. epist. 202. See book v. of Bossuet's *Variations, passim.*

of promise, and that we may hope even yet to see the dawning of a brighter day. But, dear friends, men said and hoped precisely the same things three hundred years ago. The change of which you are conscious is a perpetual change, and the restoration you dream of can never come.*

Again, Protestantism has failed to reach what people nowadays call 'the masses.' It may or may not be evident *why* it has failed to do so; but from the fact itself it is fair to presume that there is inherent defect in the system. Protestantism may provide a church for the rich and the respectable; but the church of the poor and the wretched it cannot be. It is a religion of caste, a religion which has respect to the man with the gold ring in fine apparel, and which says to the poor man in mean attire, Stand thou there. Surely, if there was one thing which the Founder of Christianity proclaimed by word and action with a more startling iteration than any other, it was that he came to preach the Gospel to the poor. This was his first message at Nazareth, when he came up out of the wilderness. This was the crowning sign of his mission which he gave to John's disciples. This was the lesson of all his beneficent life. Into his kingdom would be gathered, not the Pharisee, but the publican; not the proud, but the lowly; not the fastidious and the dainty, but the beggar, the cripple, and the outcast. And now let us try an experiment. Let us get up early in the morning, and, without waiting for our comfortable meal, let us go and enquire the way to the

---

* Did you ever know a Catholic who 'worried' about his Church, who was despondent for the purity of the Faith, who looked forward with apprehension to 'the next Convention,' who went about his work in a feverish excitement, as if his Church needed his championship? This by the way; yet think it over.

nearest Catholic Church. Ah! there we find them, from the streets and lanes of the city, aye, the poor, and the maimed, and the halt, and the blind; but the rich men who were bidden, where are they?*

Once more—and here the facts are so plain that a child can do them justice—Reformed Christianity has failed, signally and hopelessly, in the work of converting the heathen. The history of Protestant Missions (let the truth be said) is a scandal and a farce. It was only at a late date that the Protestant Churches awoke to the fact that there were heathens to be converted, and that the command to teach all nations had never been revoked. Since that time there have been spasmodic efforts; but they have only proved, what it needed no experiment to demonstrate, that the mere divisions of Protestantism would alone be a fatal barrier to the success of its missionary enterprises. Christianity must come to heathen nations now as it came to the pagan world of old; it must come with authority; it must come as a direct revelation from the one true God, through his authorized and his only representatives. If it is to exhibit itself henceforth merely as an unseemly scramble for proselytes, then the conquests of Christianity are ended.

---

* "Ye daily defile the honorable Sacrament of Christ's body and blood in your most wicked, damnable, devilish, idolatrous, heathenish, vile, stinking, blasphemous, detestable, and abominable massing." So wrote that staunch Reformer, the learned Becon, Chaplain to Archbishop Cranmer. There is genuine Anglicanism for you! That trumpet has no uncertain sound. What a ring it has! How it recalls the magnificent charge of Latimer and Jewel and Barrow—*et id omne genus!* How its fearless defiance puts to shame the mincing hesitancy of these effeminate days! And how every word tells! It were bad enough to do the abominable thing once a month, but—*ye do it daily!*

This, let me say, I acknowledged to myself long ago. My heart bled at the struggles, the disappointment, the premature death, of those whom I myself had known and loved; for I felt that those men and women, so pure and so devoted, were selling their lives for naught. In a despairing way, I put off the question of the conversion of the great outlying world until the divisions of Christendom itself should be healed. But I did not see then, what is very clear to me now, that the desultory propagandism of Protestant sects is not futile merely, but destructive, that, so far as it goes, it is a cruel hindrance to the efficient working of the only agency which can ever christianize mankind. It is a fiendish device of the great enemy of souls, who has first blinded the eyes of men, and then made use of Christian zeal and Christian self-sacrifice to undermine Christianity itself. "Woe to the sects that have torn the garment without seam! *But for them the world would be Christian.*"*

This is not the place in which to speak of the missionary achievements of the Catholic Church.† I cannot, however, as we pass, withhold my tribute of homage to the sublime patience with which that Church has borne these attacks of her unnatural assailants. Without a murmur, with a love like that of her Divine Redeemer, she has set herself to bind up the wounds which her own misguided children have inflicted. She has kept on her noiseless way, numbering up her martyrs, and gathering in her many sons, doing her appointed work in the nineteenth century as she did it in the seventeenth and in the ninth. She pauses not to herald

---

* De Maistre.

† Let the candid reader consult Mr. Marshall's work on *Christian Missions;* or chapters vi. and vii. of Cardinal Wiseman's *Lectures on the Doctrines of the Church.*

her conquests. She publishes no reports. She makes no appeal. " No clamor or boast is heard within her : but she perseveres in the calm fulfilment of her eternal destiny, as unconscious of any extraordinary effort as are the celestial bodies in wheeling round their endless orbits and scattering rays of brilliant light through the unmeasurable distances of space. She leaves it to those who find the very attempt at conversion a new thing—who, in their very statements, speak of it as a fresh calling, and as an experimental effort —to blazon forth every new attempt, to hoard up, in their annual reports, every gleaning of hope, and employ the orator's skill, and the democratic arts of public appeals, to keep alive the apostolic vocation." *

Finally, Protestantism has, as a matter of fact, developed into naturalism and rationalism, and that with a regularity which seems to indicate the operation of some irresistible moral force. This gravitation has been observed by many with ill-concealed exultation, by many more it has been watched with undisguised alarm; but the fact will hardly be questioned by any well-informed man. Mr. Lecky, who ought to be an authority on such a matter, speaks of " the extraordinary strides which professed and systematized Rationalism has made in most Protestant countries." He uses familiarly the expression ' Protestant Rationalism,' and says that any one " must indeed be wilfully blind to the course of history who does not perceive that during the last hundred years these schools [of Protestant Rationalism] have completely superseded the dogmatic forms of Protestantism as the efficient antagonists of the Church of Rome." * In the Church of England this development has

* Cardinal Wiseman.   † *Hist. of Rat.* i. 181, 184, *et al.*

been retarded by the impediments of tradition, in the shape of creeds and a liturgy, and by the inertia which marks the movements of a State Church; but it has been only retarded, and every one familiar with the recent history of that Church must be aware of the rapid inroads which have been made by 'professed and systematized rationalism,' say, in the last twenty-five years.

I think that a test can without difficulty be given—though it may cost more words than I can well spare—which will show to what extent this rationalistic spirit has acquired unsuspected control over the mind of the most conservative Protestant. I have little hope, to be sure, that the argument will be treated with much respect; yet, if it were candidly considered, I believe its effect upon some minds would be very great.

The term 'rationalism' is a somewhat vague one (Mr. Lecky himself takes good care not to define it); I suppose, however, we all understand it to imply that intellectual habit which in approaching the phenomena of nature and the facts of history begins by discarding the notion of the supernatural and denying the credibility of miracles. Now, Protestants reject *in toto*, without hesitation and without examination, all miracles which are said to have taken place since the days of the Apostles. An alleged miracle in our own day is regarded with contemptuous indifference, not because it is unauthenticated, but because it is miraculous—as Mr. Lecky indeed says, adding the extraordinary admission that the assurance with which such miracles are repudiated is as "unreasoning as that with which they would have been once received." If the Lord Jesus Christ were to appear again, and do the identical mighty works which he once wrought in Galilee and Judæa, they would not even attract observation. The newspapers would chronicle a few wonderful cures and a case or two of suspended animation, and the stories would be forgotten.

What, now, has driven Protestants into this thoroughly rationalistic attitude? The answer is plain. It is *not* anything in the *reason* of the case which obliges them to receive the testimony of one age and refuse that of another. On the contrary, it is more rational to say, with the Catholic, that 'what God did once, he is likely to do again,' than to affirm, with the Protestant, that 'what God did once, he is *not* likely to do again.'* The assertion so readily made, that miracles are employed by God *solely* for the purpose of ushering in a new dispensation, and to accredit the founder of a new spiritual dynasty, is *a pure assumption*, a mere plausible theory, which has been devised to fortify a position already taken, and to justify Protestants in *not rejecting the miracles of our Lord and his Apostles*. It is without a shadow of support in those writings from which Protestants profess to draw their faith. Miracles were wrought with more or less frequency throughout the pre-Christian period; and so far was Christ himself from predicting their cessation, that when he gave mission to his Apostles, immediately before his ascension, he expressly announced the signs which should "*follow them that believe.*"† Besides, those who

---

* See Newman, *Apol.* p. 339.
† St. Mark xvi. 17. The only intimation given by our Lord of any divinely imposed limit to the power of working miracles is a significant one for these days. We are told that in his own country he did not many mighty works, "*because of their unbelief*" (St. Matt. xiii. 58), or, as St. Mark puts it, "He *could* there do no mighty work, save that he laid his hands upon a few sick folk, and healed them." After this remarkable declaration, is it possible to read without being startled that maxim of modern rationalism, "*Mira-*

make this assertion are generally guilty of an amazing *petitio principii*. They start with the divinity of the Founder of Christianity, and by it establish the credibility of his marvellous acts. They scoff at the miracles of St. Francis Xavier, because he was a Jesuit; but they believe those of Jesus Christ, because he was God incarnate. This is, of course, absurd; and the worst of it is that Protestants are not aware of the absurdity. They do not perceive, what is—or rather ought to be—exceedingly plain, that the miracles of our Lord himself and those of the humblest of his saints must be tested by the same rule of rigid and impartial *evidence*.

Is there, then, any intrinsic difference of character between the miracles of Scripture and those of ecclesiastical history, which puts them at once on a different footing? Voltaire ought to have convinced us long ago that no legend in the *Lives of the Saints* is a whit more grotesque and *irrational* (I speak as a fool) than the stories of the wonderful ark and the talking ass, of the labors of Samson and the marvels of Elisha, of Jonah's fish, or the 'possessed pigs,' or the vision of the great sheet. Is there, finally, an amount and kind of testimony in the one case which is wholly wanting in the other? Those who assume the affirmative have, I fear, never thought very much, or very candidly, about the subject. The writings of the Fathers abound in miraculous narratives, marked by an apparent sincerity and a minuteness of detail which make it impossible to distinguish between their witness to the fact of miracles and that of the Evangelists. The testimony of ecclesiastical history is sim-

---

cles cease *when men cease to believe and expect them*" (Lecky, *History of European Morals*)?

ply overwhelming. Dr. Middleton begins his *Free Inquiry* by admitting out and out that "the claim to a miraculous power was universally asserted and believed in all Christian countries and in all ages of the Church, till the time of the Reformation;" that "ecclesiastical history makes no difference between one age and another, but carries on the succession of its miracles, as of all other common events, through all of them indifferently;"* and that, "as far as the Church historians can illustrate or throw light upon anything, there is not a single point in all history so constantly, explicitly, and unanimously confirmed by them all, as the continual succession of those powers through all ages, from the earliest father who first mentions them down to the time of the Reformation; which same succession is still further deduced by persons of the same eminent character for probity, learning, and dignity, in the Romish Church, to this very day."† It may be said, moreover, with truth and force, that the miracles of recent times have had to run the gantlet of a scepticism which in earlier days had no existence. The later the miracle, the more searching has been the criticism.

What, then, is the answer which I said was so plain? Simply this. Protestants *began*, not as rationalists, but as Protestants; they rejected miracles at first, not because they were miraculous, but because they were *Romish*. They had no choice. If the miracles were real, the doctrines were true. They were compelled, cost what it might, to get rid of a divine attestation which would have condemned themselves. They could make no distinction of centuries; the testimony of one was that of another. To have admitted even a

* Introductory Chapter, p. xlv.
† Preface, p. 15. Never mind the sneer.

brief continuance of miraculous gifts would have "unwarily betrayed the Protestant cause into the hands of its enemies; for it was in those primitive ages, particularly in the third, fourth, and fifth, those flourishing times of miracles, in which the chief corruptions of Popery" were "introduced."* Middleton simply looks the matter in the face when he says: "By granting the Romanists but a single age of miracles after the time of the Apostles, we shall be entangled in a series of difficulties, whence we can never fairly extricate ourselves till we allow the same powers also to the present age."† But what began as illogical Protestantism must end inevitably—there is no possibility of escape—in logical rationalism. The human intellect cannot persist for many generations in a palpable inconsistency. The theologians of Tübingen have simply reached that point already which must sooner or later be the *reductio ad absurdum* of all Protestant theology. Those who in effect deny the possibility of miracles in the nineteenth century must end by denying their possibility in the first. If no reasonable amount of evidence can substantiate a miracle to-day, no conceivable amount can establish the credibility of one which happened centuries ago, in a distant country and a credulous age. The only way of disposing of the unanimous and circumstantial testimony of the Fathers is by charging them, as Middleton did, *en masse*, with wholesale and habitual "forgery," with a "bold defiance of sacred truth;"‡ and a scepticism (I might better say, a credulity)

---

* *Ibid.* Introd. Chap. p. li. Notice, in passing, the admission of *primitive* 'Popery.'

† *Ibid.* p. xcvi.

‡ *Ibid.* p. lxxxiv. *Falsus in uno, falsus in omnibus.* If the Fathers

which can deal thus with the Fathers, will not long continue to reverence the veracity of their predecessors. The end is not far off. Three hundred years of Protestantism have left to Christianity only the distant tradition of a supernatural revelation; and "the idea of the miraculous, *which a superficial observer might have once deemed its most prominent characteristic*, has been driven from almost all its intrenchments, *and now quivers faintly and feebly through the mists of eighteen hundred years.*"*

For myself, now that I have come to look at this matter fairly and fearlessly, I hesitate not to say that, if ever sound reason should force me to reject in a body the miracles of the Catholic Church, I will follow reason further, and enroll myself as an humble disciple of Strauss, or Spencer, or Tyndall. But I also say, and with equal confidence, that reason itself will be dethroned before I can be brought to believe that the concurrent testimony of eighteen centuries is a gigantic fraud, and the blessed saints of all ages a set of cunning and consummate knaves.

Protestantism—" Ah !" exclaimed Bossuet, " our heart beats at this name, and the Church, always a mother, can never, when she remembers it, repress her sighs and her desires."† Protestants, the Holy Father has written to you as to those who acknowledge the Lord Jesus Christ as your Redeemer, and glory in the name of Christian; he entreats you to examine anxiously whether you are in the true path marked out for us by our Divine Lord; he supplicates you

were systematic liars, where is your evidence for even the *authenticity* of the New Testament Scriptures?
* *Hist. of Rat.* i. 195. The italicizing is mine.
† Quoted by Mgr. Dupanloup.

to follow the yearnings of your souls, and to offer most fervent prayers to the God of mercy that the wall of division may be broken down and the mists of error be scattered; with hands outstretched he waits to welcome you to the fold of peace. Come, brothers, come back. The day is far spent—*majoresque cadunt altis de montibus umbræ.* Aye! it is growing dark; and reason, if it must reign alone, will soon be reigning "like the night star, over shadows which it cannot dissipate." Come back, ere it be too late—lest haply you be found even to fight against God.

    Venite, fratres, si vultis ut inseramini in vite.
    Dolor est, cum vos videmus præcisos ita jacere.
    Numerate Sacerdotes vel ab ipsa Petri Sede,
    Et in ordine illo patrum quis cui successit videte;
    Ipsa est Petra, quam non vincunt superbæ inferorum portæ.*

* St. Augustine.

CHAPTER V.

THE CHURCH AND CIVILIZATION.

WHEN a man has once worked his way out of a huge prejudice, it is interesting to him (suffer me, dear reader, to be garrulous) to look back and see how completely he continued under the control of the delusion after he was in possession of knowledge which ought to have dispelled it for ever. In an address, delivered some fifteen months ago, upon 'The Relation of the Church to Education,' I am amused to find the following passage:

"It is most instructive to observe—if we will but stop to appreciate—with what amazing forethought the Church of Rome has acted with reference to the question of education in America. With subtle instinct she seems early to have sounded the American mind, and weighed the character of American institutions: at the outset of our national career she paused to calculate the resultant of the strange forces which then went into operation; and with consummate tact she laid her plans to meet the issues of the future. Silently, but with restless energy, she went to work; and all over the broad republic schools and colleges arose bearing the abused name, the spurious title, of 'Catholic.' And now men are astonished, are bewildered, to learn for the first time that the Roman Church, instead of being the deadly enemy of popular education, is its best friend and wisest supporter; that, instead of seeking to crush out intellectual enterprise, she is the true fosterer of science, the sympathizing encourager and promoter of investigation and discussion. We ourselves are not for one moment misled by these astounding claims. *They are confuted by the history and policy of Romanism through centuries of time.* But we do pay the tribute of our cordial admiration to what seems to us a master-stroke of shrewdness on a grand scale. The Church of Rome foresaw that in the new campaign it would not do to use the old and ponderous weapons. She laid them aside, and chose new ones. And she chose wisely— as the history of the next fifty years, we believe, will show. In the debate which has already opened upon questions of national education, she will take no insignificant and retiring part. When the crash comes in the present public-school system, she will be found prepared and equipped, and will start in the race which is to follow with immense advantage in her favor."

The fact that Protestantism had been beaten on its own chosen ground, and with its own boasted weapons, was undeniable; and I seem to have been able to explain it only by some queer theory of a diabolical inspiration directing the tactics of the subtle Church of Rome. It never entered my mind to question what I took as simply axiomatic, that the traditional attitude of 'Romanism' had been one of hostility to progress and intellectual enlightenment. And yet in the very same essay occur a few words on the work of the Church in the Middle Ages which might have led me to suspect the soundness of the supposed truism:

"We do not believe that the mediæval Church is deserving of all the abuse which is sometimes so flippantly heaped upon it. Such abuse seems to us to betray a shallowness of historical appreciation. Those were dark days, God knows. The twilight was long and dreary. But let us thank the Church of God that the light did not go out altogether. It took a long time to civilize and christianize the wild hordes which poured down from the North, and almost swallowed up the Latin races of Southern Europe. Instead of being the enemy of intellectual culture, the Church of the Middle Ages, though groping in obscurity and staggering under accumulated error, did a gigantic work in lifting the mind of Europe up to a level from which it could step upon the plane of modern progress. Her school-men were scholars whose infinite research and masterly logic would, in brighter days, have won mighty conquests in the service of truth. Her universities were conducted on a scale and with a liberality which would confound the men of this generation. To her we owe the preservation of those seeds of ancient learning, which, in the fulness of time, burst their shell, and covered all Europe with a golden harvest. To her we owe it that those monuments of Christian antiquity, the writings of the Fathers, are ours, as they were hers. To her we are indebted for the transmission intact of the Holy Scriptures themselves. No! So long as the Church of Rome remained, in the providence of God, the great Catholic Church of the West, she continued to be the powerful, though corrupt, defender, the rude conservator, of learning and science. Whatever she may have to answer for in other respects, we stop not here to cast a stone at her."

Of course, the two passages are inconsistent. The latter contains a modicum of truth, however partially and grudgingly stated, sufficient to demolish the outrageous assumption of the former.

The fact is, Protestantism owes its continued existence to the belief, incessantly proclaimed and assiduously inculcated, that the Catholic Church, instead of being the cause and very foundation of modern civilization, has been the great obstruction, in spite of which, and over which, the human mind has gained its conquests. Let the contrary once be made evident, and a reformed Christianity would be without basis or excuse. Therefore, as has been admitted by one who will not be accused of a weakness for the Catholic Church, Protestantism has been compelled to rewrite all history, and to accommodate facts to its own necessities.* A belief which education has thus wrought into a man's intellectual fibre is well-nigh incradicable; it gives a cast, a coloring, to all that he sees and reads. Even a candid student is baffled and misled at every step. The continuity of history is destroyed for him. Or, rather, he views it from a wrong centre, and all his estimates are vitiated by the error of his position. But let a man, by the grace of God, be once led to change his point of view, let him be brought back to the high hill of truth,—

> Despicere unde queas alios passimque videre
> Errare atque viam palantis quærere vitæ,†—

and quickly the whole perspective changes; the distorted becomes straight, what seemed broken appears continuous, what before was retrograde is now progressive; and that which once presented only a scene of perplexing confusion, a chaos of contradictions, now unrolls in a panorama consistent in every part and shining all over with a divine

---

* "To live, Protestantism found itself forced to build up a history of its own."—Thierry.

† Lucretius, ii. 9, 10.

meaning. For the first time the Christian student finds himself in possession of an intelligible philosophy of history.

To attempt any review of Christianity in its relation to progress in civilization, art, and letters, is out of the question here. Perhaps the most serviceable thing which can be done in the brief space which I can allow myself will be to bring together a few statements and admissions, made by others than Roman Catholics, which concur in establishing one general conclusion. If a Protestant can once be led, by Protestant testimony, to suspect that the civilization of which he is now enjoying the fruits is not the product of the so-called Reformation; that its growth began in an age far more remote; that the much-abused 'Dark Ages' were not so dark after all; that the obscurity which for a while overspread the Christian world was not a decadence of Christianity, but an irruption of pagan disorder; and that in the centuries preceding the sixteenth a work of organization and illumination was accomplished for which no force that Protestantism has ever displayed would have been adequate, and compared with which the results of Protestantism would indicate only a process of disintegration;—if, I say, he can be brought even to surmise the truth of all this, he will have gotten hold of a thread of truth, which, by God's blessing, may end in the unravelling of the whole tissue of his Protestant prejudices.

Let us go back, then, to the darkest days of Christian history, to the tenth century. "True, the world was dark, very dark and very wild; and its corruptions were powerfully felt at times in the bosom of the Church itself; but no one but a simpleton or a knave will pretend to make this barbarism *her* work, or to lay it as a crime to *her* charge.

She was the rock that beat back its proud waves. She was the power of order and law, the fountain of a new civilization, in the midst of its tumultuating chaos."* "Just as she had subdued the intelligence and refinement of the old Roman Empire, it was swept away, and she was left alone with its wild destroyers. Her commission was changed: she had now to tame and rule the barbarians. But upon them the voice which had rebuked the heretic fell powerless. While they pressed into her fold, they overwhelmed all her efforts to reclaim them, and filled her, from east to west, with violence and stunning disorder. When, therefore, she again roused herself to confront the world, her position and difficulties were shifted. Her enemy was no longer heresy, but vice—wickedness which wrought with a high hand, foul and rampant, like that of Sodom, or the men before the flood. It was not the faith, but the first principles of duty—justice, mercy, and truth—which were directly endangered by the unbridled ambition and licentiousness of the feudal aristocracy, who were then masters of Europe. With this fierce nobility, she had to fight the battle of the poor and weak—to settle the question whether the Christian religion and the offices of the Church were to be anything more than names, and honors, and endowments, trappings of chivalry and gentle blood; whether there were yet strength left upon earth to maintain and avenge the laws of God, whoever might break them. She had to stand between the oppressor and his prey—to compel respect for what is pure and sacred from the lawless and powerful." †

* Dr. Nevin, *Mercersburg Review*, November, 1851; article, *Early Christianity*.
† *British Critic*, vol. xxxiii. p. 7.

What power, think you, would Protestantism have had to call order out of this appalling anarchy? Let us see now what the Catholic Church was able to do. "The Church still had, as in earlier days, her miracles, her martyrdoms, her missionary zeal, her holy bishops and saints, her works of charity and love, her care for sound doctrine, her sense of a heavenly commission, and her more than human power to convert and subdue nations."* And presently a new world began to rise out of the waste of waters. There were "five institutions," writes Chancellor Kent, "existing about the period of the eleventh century, which made a deep impression upon Europe, and contributed, in a very essential degree, to improve the law of nations. . . . Of all these causes of reformation, the most weight is to be attributed to the intimate alliance of the great powers as one Christian community. . . . The history of Europe, during the early periods of modern history, abounds with interesting and strong cases, to show the authority of the Church over turbulent princes and fierce warriors, and the effect of that authority in meliorating manners, checking violence, and introducing a system of morals which inculcated peace, moderation, and justice. The Church had its councils or convocations of the clergy, which formed the nations professing Christianity into a connection resembling a federal alliance, and those councils sometimes settled the titles and claims of princes, and regulated the temporal affairs of the Christian powers. The confederacy of the Christian nations was bound together by a sense of common duty and interest in respect to the rest of mankind."† "The

---

* Dr. Nevin, *ubi supra*.
† *Commentaries on American Law*, vol. i. lect. i. pp. 9, 10. A

Church," says Mr. Lecky, "was the very heart of Christendom, and the spirit that radiated from her penetrated into all the relations of life, and colored the institutions it did not create." "A certain unity of type was then manifested, which has never been restored." "This ascendency was gained by mediæval Catholicity more completely than by any other system before or since, and the stage of civilization that resulted from it was one of the most important in the evolutions of society. By consolidating the heterogeneous and anarchical elements that succeeded the downfall of the Roman Empire, by infusing into Christendom the conception of a bond of unity that is superior to the divisions of nationhood, and of a moral tie that is superior to force, by softening slavery into serfdom and preparing the way for the ultimate emancipation of labor, Catholicism laid the very foundations of modern civilization. Herself the most admirable of all organizations, there were formed beneath her influence a vast network of organizations, political, municipal, and social, which supplied a large proportion of the materials of almost every modern structure." "In the transition from slavery to serfdom, and in the transition from serfdom to liberty, she was the most zealous, the most unwearied, and the most efficient agent."* "It is historically certain," Dr. Nevin declares, "that European society, as a whole, in the period before the Reformation, was steadily advancing in the direction of a rational, safe liberty. The problem by which the several interests of the throne, the aristocracy, and the mass of the people were to be rightly guarded and carried forward in

somewhat similar passage occurs in the preface to the third edition of Wheaton's *Elements of International Law*.

* *History of Rationalism*, vol. ii. pp. 36, 37, 209.

the onward movement of civilization, so as by just harmony to serve and not hinder the true welfare of all, was one of vast difficulty; which, however, in the face of manifold disturbing forces, we may see still approximating, at least, more and more towards its own full and proper solution. The simple position of these several elements relatively to each other, at the going out of the Middle Ages, is of itself enough to show how false it is to represent the old Catholicity as the enemy of popular liberty; for we see that European civilization, at this time, after having been for so many centuries under the sole guardianship of that power, presented no one of these interests as exclusively predominant."*

The same superhuman force which is thus apparent in the reorganization of the moral and social world is visible also in a marvellous quickening of the intellectual powers. "The more carefully," says Lecky, "the history of the centuries prior to the Reformation is studied, the more evident it becomes that the twelfth century forms the great turning-point of the European intellect. Owing to many complicated causes, which it would be tedious and difficult to trace (!), a general revival of Latin literature had then taken place, which profoundly modified the intellectual condition of Europe."† Dr. Nevin again adds his testi-

---

* *Mercersburg Review*, March, 1851; article, *Modern Civilization*.
† *Hist. of Rat.* i. 70. No wonder the historian of rationalism found the causes of this wonderful revival *tedious and difficult to trace!* Elsewhere, in a moment of unguarded enthusiasm over the grandeur of St. Peter's at Rome, Mr. Lecky exclaims: "There lie those mediæval pontiffs who had borne aloft the lamp of knowledge in an evil and benighted age, who had guided and controlled the march of nations."

mony: "It is a most childish fancy, certainly, to suppose that the revival of learning began properly with the sixteenth century. It dates at least from the eleventh; and there is abundance of evidence that the progress made between that and the age of the Reformation was quite as real and important as any that has since taken place. All sorts of learning were in active exercise before Protestantism came in to share their credit with the Roman Church."* So rapidly did the movement advance, that of the period after the middle of the thirteenth century Hallam is able to say: "It is an age in many respects highly brilliant; the age of poetry and letters, of art, and of continual improvement."† Hallam repeatedly acknowledges the great debt which the world owes to Italy for her renewal of classical learning. "It would be difficult," he says, "to find any man of high reputation in modern times who has not reaped benefit, directly or through others, from the revival of ancient learning. We have the greatest reason to doubt whether, without the Italians of those ages, it would ever have occurred."‡ And Italy was the seat and home of the Papacy. Of the sixteenth century Hallam remarks, very quietly: "It is probable that both the principles of this great founder of the Reformation [Luther], and the natural tendency of so intense an application to theological controversy, checked for a time the progress of philological and philosophical literature on this side of the Alps."§

---

* *Mercersburg Review, ut sup.*
† *Middle Ages*, ch. iii. pt. ii.
‡ *Literature of Europe*, vol. i. ch. ii. n. 49.
§ *Ibid.*, ch. iv. n. 61. Frederick Schlegel, in his *Philosophy of History*, calls the period of the Reformation "truly a barbarous

Gibbon, I think, somewhere puts the number of universities in Europe at the end of the fifteenth century at "about

era." The lamentations of Erasmus over the injury done to letters by the Reformation are well known. But the testimony of Erasmus is perhaps out of order here.

M. Littré, of the French Institute, who is far from being a Catholic, has lately added his learned tribute to the regenerative work of the Church during the Middle Ages, in his *Etudes sur les Barbares et le Moyen Age*. The following spirited sentence, from a writer who still *continues a Protestant*, will be fresh in the memory of many of my readers: Dr. Ewer says that the real cause of the light and progress of modern times is "a general awakening of mind, which began far back in the Middle Ages, four hundred years before the Protestant dogma was ever thought of—an awakening of mind, of taste, of the genius of invention, which, abandoning the rude structures of the seventh, eighth, ninth, and tenth centuries, brought out, long before the Continental [why *Continental?*] Reformation, the most ornate specimens of architecture the world ever saw; which, in the eleventh century, invented paper, and, before John Calvin and Martin Luther [and Thomas Cranmer and Henry Tudor?] ever saw the light, produced the art of printing—paper and printing, the two conservers of human intelligence ; which, in the twelfth century, devised banks of exchange and discount, and, not long after, invented gunpowder, conceived the idea of the post-office, and discovered and applied the principle of magnetism in the mariner's compass, thus giving such a start to commerce and magnificent geographical discovery as they had never had before ; which, in the tenth century, contrived clocks ; which invented painting in oil-colors before Luther was born ; which, in the thirteenth century, introduced astronomy and geometry into Europe, and, not long after, brought in algebra, and fostered all three sciences; which discovered America a quarter of a century before the Continental Reformation so-called opened ; which, centuries before Luther, produced a Dante, and a Petrarch, and a Chaucer, and a Boccaccio, and a Roger Bacon—Roger Bacon, who, three centuries before his successor, Lord Francis Bacon, announced to the world the very method of legitimate investigation in accordance with which all modern science is pursued, and upon which Lord Bacon afterwards built his fame—Roger Bacon of the so-called

fifty." Dr. Helfenstein* has given a list of sixty-six which were in operation at the beginning of the Reformation.† Two of these (those of Edinburgh and Alcalá) were opened early in the sixteenth century. The oldest, those of Bologna, Paris, and Oxford, were founded in the twelfth, or perhaps in the eleventh century. But all of these *Studia Generalia* grew out of monastic and cathedral schools which had existed long before. We have abundant evidence, in the decrees of councils and the letters of popes and bishops, that from the very earliest ages the Church had labored, in the most thorough manner, to provide instruction—and gratuitous instruction—for her children. The work accomplished by these mediæval universities is simply magnificent. The Catholic youth of Europe were seized with a rage for letters, and they crowded to the great academies by scores of thousands.‡ They sat by thousands at the feet of the great masters.§ The courses of studies pursued at the

---

dark ages, who had this immense advantage over the Bacon of the sixteenth century, in that he personally put his method into practice."—*Failure of Protestantism*, pp. 142, 143.

* *Contemporary Review*, Feb., 1867; art. *Mediæval Universities*.

† Of these, Italy claimed eighteen, Germany fifteen, France twelve, Spain and Portugal ten, England and Scotland six, and five belonged to other countries.

‡ The numbers of the students at the larger universities seem now almost romantic. In 1262, Bologna counted 10,000; the University of Paris contained, in 1394, an equal number; Salamanca and Vienna boasted of 7,000 each. Wood, in his history of the University of Oxford, says that, in 1250, it numbered 30,000 members. Huber defends this estimate, though it is doubtless exaggerated.

§ Abelard, for instance, and Albertus Magnus, lectured to several thousand auditors. They were forced to deliver their courses in the open air. The Place Maubert (Magni Alberti), in Paris, still remains an interesting memento of this scholastic enthusiasm.

schools, if we had time to speak of them, would challenge our admiration no less than the whole scale upon which the schools were administered.

Then, too, look at the testimony furnished by the libraries of Europe. We need not go to Florence, nor the Vatican. We are collecting Protestant contributions; so let us follow a charming *cicerone*, who will introduce us to a corner of the great library of Protestant England. Mr. Matthew Arnold gossips thus over the collection of the Abbé Migne: " In spite of all the shocks which the feeling of a good Catholic has in this Protestant country inevitably to undergo, in spite of the contemptuous insensibility to the grandeur of Rome which he finds so general and so hard to bear, how much has he to console him, how many acts of homage to the greatness of his religion may he see, if he has his eyes open! I will tell him of one of them. Let him go, in London, to that delightful spot, that Happy Island in Bloomsbury, the reading-room of the British Museum. Let him visit its sacred quarter, the region where its theological books are placed. I am almost afraid to say what he will find there, for fear Mr. Spurgeon, like a second Caliph Omar, should give the library to the flames. He will find an immense Catholic work, the collection of the Abbé Migne, lording it over that whole region, reducing to insignificance the feeble Protestant forces which hang upon its skirts. Protestantism is duly represented, indeed; Mr. Panizzi knows his business too well to suffer it to be otherwise; all the varieties of Protestantism are there; there is the library of Anglo-Catholic Theology, learned, decorous, exemplary, but a little uninteresting; there are the works of Calvin, rigid, militant, menacing; there are the works of Dr. Chalmers, the Scotch thistle, valiantly doing duty as the rose of Sharon, but keeping something very Scotch about it all the time; there are the works of Dr. Channing, the last word of religious philosophy in a land where every one has some culture, and where superiorities are discountenanced—the flower of moral and intelligent mediocrity. But how are all these divided against one another, and how, though they were all united, are they dwarfed by the Catholic leviathan, their neighbor! Majestic in its blue and gold unity, this fills shelf after shelf and compartment after compartment, its right mounting up into heaven among the white folios of the *Acta Sanctorum*, its left plunging down into hell among the yellow octavos of the *Law Digest*. Everything is there, in that immense *Patrologiæ Cursus Completus*, in that *Encyclopédie Théologique*, that *Nouvelle Encyclopédie Théologique*, that *Troisième Encyclopédie Théologique ;* religion, philosophy, history, biography, arts, sciences, bibliography, gossip. The work embraces the whole range of human interests; like one of the great Middle-Age cathedrals, it is in itself a study for a life. Like the net in Scripture, it drags everything to land, bad and good, lay and ecclesiastical, sacred and profane, so that it be but matter of human concern. Wide-embracing as the power whose product it is! a power, for history, at any rate, eminently *the Church ;* not, I think, the church of the future, but indisputably the church of the past, the church of the multitude."*

We will not stop to quarrel with this graceful writer for his somewhat hesitant opinion about the future. His confident testimony to the past is all that we require. If Mr. Arnold fancies that he, or anybody else, can con-

---

* *Essay on Pagan and Mediæval Religious Sentiment.*

struct a new Church and a better, by all means let him amuse himself with the experiment.

And now, I think, we have had enough—enough, at any rate, to mitigate our surprise at the curt indignation of the German historian and Protestant vindicator of Innocent III., when he bluntly says: "Only superficial minds, that disdain the study of documents, and are blinded by the pretended superiority of our epoch, or by systematic hatred, dare accuse the Church of having favored ignorance;"* and to enable us to understand how an English political reformer, writing to a Pope of Rome, could confess his shame at having been for fifty-two years of his life a reviler of the religion of his fathers, " of that religion which fed the poor out of the tithes and other revenues of the Church, of that religion which had inspired men with piety and generosity to erect every edifice now remaining in the country worth the trouble of walking a hundred yards to see, and had created every seminary of learning, and caused to be enacted every law, and to be framed every institution, of which England has a right to be proud."†

---

* Hurter, *History of Innocent III.*, book xxi.
† William Cobbett, *Letter to Pope Pius VIII.*, Nov. 10, 1828.

CHAPTER VI.

THE CHARGE OF PERSECUTION.

THERE is no chapter in the history of the human race which is to me so painful as that afforded by the annals of persecution. It is hard for me to recur without a feeling almost of physical faintness to the records of those stern days when men deemed the infliction of suffering upon the body an effective stimulus for quickening the conscience and a legitimate argument in compelling the assent of the understanding. I shudder as I find myself involuntarily attempting to calculate the incalculable sum of mortal agony which has been worked out in the cause, or in the name, of religion; and I turn away from the thought with a thanksgiving to Almighty God that the ages of coercion seem to have passed, or almost passed, away. Let me follow up this brief preface by three brief observations.

First, if every one of all the ancient and dreary stories which have done such gallant service in the polemics of Protestantism were just and true, they would have no place whatever among the arguments which must determine the great question of the identity of the Church. They would prove nothing against the fact that the Catholic Church in communion with the See of St. Peter is the one only Church of our Lord Jesus Christ. The doctrine of physical coercion is no part of the Catholic faith. It finds no place either in Scripture or divine tradition. If Catholics persecuted in the sixteenth century, they persecuted, not because they were

Catholics, but because they lived in the sixteenth century. In an iron age men will do hard things, and things which do not lose in horror because tested by the standards of more humane times. In one sense, it is true, the Church is, and always must be, intolerant. Truth is intolerant of falsehood. The mission of the Church is to condemn error, and to eradicate it. But the weapons of her warfare are not carnal, but spiritual; and her judgments receive their sanction, not from them that kill the body, but from Him who is able to destroy both soul and body in hell. To say, as I have seen it gravely said, that persecution has by the Church of Rome been elevated to a dogma, is ridiculous—or would be so, if it were not mournful. Men who have the face to make such an assertion as this are merely persisting in one of those imputations which Bossuet, as I have said, calls calumnious; and their persistence is only an unconscious tribute to the immutability of that divine Church which in their souls they believe to be so unchangeable that the very tempers and manners of the times through which she has passed must, so far as she is concerned, remain the same from generation to generation.

But, secondly, so far are the well-worn charges of Protestants from being deserved, that they are often either irrelevant or so exaggerated as to be essentially untrue. I say this with the less reserve because I could have used almost the same words a year ago. As a Protestant, I do not see how any man who is at the same time decently educated and fairly disposed can lay to the account of the Catholic Church such items as the Spanish atrocities in the Netherlands, the Dragonnades of the Cévennes, and the Massacre of St. Bartholomew. It would be as fair to hold the Orthodox Church of Russia responsible for all the woes of Poland, or to assert that the wrongs of Ireland are the necessary consequence of the theology of the Thirty-nine Articles. The *Te Deum* of Gregory XIII. is certainly a morsel for Protestant controversialists; but it is mere churlishness to refuse to believe that the Pope had been deceived as to the facts. "He received a hurried despatch from the French court that a murderous attempt had been made on the lives of the king and of his family, and that they had been delivered from the hands of the Huguenots, and the assassins had been punished; whereupon the Pope went to St. Peter's, and returned public thanks to God. He did not know the lamentable truth of that night."*

The Spanish Inquisition, as its name implies, was not a Catholic, but a national and local tribunal. It was an institution more political than religious, authorized, it is true, by the Pope, but solicited and maintained by the royal power, an institution devised to protect the unity of the Spanish kingdom, and founded upon the principle that heresy was a crime against the peace of society, and, as such, punishable by the civil power.† Mr. Lecky, and even Llorente himself,‡ admit that the Roman Pontiffs more than

---

* Mgr. Ségur ('*Plain Talk*'); who quotes the following from the *North British Review*, of June, 1863: "The See of Rome was imperatively called upon for immediate action before the true facts of the case could by any possibility have been really known, *if, indeed, they were not designedly concealed.*"

† Voltaire, Ranke, Guizot, Schlegel, and others, might be cited on this point.

‡ Protestants, by the bye, quote Llorente on the Spanish Inquisition with the same composure that they cite the *Provincial Letters* as proof of the morality of the Jesuits. But Llorente is evidently a very worthless authority. He was dismissed in disgrace from the secretaryship of the institution of which he afterwards became the historian. He was a traitor to his country, and a bitter enemy

once endeavored to mitigate its severities, and protested against the horrible excesses of Torquemada. And when Charles V. and Philip II. attempted to impose the tribunal upon Italian cities, the Popes encouraged the Italians in resisting the imposition.

As for the Roman court, I am not aware that the smallest proof has ever been given that its proceedings were other than mild and conservative. As Balmes well observes, "the conduct of Rome in the use which she made of the Inquisition is the best apology of Catholicity against those who attempt to stigmatize her as barbarous and sanguinary."* The records of the Roman Congregation were carried off to Paris by Napoleon, early in the present century; a French translation of a portion was made by order of the Emperor; and it was not till 1846 that the last of the plundered documents were returned to the Vatican. In 1849, the Roman archives were again pillaged; and seventy folio volumes of the Inquisition are at present in the library of Trinity College, Dublin. Nothing, however, has ever been discovered which could bring discredit upon the proceedings of the tribunal.

The publicity given to these Roman records has had the good result of disposing of the old myth of the woes of starry Galileo. An immense amount has been written on the Galileo trial within the last thirty years; and any one who will take the trouble to do a little reading will speedily convince himself that the astronomer never suffered the

---

of the Pope and the Church. And when Joseph Bonaparte put the records of the Inquisition at his disposal, he took good care to burn such as it might be inconvenient to preserve.

* *Protestantism and Catholicity Compared*, c. xxxvi.

torture, and that the *E pur si muove* is, as has been pithily said, 'un de ces mots de circonstance inventés après coup.' All that the Inquisition ever did was to tell the man of science to stick to his science, and leave the Church to take care of the interpretation of Scripture. To say that the Catholic Church ever committed itself against the Copernican system—or any other system—of astronomy, is rodomontade. Copernicus himself was a Catholic priest, for many years an honored professor in the city of Rome itself, and, in 1543, dedicated his great work, *De Revolutionibus*, to the head of the Church, Pope Paul III.*

The third remark is one which I have hesitated to make, but which I trust no generous friend will judge unfairly. It is that for a Protestant to talk loudly about toleration, and to arraign the Church of his forefathers on a charge of persecution, is, on the whole, the most naive piece of effrontery in the annals of controversey. Recrimination is not argument—nor have I found that Roman Catholics in general are in the habit of rendering railing for railing; but I am not sure that a little unpleasant truth, spoken by one who is not a Catholic, may not be of some service in checking for a moment the flow of this everlasting vituperation. I say, by one who is not a Catholic. I am not going to take upon myself the odious task of uncovering the ghastly record of that haughty Church which well deserved the taunt of the old persecuted Puritan, that she had been " planted in the blood of her mother." I am not going to furnish an

---

* In 1616, the chair of astronomy in the Pope's own university at Bologna was tendered to Kepler, a Protestant, and the ablest advocate of Copernicanism. The trial of Galileo took place in 1633. An excellent review of the case may be found in the *Catholic World*, of December, 1868, and January, 1869.

essay on the writ *De Hæretico comburendo*, nor the laws for the 'hanging and embowelling' of Papists. Let us leave all that to history.* I will merely quote a few passages on the nature of Protestant toleration in general from one who has attempted a systematic history of Persecution, and who has not hesitated to write many hard sentences against the Roman Catholic Church, as will abundantly appear in the words which I shall copy. Passing by the details of the evidence which, as the writer says, is " sufficient to show how little religious liberty is due to Protestantism considered as a dogmatic system," let us give his reflections on the bearing of that evidence.

" Catholicism," he writes, " was an ancient Church. She had gained a great part of her influence by vast services to mankind. She rested avowedly upon the principle of authority. She was defending herself against aggression and innovation. That a Church so circumstanced should endeavor to stifle in blood every aspiration towards a purer system,† was indeed a fearful crime, but it was a crime which was not altogether unnatural. She might point to the priceless blessings she had bestowed upon humanity, to the slavery she had destroyed, to the civilization she had founded, to the many generations she had led with honor to the grave. She might show how completely her doctrines were interwoven with the whole social system, how

---

* See Hallam's *Constitutional History*, Macaulay's *History*, and *Review* of Hallam, Lecky's chapter on *Persecution*, Milner's *Letters to a Prebendary*, Challoner's *Memoirs of Missionary Priests*, etc. The writ 'De Hæretico comburendo' was in force until 1677. Palmer, *On the Church*, i. 382.

† The 'purer system' referred to, be it remembered, *is not Protestantism*. That was only an '*aspiration*.'

fearful would be the convulsion if they were destroyed, and how absolutely incompatible they were with the acknowledgment of private judgment. These considerations would not make her blameless, but they would at least palliate her guilt. But what shall we say of a Church that was but a thing of yesterday, a Church that had as yet no services to show, no claims upon the gratitude of mankind, a Church that was by profession the creature of private judgment, and was in reality generated by the intrigues of a corrupt court, which, nevertheless, suppressed by force a worship that multitudes deemed necessary to their salvation, and by all her organs, and with all her energies, persecuted those who clung to the religion of their fathers? What shall we say of a religion which comprised at most but a fourth part of the Christian world, and which the first explosion of private judgment had shivered into countless sects, which was, nevertheless, so pervaded by the spirit of dogmatism that each of these sects asserted its distinctive doctrines with the same confidence, and persecuted with the same unhesitating virulence, as a Church which was venerable with the homage of more than twelve centuries? What shall we say of men who, in the name of religious liberty, deluged their land with blood, trampled on the very first principles of patriotism, calling in strangers to their assistance, and openly rejoicing in the disasters of their country, and who, when they at last attained their object, immediately established a religious tyranny as absolute as that which they had subverted? These were the attitudes which for more than a century Protestantism uniformly presented; and so strong and so general was its intolerance that for some time it may, I believe, be truly said that there were more instances of partial toleration being advocated by Roman Catholics than by orthodox

Protestants. . . . Hôpital and Lord Baltimore, the Catholic founder of Maryland, were the two first legislators who uniformly upheld religious liberty when in power; and Maryland continued the solitary refuge for the oppressed of every Christian sect, till the Puritans succeeded in subverting the Catholic rule, when they basely enacted the whole penal code against those who had so nobly and so generously received them. But among the Protestants it may, I believe, be safely affirmed, that there was no example of the consistent advocacy or practice of toleration in the sixteenth century that was not virulently and generally denounced by all sections of the clergy,* and scarcely any till the middle of the seventeenth century. . . . Nothing can be more erroneous than to represent it [persecution] as merely a weapon which was employed in a moment of conflict, or as an outburst of natural indignation, or as the unreasoning observance of an old tradition. Persecution among the early Protestants was a distinct and definite doctrine, digested into elaborate treatises, indissolubly connected with a large portion of the received theology, developed by the most enlightened and far-seeing theologians, and enforced against the most inoffensive as against the most formidable sects. It was the doctrine of the palmiest days of Protestantism. It was taught by those who are justly esteemed the greatest of its leaders. It was manifested most clearly in those classes which were most deeply imbued with its dogmatic teaching."†

---

* " Persecution is the deadly original sin of the Reformed churches, that which cools every honest man's zeal for their cause in proportion as his reading becomes more extensive."—Hallam, *Constit. Hist.* v. i. c. 2. (Note *in loc.*)

† Lecky, *Rationalism in Europe*, v. ii. pp. 57, 59, 61.

All of which may be conveniently summed up in the epigrammatic remark of D'Alembert: "Les Réformés, qui reprochent tant l'intolérance à l'Eglise Romaine, ne haissent la persécution, que quand elle les regarde,—et nullement quand ils l'exercent."

Mr. Lecky's thesis, in support of which, be it said, he writes with excellent temper as well as with rare grace of language, is that while religious toleration is in no sense due to Protestantism considered as a system of positive belief, it *is* due to the spread of that rationalistic spirit to which dogmatic Protestantism sooner or later gives place. If the exercise of private judgment is both a right and a duty, it is certainly absurd, as Mr. Lecky says, to prescribe beforehand the conclusion to which a man must arrive, and no less absurd "to denounce the spirit of impartiality and of scepticism as offensive to the Deity." While, however, I am happy to agree with Mr. Lecky in his judgment that dogmatic Protestantism is an absurdity, I venture to dissent from his opinion that the spirit of infidelity (or rationalism, if Mr. Lecky prefers) is really tolerant, much less that it is mild and merciful. Doubtless it is absurd for men who have once claimed the right of private judgment to denounce either indifferentism or incredulity; but it is by no means so unnatural that men who assert the right to believe nothing should denounce, assail, and conspire to extirpate a Church which claims to speak with divine authority, and therefore condemns with the same voice both misbelief and unbelief. And I have read the history of the last hundred and fifty years to very little purpose if it be not a fact that no persecution which that Church has ever been called to endure has been so savage, no spirit by which she has ever been threatened so truculent and pitiless, as that which has been meted out to her, and that in which she is now menaced, by the rationalists, the free-thinkers, the so-called liberals of modern Europe. At the beginning of this chapter, I intimated a doubt whether the days of proscription and violence were yet over. Perhaps some of us may live to see the doubt justified;—quod avertat Deus. However much I may think Mr. Lecky mistaken, I have no desire to witness such a practical demolition of his theory.

Meanwhile let me record my own conviction that genuine toleration is not and cannot be the offspring of that rationalistic spirit which, while it grants the liberty of doubting, has always denied the liberty of believing, but rather that it is the fruit of Christian love, of that supernatural charity which suffereth long and is kind. But Christian charity can only exist in company with Christian faith. And faith must rest upon authority. Whether, supposing a divine authority to have been created among men, it be or be not rational to believe, whether the exercise of private judgment in matters of revelation be either a duty, a right, or an act of common sense, is a question which has been suspended in these pages hitherto, but which can be deferred no longer. I shall at once address myself to its discussion. And as I am writing not for fully developed rationalists, but only for Protestants, I shall begin by assuming the fact of the Incarnation.

Before, however, leaving this subject of persecution, I cannot resist the impulse to put a question, the very asking of which (it makes me smile to think) will rouse a quick suspicion in more than one honest Protestant bosom. Dear, good reader, do not be too clever—do not probe *too* keenly. I am only going to quote from the English Bible, and leave the interpretation to your own quiet conscience. St.

Peter, as you remember, after telling us that our dear Lord "suffered for us, leaving us an example that we should follow in his steps," reminds us that, "when he was reviled, he reviled not again; when he suffered, he threatened not." And our Divine Master himself pronounced this remarkable declaration to his disciples: "Blessed are ye when men shall hate you, and when they shall separate you from their company, and shall reproach you, and cast out your name as evil, for the Son of man's sake. Rejoice ye in that day, and leap for joy; for, behold, your reward is great in heaven." Now, cast your eyes over the wide world, and back through three centuries of time, and ask yourself what Society of men has, on the whole, been most signally called to fulfil the precept of the great Apostle, and has most amply inherited the benediction of our blessed Lord and Saviour.

PART II.

THE CHURCH CONSIDERED AS A DIVINE CREATION.

CHAPTER I.

THE INCARNATION AND THE MISSION OF THE HOLY GHOST.

THE loftiest of the ancient philosophers confessed the incompetence of reason to determine spiritual truth, and looked forward, with an instinct of prophetic anticipation, to the advent of a God who might remove uncertainty by the word of divine authority.* It is time for Protestants to ask themselves whether they are any better off than Plato was. For them a God has come—and gone. *Ad superos Astræa recessit.* The Divine Word walks the earth no more; and for the ascertaining of truth it is as if he had never descended from heaven. Christianity has furnished many new and glorious ideas, so novel indeed and so beautiful that men call it a revelation. But when we come to sift the meaning of this expression, it only signifies that a new domain of speculation has been thrown open, in which the human intellect may wander up and down, and admire—and doubt. The relation of truth to reason, the appeal which it makes to the mind, is the same now as before. The reception of what are called Christian

---

* Εἰ μὴ Θεὸς ὑφηγοῖτο. Plato, *in Epinomide.* So also in the Second Alcibiades. The thought seems to run through the Phædo like an undertone; *e.g.* (§ 85), we are told that if to discover truth be impossible, yet a brave man "will take at any rate the best of human words, and that which is most irrefragable, and carried on this as on a raft sail through life in perpetual jeopardy, *unless one might make the journey on a securer vessel, some divine word, if it might be, more surely and with less peril.*"

doctrines is simply the assent of the understanding to propositions the truth of which appears probable.*

Men have what they call faith. But it is evident that this belief is only a number of opinions, more or less strong, and differing from any other intellectual judgments only in this, that they are of such a nature as to excite emotion, suggest comfort, and inspire hope. The very hope thus awakened in the mind is of a sort which shows the character of the belief from which it springs; for it is a looking anxiously forward—I am speaking, be it remembered, of Protestants—to a future state, in which present doubt shall be exchanged for knowledge, and the mists of uncertainty be dissolved in the effulgence of light. This is in effect precisely what Plato did. 'And exactly what St. Paul did,' you quickly exclaim. Ah, dear friend, how clearly, if you could only see it, this very appeal of yours shows how utterly you have failed to comprehend the nature of Catholic faith! You quote St. Paul as if he had said, 'Now I *doubt*, but then shall I *know*.' St. Paul was a Catholic, and he spoke as a Catholic. And his words were: "Now I KNOW"—I know now, and I shall know then; the assurance is the same, the *measure* of cognition alone is different; "now I know in part, but then I shall know even as I am known."

Protestant faith is an intellectual *effort*. It is a struggle to hold fast truth, the tenure of which is acknowledged to be difficult, and the precise limits of which are felt to be indeterminate. The confidence with which the mind reposes upon its belief varies; it rises and sinks; the least intellectual commotion startles it; at times it is ready to vanish

---

* As Chillingworth has not only admitted, but endeavored to prove.

away. There are moments when the mind becomes aware how purely subjective (if I may thus employ the word) is the foundation upon which it has built. It sees that both of the premises of its grand argument are expressions of opinion only, are, as such, uncertain and possibly false. Protestant theology is summed up in the following syllogism:

> All doctrines contained in Scripture are true.
> This doctrine is contained in Scripture.
> Therefore it is true.

But it is impossible for a Protestant to establish the certainty of either of the propositions upon which this conclusion rests.* And so faith becomes a kind of spiritual *strain;* men feel that they ought to believe, and are unhappy and filled with reproaches because they do not and cannot believe as they ought. They find a melancholy consolation in the theory that doubt is one of the trials—and the greatest—of our present state of probation, that it is the crowning test of Christian perseverance, a virtue which is exhibited in perfection when men who have lost all confidence shut their eyes and imagine themselves confident still, and which might therefore not inappropriately be called the triumph of hope over faith.

Protestants have hope: so had Plato, a "mighty hope," and the "prize" he looked forward to was "glorious"— καλὸν τὸ ἆθλον καὶ ἡ ἐλπὶς μεγάλη.† There is no intelli-

---

* Indeed, upon the minor premise, one-half of the Protestant world has always contradicted the other half; and as to the major, it is already extensively called in question. In other words, Protestants are rapidly ceasing to have any theology, and, therefore, any faith at all.

† *Phædo,* § 112.

gent Protestant, be he ever so devout, who, in his calmer moments, would presume to use language more strong than the words which the heathen philosopher puts into the mouth of Socrates: "To confidently affirm that [the truth] is such as I have described becomes no reasonable man. But I do think that it becomes him to believe that it is either this or like this, if at least the soul is shown to be immortal; and that it is worthy of him to face peril boldly in such a belief, for the peril is glorious; and such thoughts he ought to use as a charm to allay his own misgivings."[*] That which the faith of Plato lacked, and to which he looked forward with a lofty yearning, is precisely that in which the faith of Protestants also fails, and for which they, too, are ever vaguely longing; and that is, certainty. But certainty is of the essence of faith. Faith and doubt are contradictory terms. Protestant faith, therefore, is only something which, as I have said, goes by the name of faith. Protestants believe their own opinions. But faith is the submission of the understanding to an authority, external to ourselves, which can neither deceive nor be deceived.

If Plato had heard the word of God coming to him with power, the character of his belief would immediately have changed. Verisimilitude would have given way to absolute assurance. And this certitude would have been, not a number of conclusions deduced from premises however probable, but the reasonable and joyful assent of the understanding to the declarations of Omnipotence. He would not have stopped to question; he would not—he could not—have waited to decide whether the truths made known to him were in accord with his own tastes or antecedent

---

[*] *Ibid.* § 114.

notions of spiritual things; he would have listened and believed. Whereas, before,

> "The intellectual power through words and things
> Went sounding on, a dim and perilous way,"

now it would make haste to bow in glad submission to the utterances of a divine and therefore infallible voice.

If the Lord Jesus Christ were to come back again to *us*, in the glory of his majesty, how quickly would we cease our dogmatizing, and hush our disputings. With one accord we would exclaim, 'the Messias is come, and he will teach us all things.' Dear friend, he is here now; he is here to-day in the midst of us, radiant with the irresistible tokens of divinity, addressing us in awful tones of authority; in the person of his Church he comes and lays his hand upon you, and says, "I that speak unto thee am he."

This is not a fiction of speech. It is no bold metaphor. The Church is the voice of God, speaking to the world now as it spoke eighteen hundred years ago. The God whose possible coming was dimly conceived by the intuition of the Greek philosopher has actually come. And has the meaning of that advent ever shone in upon your mind? Have you ever apprehended, have you ever begun to apprehend, the appalling fact of the Incarnation? The infinite, eternal God brought himself within bounds; he took unto him a reasonable soul and human flesh; he suffered death as a sacrifice for the sins of the world; he created a Church, and built it upon a rock, and said, "the gates of hell shall not prevail against it;" he chose his representatives, and in words of omnipotence he invested them with their awful commission; to one of them he gave the keys of the kingdom of heaven; to all of them he said: "whatsoever you shall bind upon earth, shall be bound in heaven, and whatsoever you shall loose upon earth, shall be loosed in heaven;" he breathed upon them, saying, "receive ye the Holy Ghost: whose sins you shall forgive, they are forgiven, and whose sins you shall retain, they are retained;" he pronounced upon them those sentences of unutterable import: "as the Father hath sent me, even so send I you:" "he that receiveth you receiveth me, and he that receiveth me receiveth him that sent me:" "all power is given to me in heaven and in earth: go ye, therefore, and teach all nations, baptizing them in the name of the Father, and of the Son, and of the Holy Ghost, teaching them to observe all things whatsoever I have commanded you; and, behold, I am with you all days, even to the consummation of the world."

This is not all. The incarnate God, who thus declared that he would himself in an ineffable manner be perpetually present in the midst of his Church, announced the speedy coming of a divine Paraclete, even the eternal Spirit of God, who should descend upon his chosen ministers, and for a special purpose should abide with them for ever. This was the Spirit of Truth, and his mission was to teach all things and to guide into all truth. And on the day of Pentecost the Holy Ghost came down, took up his abode within the Church, and began his work of supernatural guidance and instruction.

Once, the facts of the Incarnation and the descent of the Holy Ghost were to me dead truths. They were doctrines, and not living facts—truth in words merely, shut up within the covers of a book.* When their real meaning first flashed

---

* 'Notional' and 'real' apprehension?

upon my apprehension, it was as if a breath from another world had swept across my soul, and stirred into action faculties of which I had never been conscious. I saw what I had not seen before; I felt the motions of new spiritual forces; my ears were opened, and I heard the mighty voice speaking to me which has been speaking in the ears of other sleepers through the long ages. The Church of God stood before me, a divine creation; sustained, not by the efforts of man, but by the hand of the Almighty; guided, not by human counsels, but by the Infinite Spirit which pervades it; indefectible, incorruptible, indivisible; knowing no lapse of time nor flux of change;—the temple of God upon earth, from whose celestial entablature the light of truth shines out upon a world of darkness and commotion, at whose ever-open gates stand the heralds who call aloud to the generations as they pass, and from within which comes the sound of many voices chanting the alleluias which echo through the ages of eternity.

The Church is the perpetuation of the Incarnation. To say that the Church had hardly been founded before it became corrupt, is to deny the reality of the Incarnation.* To say, as Luther said, "what is the use of reason if it be not that men may judge for themselves? Therefore, judge for yourselves; and, spite of popes, and councils, and canons, decide as your reason prompts you; this is Christian liberty, this is Christian wisdom," is to set aside the office of the Spirit of God. To say, as the English Reformers said, that "not only the unlearned and simple, but the learned and wise, not the people only, but the bishops,

---

* "He that is able to prevent subtractions, why must he not be able to prevent dangerous additions?"—Bossuet, *Variations*, l. xv. § 84.

not the sheep, but also the shepherds themselves, . . . being blinded by the bewitching of images, as blind guides of the blind, fell both into the pit of damnable idolatry; in the which all the world, as it were, drowned, continued until our age, by the space of above eight hundred years; . . . so that laity and clergy, learned and unlearned, all ages, sects, and degrees of men, women, and children, of whole Christendom (a horrible and most dreadful thing to think), have been at once drowned in abominable idolatry, of all other vices most detested of God and most damnable to man, and that by the space of eight hundred years and more,"*—is to utter words against the divinity of the Holy Ghost the very reading of which excites a shudder.

On the other hand, reason assures me that a divinely instituted society supposes infallibility.† When, therefore, the Catholic Church addresses me, and says that her words are the words of God, speaking not once but always; when she proclaims that her saints and fathers are not her teachers, but her children and her pupils;‡ when she declares that her doctrines are the truth, in the unerring enunciation of which she has been guided by the Holy Ghost; the call is such as reason has led me to anticipate. When men assail the Church because of her lofty claims; when they say that her attitude is one of towering and imperious presumption; when they characterize her as exclusive, and stigmatize her demands as stern and peremptory; when they complain

---

* *Homily against Peril of Idolatry*, part iii.

† Malebranche, quoted by De Maistre.

‡ " The only Father in whom, it is said, the Church has noted no error, is St. Gregory of Nazianzum. The Church can freely criticise the works of its own disciples ; for, while they may err, it cannot."—Manning, *Temporal Mission*, p. 208.

that she will make no concession nor compromise, that she will not give up one iota of dogma for the sake of peace and reunion—I see in this the tribute which the self-will of fallible man pays to the inerrancy of the interpreter of the will of God. If the Church be divine, this *must* be her aspect, such must be the tone in which she speaks. To submit is to obey, not man, but God.

"The Church," says St. Chrysostom, "is more firmly fixed than heaven itself. Perhaps some Greek charges me with madness; but let him wait for the truth of the matter, and learn the force of the truth that it is easier that the sun should be extinguished than that the Church should be obscured. Who is it, he asks, that proclaims this? He who has founded her. 'Heaven and earth shall pass away, but my words shall not pass away.'"* The Church is still fixed and shining; and through all these years of my life I had not seen it! Alas, my blindness! It has been like that of the wretched owlet of the English poet, which,

> "Sailing on obscene wings athwart the noon,
> Drops his blue fringed lids, and holds them close,
> And hooting at the glorious sun in heaven,
> Cries out, 'Where is it?'"

Pope Pius IX., in a letter to the Archbishop of Munich, has condemned the irrational procedure of those who, *ad-*

---

* *Hom. in illud vidi Dominum*, iv. 2. Contrast with this passage the language of the Continental Reformers, in their letter already referred to, giving license to the Landgrave Philip to commit bigamy: "Your Highness sees that our poor, little, miserable Church is feeble and abandoned, and in need of virtuous princes to protect her." "Prout Celsitudo vestra videt, paupercula et misera Ecclesia est exigua et derelicta, indigens probis Dominis Regentibus"!

mitting the fact of a divine revelation, make the ineffable truths proposed by that divine revelation subject-matter for the decisions of their private judgment.* This has been the utterance of the Catholic Church ever since the first assertion of that vaunted principle which is the common foundation of *all* the reformed churches. The right of private judgment in matters of revelation is, in the end, the sole dogma of Protestantism—and a more irrational one cannot be found in the history of the human intellect. The Catholic is logical; he is convinced that God has spoken, and he believes without question or reservation. The infidel is at least consistent; he refuses to believe that God has spoken. But the Protestant, who admits that God has spoken, and then proceeds to make up his mind how far it will be reasonable to believe what God has said, is inconsistent, illogical, and guilty of a presumption which is as perilous as it is absurd.

Thank God that I have come at last to understand the meaning of that watchword of the true Catholic, 'Credo ut intelligam.' "Understand my words," says St. Augustine, "that you may believe them, but believe the word of God that you may understand it"—" Intellige ut credas verbum meum, sed crede ut intelligas verbum Dei." O sublime harmony of reason and faith! In human things, understanding comes first and belief afterwards. But when God speaks, he speaks with authority; and as soon as reason

---

* "— recentem illam ac præposteram philosophandi rationem, quæ etiamsi divinam revelationem veluti historicum factum admittat, tamen ineffabiles veritates ab ipsa divina revelatione propositas humanæ rationis investigationibus supponit." The entire passage is given in a note by Archbishop Manning, *Temporal Mission*, p. 124.

recognizes the voice of God, faith comes—faith first—and comprehension follows. I bow, I tremble, I believe; then, like a little child, I begin to learn the wondrous lessons of the Church at the feet of my divine instructress; and one by one the eternal truths of God break radiantly upon my entranced conception. I do not stop before the shining temple to ask what pictures hang upon its walls, or what jewels glisten on its altar; I enter there, and worship.

CHAPTER II.

INFALLIBILITY.

F there be a Church of God upon earth, that Church, as we have seen, must be supernaturally protected against error. If the Church has ever gone astray, if it can *possibly* depart from the truth, it does not cease to be divine—which is an absurdity—but it never was divine. Those who assert the fallibility of the Church must end by denying the facts of the Incarnation and the descent of the Holy Ghost. Sooner or later all Protestants must come to look upon these primary truths of the Church as those remorselessly logical Germans already do—merely as beautiful myths in the great poem of Christianity. On the other hand, those who admit the existence of a Church founded and sustained by Almighty power, must, if they would escape inconsistency, acknowledge that it can never lose or be in doubt about the truth which it has always possessed. But there can be only one infallible Church. And there is only one Church which claims infallibility.

The assertion of such a claim puts instantly an infinite distance between the Church which makes it and all other institutions whatsoever. A society which admits its fallibility confesses itself human; an organization which assumes its own inerrancy claims to be divine. Claims, did I say? The very fact of such a claim is proof of its validity. No human society would dare to put forth such a pretension. No human voice could sustain such a tone without faltering. But look at the Catholic Church. Her attitude is the most astounding thing in history. Has she ever flinched, or been irresolute? Has she ever forgotten herself? Never for an instant. There has been no tremor in her voice; through the long centuries it has sounded like a ceaseless roll of thunder.* She came forth from God, and her supernatural consciousness has never failed her. She has carried herself with the lofty instinct of divinity. Vera incessu patuit dea!

It is passing strange to me that I did not sooner see that infallibility is of the very essence of the Church, and how those who attempt to get rid of it, and to conceive of a fallible divine Church, are inevitably involved in hopeless contradictions. Let us go back to the beginning of the sixteenth century. Either there was a Church of God then in the world, or there was not. If there was not, then the Reformers certainly could not create such a Church. If there was, they as certainly had neither the right to abandon it nor the power to remodel it.† The Reformers admitted the existence of such a Church; in the Apostolic symbol they daily made an act of faith in the Holy Ghost and the Holy Catholic Church. And yet they proclaimed that the Church which they professed to believe, instead of being by the Holy Ghost preserved from error, had become foul with falsehood and deadly contagion. Their action belied

---

* 'Videor mihi non verba sed tonitrua audire.'—St. Jerome (spoken of St. Paul).

† St. Augustine put the same dilemma to the would-be reformers of his day: " Quod si erat etiam tunc Ecclesia, et hæreditas Christi non, interrupta, perierat, sed per omnes gentes augmenta accipiens permanebat, tutissima ratio est in eadem consuetudine permanere quæ tunc bonos et malos in una complexione portabat. Si autem tunc non erat Ecclesia, quia sacrilegi hæretici sine baptismo recipiebantur, et hoc universali consuetudine tenebatur; unde Donatus apparuit? de qua terra germinavit? de quo mari emersit? de quo cœlo cecidit?"—*De Bapt. cont. Donat.* l. iii. c. 2.

their profession. They did not really believe either in the Holy Ghost or the Holy Catholic Church.

Well, as they could not have their way with the old Church, they went forth and founded a new one—a hundred new and improved churches. And having set up their churches, they furnished them each with well-digested and elaborate confessions of faith. The new churches and articles were based upon the assumed failure and corruption of the old. But the fact of such a failure would have rendered all churches henceforth impossible, and all creeds for ever worthless. Of what value to me is the teaching of a Church which approaches me with words such as these: 'My child, I admit frankly that I may be mistaken. God forbid that I should arrogate to myself what it would be impious madness for a human institution to assert. The Church of Rome has erred. All churches have erred. To err is human. Nevertheless, I represent to you in some way the visible Church. And, somehow or other, I have authority in controversies of faith. Here are my Articles of Religion. You may interpret them, I am happy to say, in any way you please; for they are rather articles of peace than articles of faith; I do not oblige you to believe them, but only not to contradict them. They are supposed to be in accordance with God's Word written, which is also supposed to contain all necessary truth—although I can give no reason for supposing so. If, however, you should be convinced of a discrepancy, you are not only at liberty, but it will be your bounden duty utterly to repudiate them. In which event, nevertheless, it will be *my* painful duty—theoretically, at least—to eject you from my communion'?*

---

* See XXXIX. Articles; Arts. VI., XIX., XX. Also, Arch-

This is rather mournful than amusing. When, however, a Church which confesses itself fallible undertakes to arraign one which claims infallibility, the case becomes purely ludicrous. The Church of Rome says: 'I come from God, and God is ever with me; and therefore I speak with authority.' The Church of England answers: 'I make no such preposterous pretension. I have nowhere been so indiscreet as to give the slightest intimation that I either came from God, or that God is with me. I am fallible. And I stake my reputation for fallibility on the assertion that the Church of Rome has erred.'*

> Eheu,
> Quam temere in nosmet legem sancimus iniquam!

But the crowning absurdity is yet to come. In the new bishop Bramhall, *Schism Guarded*, p. 190. De Maistre's sentence on the Anglican Articles is famous: "The Anglican Church is the only association in the world which has declared itself null and ridiculous by the very act which constitutes it. . . . The Anglican Church declares to her children that she is, indeed, entitled to command them, but that they are equally entitled to refuse her their obedience. At the same moment, with the same pen and ink, on the same paper, she enunciates dogma, and declares she has no right to do so. I think I may be allowed to entertain the conviction that, of the interminable catalogue of human follies, this is one which will always hold a distinguished rank."—*Du Pape*, l. iv. ch. xi. § 5.

* Mr. Palmer, of Worcester College, one of the most scholarly as well as conservative of modern Anglicans, seems to have felt the awkwardness of this assertion on the part of the Church of England, and explains it thus: "The article only affirms that the Roman Church *has erred* in matters of faith, *e.g.*, in the case of Liberius and Honorius; there is no assertion that it *does* now err in faith."—*On the Church*, vol. i. p. 242. Bravo! This is exquisite! So even the XXXIX. Articles do not deny that the Church of Rome may have been infallible *in the long run!*

confessions of faith it was necessary to give some definition of that without which no confession would be possible—the Church. Let us see whether our clever Reformers were able to get over the difficulty without compromising themselves. The Thirty-nine Articles give two notes as of the essence of the Church, viz.: the pure preaching of the Word, and the due administration of the Sacraments according to Christ's ordinance. The Augsburg Confession (a more respectable manifesto, by the way) gives the same characteristics, and adds that the Church is one, holy, and indefectible.* The confessions of all the Protestant churches unite upon these same two essentials of the visible Church. In the true Church the pure faith is preserved, and the sacraments are rightly administered. If otherwise, the Church does not answer its definition; it has failed in its very essence. But a definition which was good in 1550 was good in 1500. The true Church was then in existence, otherwise the nascent Reformers must give the lie to their profession of belief in the Holy Catholic Church; and in this true Church, because it *was* the Church, the pure faith was necessarily preserved, and the sacraments were rightly administered. There is no escape from this. The fact is, that in conceiving of the Church it is impossible really to eliminate the notion of infallibility. It lurks—nay, it stares us in the face—in the very confessions of the Protestant churches. The definition of the Reformers will for ever remain a monument of their folly, and a memorable vindi-

---

* " Item docent, quod una sancta ecclesia perpetuo mansura sit. Est autem ecclesia congregatio sanctorum in qua evangelium recte docetur, et recte administrantur sacramenta."—*Confess. August.* Art. VII.

cation of the infallible Church against whose teaching they presumptuously rebelled, and whose holy sacraments they wantonly mutilated.

But we do not need to go back three hundred years in order to discover in what a tangle of perplexities men find themselves when they profess to believe in the Church, and yet deny its infallibility. There is a singular instance close at hand—and a very interesting one I, at least, have found it. It was impossible that, as a Protestant, feeling my way towards the Catholic Church, my attention should not have been attracted by the recent and somewhat notorious letter of Mr. Ffoulkes to the Archbishop of Westminster. Here was a case, not of a Protestant arguing against Catholicism, but of a man who professed to be a Catholic accusing his own Church, and that in a tone which a Protestant might envy. Well, I read Mr. Ffoulkes's letter; and found it a melancholy exhibition of the assertion of personal infallibility as against the infallibility of the Church. It was bad enough for the Reformers to leave the Church because they thought she had erred; but when a man turns Catholic, not because he submits to the Church's divine authority, but because for some inscrutable reason he takes a fancy to, he does an irrational thing, which very naturally results in a conspicuous and mortifying blunder.

Addressing the Archbishop, Mr. Ffoulkes says: "Your argument, I presume, would be that the Church of Rome claims to be infallible; that you submitted yourselves to it as such, in the fullest confidence that its decisions can never mislead you; that they are God's voice speaking to you, which you are bound at the peril of your salvation never to mistrust, much less dispute. I joined the Roman Communion on other grounds, and was accepted."* What the "other grounds" were I have been at a loss to discover; but it matters not; Mr. Ffoulkes entered the Roman Catholic Church without in his heart submitting to her infallible authority. At the same time he was perfectly aware of her claim to possess such authority. In the sentence immediately following that just quoted, he says: "Practically, no doubt, the Church of Rome claims to be infallible;" and later, he admits, without any reservation, that, on questions both of Faith and Morals, "Rome claims to be infallible."† Of the honesty of this procedure I have nothing to say; we are only concerned with its logical consequences.

Mr. Ffoulkes, finding himself safe inside the infallible Church in undisturbed possession of his private opinion on questions both of faith and morals, proceeds to apply his measuring-rod. Perhaps he will believe the infallibility of Rome, after all, if he finds it to coincide with his own. "I said to myself," says he, "if she is really infallible, she can stand much more searching criticism than the [church] which I am leaving for her sake, on behalf of which no such claim has ever been made:" "I felt that if I found the claims of the Church of Rome to be thoroughly in accordance with facts, I should ever afterwards regard her with tenfold reverence from having verified them myself."‡ (It is really hard to copy these sentences without a smile.) Mr. Ffoulkes has his own notions about Reunion and the Filioque, and the Athanasian Creed; and, after a "dozen years or more" of constant study, he comes to the conclu-

---

* *The Church's Creed, or the Crown's Creed? A Letter*, etc. (New York, Pott & Amery), p. 4.
† *Ibid.* p. 32.   ‡ *Ibid.* p. 5.

sion that Rome does not by any means agree with him on these points, so he turns and rails on her in good set terms: "Therefore, my Lord, with the facts of this controversy before me, I find this conclusion inevitable: that, whether absolutely inerrant or not in matters of faith herself, Rome has abundantly proved, during the last 1,000 years, that she can be a most negligent, hesitating, fickle, self-seeking, hypocritical guide to others, even where the faith is concerned."* He knew at the outset that Rome professed to teach and not to be taught; and because she persists in her unreasonable attitude, notwithstanding the lessons he has read her, he exclaims, in a tone of querulous disappointment: "Rome has spoken; but I can discover nothing in what she has said like a confession of sins, or of the justice of God in punishing them—expressions of regret for the past, or promises of amendment in future. All Christendom has gone astray save she. Of all institutions, the Popedom alone stands erect; has never erred on any subject whatever; has never been otherwise than what it is now; has preserved its integrity, as well as its faith, unsullied." † What a blessed thing, to be sure, it would be for us all if Rome would only confess that she too had gone astray! We would all be then in the same boat. There would then be no uncomfortable authority perpetually staring our pride in the face. And we would have the unspeakable satisfaction of knowing that in all the world there was no more truth, no certainty, and no means of recovering what we had for ever lost. Thank God, that, though "all Christendom has gone astray," the "Popedom" still "stands erect"! Thanks be to his eternal mercy, that there is one Church at least which, after

---

* *Ibid.* pp. 26, 27. † *Ibid.* p. 80.

all our wanderings and failures, can still turn to us and say that as our divinely guided Teacher she " has never erred on any subject whatever, has never been otherwise than what she now is, has preserved her integrity as well as her faith unsullied." *

---

* It is evident that Mr. Ffoulkes is not the only man who has entered the Roman Catholic Church "on other grounds" than because she claims obedience, and who has discovered too late that she is really in earnest in making the claim, and arrogant enough to insist upon it. Witness the following paragraph from the 'Installation Address' of the newly appointed Dean of the General Theological Seminary of the Protestant Episcopal Church : " But the most serious charge we have to bring against this body (the Church of Rome) is the way in which she treats her own children. SHE DEMANDS OF THEM A BLIND OBEDIENCE, A SLAVISH SUBMISSION. This with her is the one great virtue. If you possess this, anything may be forgiven you ; if you fail in this, not angelic virtues will save you. And this rule prevails in her monasteries alike and convents, among her priesthood, in her councils, everywhere. The more perfectly you would become her dutiful child, the more thoroughly you must unman yourself; reason, conscience, will, judgment, all must submit ; the holiest affections must be sacrificed, the most sacred ties be disregarded—and all for what ?—to become a perfect Christian after the model of Rome !"

And yet, a moment later, the Dean turns round to the young gentlemen committed to his pastoral care, and says : " You are now preparing yourselves to become ministers of Christ's Church. Begin then early to pursue the road which the Church dictates. YOU MUST NO LONGER THINK YOUR OWN THOUGHTS, OR FORM YOUR OWN PLANS, BUT LEARN WHAT THE CHURCH TEACHES, AND OBEY WHAT SHE COMMANDS. You may think that at some time something is left in that Church undone which should be done, something done which should be left undone ; but you should know also that it belongs not to *you* to remedy or supply the deficiency. You know that God, under whose especial guidance we believe the Church to be, may indeed permit evil for a time ; but his good Spirit will rectify what is wrong, and supply what is wanting, *in the appointed way,* and in due season. Your one aim, therefore,

Infallibility.   129

Heresy is only the practical denial of infallibility. It is the choosing one's own faith, instead of receiving without reservation the faith of the Church. Heresy may exist

> should be to understand fully what the spirit of the Church is, and your one duty to fulfil it. If any of you are about to become the ministers of God thoughtlessly, and with indifference to your profession, or if any of you are about to become such without duly considering the sacrifice of *self-will* it involves, be persuaded to renounce your intention."—*Church Journal,* March 2, 1870.

To a simple-minded reader it might perhaps seem as if nothing but infatuation could have put two such passages upon the same sheet of paper. A logical but doubtless too hasty reader, on the other hand, might infer that the Dean, speaking from personal experience, means to say that the Church of Rome, being fallible and void of divine authority, has no right to make perfect Christians after her model ; whereas the Protestant Episcopal Church, being infallibly directed by the Holy Spirit, has the highest right to control the thoughts, words, and actions of her children. But the reader who has formed some acquaintance with the beautiful elasticity of Anglican theology is able to do the Dean better justice. The Church of Rome teaches in only one way, and allows her children no *choice ;* therefore she is a tyrant. But the Protestant Episcopal Church is 'Catholic' enough to teach in a hundred different ways, and liberal enough to offer them all alike for our acceptance ; so that when she seems to command she is really inviting us, as it were, to a goodly feast, where viands have been spread which cannot fail to meet the eccentricities of the most fastidious palate. Happy students of the General Theological Seminary ! You are indeed no longer to think your own thoughts ; you are to learn what the Church teaches, and obey what she commands. But know that the thoughts of your Church are, by the provision of a munificent Providence, exactly as multifarious as your own ; and her commands, by the same bountiful forethought, tally to a marvel with your individual preferences. Your profession involves, it is true, a sacrifice of self-will, so complete, indeed, that if you have not duly considered it, you had better relinquish your sacerdotal intentions ; but remember that the sacrifice consists in obediently acknowledging the *laisser faire* of Protestant Episcopal theology. *This* is the spirit of your Church, which you

within the Church, but it is not of the Church; and by and by, if the error attains such strength as to be dangerous, the Church takes note of it, and casts it out. Each time that the Church thus expels falsehood, she renders the statement of her own faith more precise. For the condemnation of an error is also the assertion of a truth. And as the Church proscribes one false opinion after another, by a natural process she gives definite expression to doctrine which before was believed, indeed, but believed implicitly; and thus faith assumes articulate form in the dogmas of a creed. The definition of dogma is an exercise of infallibility. Development is not the creation of truth, but the systematic evolution of its formula.*

must make it your one aim fully to understand. And your one duty towards her will be best fulfilled by availing yourselves without scruple of the generous accommodations which she offers. For you have been told, only five minutes ago, that, " on the broad platform which she presents, the High Churchman and the Low Churchman, the Broad Churchman (if he be represented by men like Dr. Arnold and Dean Stanley), the Ritualist (if he will but confine himself within her limits, and not seek covertly to change her doctrines and her usages), may stand and feel himself at home."

I would most gladly have avoided even this marginal reference to events which are too near home to be touched upon without exciting bitterness. I have no wish to plant more thorns in my path than will grow there without my sowing. But the prominence that has recently been given to testimony which will have an adventitious influence on the *experto crede Ruperto* principle, has challenged at least a passing comment upon an inconsistency, compared with which the vagaries of Mr. Ffoulkes seem, for a moment, to have all the rigidity of logic.

* " The dogma of the Trinity was not perfectly brought out till the Arians declaimed against it ; nor was penance, until attacked by the Novatians ; nor the efficacy of baptism, until questioned by rebaptizers. Nay, what regarded the unity of the body of Jesus Christ was not discussed with minute exactness until the weak,

Truth is immutable, but error is never fixed. Thus variation becomes a mark of heresy, and has been so noted from the first. "There are heretics everywhere," writes St. Augustine, "but not the same heretics everywhere. For there is one sort in Africa, another sort in the East, a third sort in Egypt, and a fourth sort in Mesopotamia, being different in different countries, though all produced by the same mother, namely, pride. Thus also the faithful are all born of one common mother, the Catholic Church; but though they are everywhere dispersed, they are everywhere the same."* "Heresy," says Tertullian, "never changes its proper nature in never ceasing to innovate; and the progress of the thing is like to its origin. What is permitted to Valentinus is allowed to the Valentinians; the Marcionites have equal power with Marcion; nor have the authors of a heresy more right to innovate than their disciples. Everything changes in heresy; and, when examined to the bottom, it is found in course of time entirely different in many points from what it was at its birth." † But so often as the Church speaks—be it in the fourth century or in the nineteenth—she speaks once for all. Guided by divine intuition, she knows when to give her judgment, and how much she needs to say; and she pronounces her decree with a precision

being exposed to danger, . . . compelled the teachers of truth to examine these truths to the bottom. . . . Thus the errors of heresy, instead of injuring the Catholic Church, have really fortified it; and those who thought wrong were an occasion of ascertaining those who thought right. What had been but piously believed became afterwards fully understood."—St. Augustine, quoted by Dr. Ives.

* *Lib. de Pact.* c. 8.
† *De Præter.* c. 42. The words of Pius IX., in the Letter of September 13, 1868, are very similar.

which admits of no evasion and a peremptoriness against which there is no appeal. For heretics to wait until the Catholic Church shall rescind or modify her decisions upon the faith is madness. As soon could the hand of man tear from the vault of heaven a star which Almighty power has suspended there, as pluck from its place a single truth which the Spirit of God has set to shine for ever in the Church's everlasting creed.

The assertion of infallibility is—as has been abundantly implied—a note of the true Church. The Church which claims now to be supernaturally directed must be identical with that which from the beginning knew itself to be the mouth-piece of the Holy Ghost. Do we need any assurance that the Catholic Church *has* always believed herself divinely guided? Is it possible that we can amuse ourselves with the notion that, because men began a few centuries ago to *talk* about infallibility, the Church then first discovered herself to be infallible? We might as well say that she awoke to her faith in the divinity of the Son of God when Arius began to discuss his eternal generation. Why! as a distinguished English convert has well said, " not a Council which ever sat, not a Father who ever wrote, not a martyr who ever suffered, but believed in a perpetual illuminating grace of the Holy Spirit dwelling in the Church of God to the end of time. Without it Councils and Fathers would not have existed, and still less martyrs."* Could the Bishop of Orleans—or of Westminster, speak more strongly in the nineteenth century than did the Bishop of Lyons in the second? "We guard the faith," writes St. Irenæus, "which we have received from the Church, and which proceeds

---

* Allies, *See of Peter*, p. 163.

perpetually from the Holy Spirit, as though it were some precious deposit, in an excellent vessel, which can renew itself, and can make new the vessel which contains it. For this is the office committed to the Church of God, that it should, as it were, breathe inspiration into his creatures, so that all its members should receive the gift and live. And here lies the principle of our communication with Christ, that is, the Holy Spirit, the pledge of incorruption; . . . of which Spirit they are not partakers who do not betake themselves to the Church, but defraud themselves of life by ill-thinking and worse deeds. For where the Church is, there is the Spirit of God, and where the Spirit of God, there is the Church and all grace; and the Spirit is truth."* So possessed were the Fathers with the belief in the perpetual preservation of the Church from error, that they saw a reference to that truth in the most incidental events of our Lord's life on earth. Thus St. Ignatius, the contemporary of the Apostles, speaking of the precious ointment, says: "On this account our Lord received the myrrh upon his head, that he might infuse into his Church incorruptibility." †

And what the Fathers believed of the Church, the Church proclaimed of herself. The key-note of all the Councils of the Catholic Church was struck at the Apostolic Council of Jerusalem, when the decree was sent to Antioch sealed with the sentence: "It hath seemed good to the Holy Ghost and to us." When the 318 Fathers of Nicæa drew up the first œcumenical Creed of the Church, they gave it sanction in the memorable words: "And for them that say concerning the Son of God, There was a time when he

---

* *Adv. Hæres.* l. iii. c. 24.
† *Ad. Ephes.* xvii. Ἵνα πνέῃ τῇ ἐκκλησίᾳ ἀφθαρσίαν.

was not; and, He was not before he was produced; and, He was produced from things that are not; and, He is of another substance or essence; or that the Son of God is subject to conversion or mutation; the Catholic and Apostolic Church saith, Let them be anathema." No hand but one nerved with power from heaven could hurl such a thunderbolt as that. Well might the great St. Athanasius, when writing to the African bishops, say of the Council in whose human deliberations he had played so conspicuous a part: "The Word of the Lord which was given in the Œcumenical Council of Nicæa remaineth for ever." *

When we come down to the great Council of the sixteenth century, in which more than in any other Protestants are interested, we are arrested immediately by the same tone of superhuman authority which startled us at the beginning. It is a tone which cannot be counterfeited, which no merely human assembly has ever dared to imitate. The Council opens its decrees in every Session with the preface: "The sacred and holy, œcumenical and general Synod of Trent, lawfully assembled in the Holy Ghost." Over and over

---

* *Verbum Dei per Œcumenicam Synodum Nicænam manet in æternum.* Bishop Bull undoubtedly asserted the infallibility of the Nicene Council (*Defensio Fidei Nicænæ*, pp. 3, 4). When pressed by Bossuet with the logical consequences of his admission, he replied by a letter on the *Corruptions of the Church of Rome*, in which he managed to say as many hard things as could well be put into into a few pages. But the great Bishop of Meaux only answered: "May the blessing of God light on the learned Doctor Bull! and, in recompense of this sincere acknowledgment, and withal of that zeal he has shown in defence of Jesus Christ's divinity, may he be delivered from the prejudices which prevent him from opening his eyes to the lights of the Catholic Church, and to the necessary consequences of that truth he has confessed."—*Hist. of the Variations*, etc., l. xv. § 103.

again are these words repeated;—and others like them: "assembled, not without the special guidance and governance of the Holy Ghost;" "not confiding in human strength, but relying on the succor and assistance of our Lord Jesus Christ, who has promised that he would give to his Church a mouth and wisdom." And then come the great Canons.

"If any one saith, that man may be justified before God by his own works, whether done through the teaching of human nature, or that of the law, without the grace of God through Jesus Christ; let him be anathema.

"If any one saith, that the grace of God through Jesus Christ is given only for this, that man may be able more easily to live justly, and to merit eternal life, as if by free will without grace he were able to do both, though hardly indeed and with difficulty; let him be anathema.

"If any one saith, that without the prevenient inspiration of the Holy Ghost, and without his help, man can believe, hope, love, or be penitent as he ought, so as that the grace of Justification may be bestowed upon him; let him be anathema.

"If any one saith, that man's free-will moved and excited by God, by assenting to God exciting and calling, nowise co-operates towards disposing and preparing itself for obtaining the grace of Justification; that it cannot refuse its consent, if it would, but that, as something inanimate, it does nothing whatever and is merely passive; let him be anathema."*

One after another they follow in stately order, page after page of resistless, of divinely sanctioned legislation. At every sweep of that majestic scythe a fresh growth of noxious

---

* Session VI. Canons I.–IV.

error falls. Socinian, Calvinistic, Lutheran, Anabaptist, Anglican—ah! my little garden of weeds, too, has been laid low. And I—yes! I am glad to see them go. O mighty Church! O Bride of Christ! I come to thee. To thee I bow. Take me; teach me; lead me by the hand; and let me never wander more.

What the Council of Nice was to the Arians, and of Ephesus to the Nestorians, and of Chalcedon to the Eutychians, that the Synod of Trent is to Protestants of every name. And when Protestants declaim against the Council which condemned them, they only follow the example of their predecessors in rebellion. Their abuse is no proof that the Council was null and void, but an excellent sign that they themselves are condemned heretics. Anglicans distinguish oracularly between doctrines which are 'Tridentine' and doctrines which are 'Catholic.' At the Council of Trent, they say, the Roman Church committed herself to heresy and innovation. "The assembly at Trent," says Bishop Bull, "is to be called by any other name rather than that of a General Council."* He calls a Roman Catholic a "miserable Trent Papist."† He speaks of the "egregious prevarication of the Trent Fathers;" and declares that in following " the pattern, forsooth, of the ancient Fathers and Councils," they "have imitated them not half so well as an ape doth a man."‡ Barrow says that the Synod of Trent was called "to settle a raff of errors and superstitions." § He announces that "the Pope with his pack of mercenary clients at Trent did indeed establish a scholasti-

---

* *Defensio Fidei Nicanæ*, p. 12.
† *Vindication of the Church of England*, ch. xxx.
‡ *Ibid.*
§ *Discourse concerning the Unity of the Church.*

cal or sophistical, rather than a Christian theology."* The doctrines defined by the Council, according to this astute theologian, "were before disputed by wise men, and will ever be disputed by those who freely use their judgment!" † In short, "there was no need of defining many of them!" ‡ What need, cries the Arian, of defining that the Son is of one substance with the Father! What need, echoes the Nestorian, of defining that the Virgin Mary is Mother of God! §

But it is time to turn away from all this outcry and tirade, and to listen to the Church herself, as by the mouth of this same Council she addresses us: "Forasmuch as this said holy Synod heartily desires, and earnestly beseeches

---

* *Supremacy*, conclusion. † *Ibid.* ‡ *Ibid.*

§ It may be not without interest to read the opinion, not of a 'heated theologian,' but of a philosophic historian upon the character of the Council of Trent. "No general Council," says Hallam, "ever contained so many persons of eminent learning and ability as that of Trent; nor is there ground for believing that any other ever investigated the questions before it with so much patience, acuteness, temper, and desire of truth. The early councils, unless they are greatly belied, would not bear comparison in these characteristics. Impartiality and freedom from prejudice no Protestant will attribute to the fathers of Trent; but where will he produce these qualities in an ecclesiastical synod? But it may be said that they had only one leading prejudice—that of determining theological faith according to the tradition of the Catholic Church, as handed down to their age. This one point of authority conceded, I am not aware that they can be proved to have decided wrong, or, at least, against all reasonable evidence. Let those who have imbibed a different opinion ask themselves whether they have read Sarpi through with any attention, especially as to those sessions of the Tridentine Council which preceded its suspension in 1549."— *Literature of Europe*, part ii. ch. 2, § 18, note. This, too, though Sarpi (as Hallam frankly allows) was the enemy and detractor of the Council whose history he wrote.

God for the things that are for the peace of the Church, that we all, acknowledging our common mother on earth, who cannot forget the sons of her womb, with one mouth may glorify God and the Father of our Lord Jesus Christ; It invites and exhorts, by the bowels of the mercy of our same God and Lord, all who hold not communion with us, unto concord and reconciliation, and to come unto this holy Synod; to embrace charity, which is the bond of perfection, and to show forth the peace of Christ rejoicing in their hearts, whereunto they are called, in one body. Wherefore, in hearing this voice, not of man, but of the Holy Ghost, let them not harden their hearts, but, walking not after their own sense, nor pleasing themselves, let them be moved and converted by this so charitable and salutary an admonition of their own mother; for, as the holy Synod invites, so will It embrace them with all proofs of love." *

Can we resist any longer the transcendent pathos of this appeal? Shall we still dare to stop our ears to a voice which is "not of man, but of the Holy Ghost"?

* Session XVIII. Decree of Invitation.

CHAPTER III.

THE APPEAL TO SCRIPTURE.

PROTESTANTS in general appeal from the voice of the living Church to the written text of Scripture. In doing so, they of course deny that there is now in the world any visible divinely established tribunal to whose authority they are bound to submit their own opinions in matters of faith. A more suicidal proceeding on the part of men who desire to know and do the will of God could not be conceived.

Good friend, let me entreat you to ask yourself a few questions. Who told *you* that the Bible is the Word of God? Who told Cranmer and Ridley that "Holy Scripture containeth all things necessary to salvation; so that whatever is not read therein, nor may be proved thereby, is not to be required of any man, that it should be believed as an article of the Faith"? And how am I to know whether Cranmer's notions, or somebody else's notions—or, shall I say, my own notions—as to what Scripture does or does not teach, are correct? Let us try to meet these three questions fairly. We are going to discuss, 1. The Inspiration of Scripture; 2. The Sufficiency of Scripture; and, 3. The Interpretation of Scripture.

I. Who told you, then, that the various writings which you now have in your possession, bound together in one volume, and published by the American Bible Society, are the inspired Word of God, supernaturally free from error, written from cover to cover under the immediate guidance of the Holy Ghost? Nobody—but some poor, fallible mortal, whose opinion is worth exactly as much as your own. You have been taught so; and you believe what you have been taught. And you do so blindly, without being able to give a satisfactory, or even intelligible account of your belief. Your own heart is witness to this; for—if you have done any thinking at all—there have been moments when you have been frightened by a sudden doubt as to the security of your foundation. The crust beneath your feet has opened for an instant, and you have gazed down into the blackness of vacancy. You have hurried away; you have smothered your doubt, and quickly hushed your fear; you have said to yourself, ' the Bible *must* be inspired, for, if there be any uncertainty about that, my peace is fled.' Your hope, then, is based upon your faith, and your faith reposes upon the fact of inspiration; but the fact of inspiration is supported by—what? Your little world, like the Hindoo's, rests upon the elephant, and the elephant rests upon the tortoise, and the tortoise rests upon nothing.

But perhaps you may say that you are convinced of the inspiration of Scripture by your own study of Scripture; that it has borne evidence to its own inspiration by its action upon your life and character. This is only saying that your faith rests upon inspiration, and inspiration is proved by your faith. If you will look again, you will doubtless see that you *began* by making an act of faith in inspiration, and that the reflex influence of which you speak is subsequent to that act. Besides, call your belief by whatever name you choose—conviction, assurance, experience—it is only your *own* faith after all; and however comforting it may be to you, it is absolutely worthless to any one else. Men will not accept inspiration on your authority. The fact of inspiration is a supernatural fact, a divine fact, and can only be attested by a divine witness, which you certainly are not. As for saying that the Scriptures prove their own inspiration, you will never be able to convince the world of that. The Scriptures do not propose themselves. And men cannot know them to be divine until they have been told so, and told so by a messenger from God himself.

Pardon me, also, for saying that you cannot be supposed to understand the force of your own assertion. Do you mean to say that your private investigation has convinced you, beyond the possibility of doubting, that the Letters of St. James and St. Jude were written under the dictation of the Spirit of God, while those of St. Barnabas and St. Clement are ordinary human compositions? And can you look back through your life, and trace the visible and unmistakable effects which have followed the divine teachings of the book of Esther, or Leviticus, or the Canticle of Canticles? The Bible is not one book, but many, composed in different tongues, among divers peoples, and by writers who were separated by long centuries of time. Who gathered together into one these scattered and multiform scriptures? Who set them apart from all other writings whatsoever? Who placed the seal of a divine authority upon them, and proclaimed to the world, and for all time, that they—they all, and all alike, and they alone—are not the mere productions of the human agents through whose instrumentality they were drawn up, but as truly the work of a Divine Author as though every page had been traced by the finger of God himself?

Possibly you are one who would answer as I myself would have done a little while ago. You begin with the four Gospels, as simple historical documents, proved to be authentic and trustworthy by the cross-fire of centuries of criticism. You take them as you would the histories of Tacitus or Thucydides. Strictly speaking, it is as if Thucydides and Tacitus and two others like them had left independent accounts of the same events, of which two of the writers had been eye-witnesses, and concerning which the remaining two had possessed the most ample means of information. The study of these records convinces you that Jesus Christ was what he claimed to be—God incarnate. This, of course, does not prove to you that the evangelists wrote under immediate divine supervision. They nowhere themselves assert the fact of such an influence; and, logically, there can be no suggestion of such an inference. Still less does it follow that all the writers of what are now called the Old and New Testaments were supernaturally moved and directed. The testimony of the evangelists does, however, convince you that Jesus Christ organized a Church; that he delegated to it his own authority; and that he gave it the warrant of perpetual guidance in the truth. Subsequent history tells you that, after some centuries had passed, and many books had been written, this Church proceeded to sift the documents in its possession, collected together a number, new and old, and, in Council assembled, solemnly pronounced them to be different in kind from all other writings, and in a peculiar sense the work and word of Almighty God. You accept the fact of inspiration upon the authority of the Church which God founded.

Well, this is good reasoning. Any one who calls it 'arguing in a circle' only shows that he has not a very clear head, and does not precisely know what arguing in a circle means. It is open to only two objections. First, the Canon of Scripture which you would receive on such grounds would be, not that which you now recognize, but that which the Council of Trent defined to be the product of inspiration—'omnes libros tam Veteris quam Novi Testamenti, quum utriusque unus Deus sit auctor;'* for *it was this identical Tridentine canon* which was first established at the Council of Carthage, where St. Augustine assisted, in the year 397, and which was afterwards confirmed by the decisions of Pope Innocent, and of the Council of Rome, under Pope Gelasius, in the fifth century, by the Council of Constantinople in the sixth, and of Florence in the fourteenth.† And secondly, no man can reason in this way, and for another hour consistently remain a Protestant.

II. What authority had the Reformers for asserting that the Written Word is, and was intended to be, the complete revelation of divine truth, containing, therefore, everything which a Christian need believe? None whatever. In their haste to find some ground from which they might assail the ancient Church, they ventured a bold and plausible assumption, which multitudes have thoughtlessly accepted because of the very assurance with which it was proclaimed, but which was not supported by a semblance of proof, which no Protestant since the Reformation has ever demonstrated, and which is devoid of any foundation, whether in pure reason, or in the declarations of Scripture itself.‡ Chilling-

---

* Sess. IV. 'Spiritu Sancto dictante.' *Ibid.*

† See Waterworth, *Origin and Development of Anglicanism*, pp. 221-228.

‡ "There must be texts, at least equally strong, brought against us, as what we adduce for our system; not merely such as say that the Scripture is useful, good, and profitable, but such as positively assert that the Scripture is *sufficient;* not such as tell us to search

worth has said all that can be said in such a cause, and Chillingworth's argument is no demonstration at all. The most which he succeeded in proving was that the Bible alone (whatever that may mean) is *the religion of Protestants.* From which ingenious conclusion Protestants must derive a vast amount of support and satisfaction. We shall have more to say on this point before the end of the chapter.

III. Who is to determine for us, as Protestants, the real meaning of the written record? Of course there can be only one true interpretation. The truth of Scripture, as St. Jerome well says, is not in the words, but in the sense— 'nec putemus in verbis Scripturarum esse Evangelium, sed in sensu.'* 'How is it, then, brethren? When ye come together, every one of you hath an interpretation.' Quot homines, tot sententiæ. Which of these constructions is the divine one?

There is a sad deal of nonsense current about ' the Bible and nothing but the Bible.' There is not one of the end-

---

the Scriptures for particular objects, but such as command us to seek *all things* therein. There must be texts, the words of Christ or his Apostles, to command us to make use of no rule but the written word; for observe, that in sanctioning any rule or principle whereby man is to be guided, it is necessary that the principle be somewhere laid down and explicitly defined, so that he should know what is to be the rule of his life, and the law whereby he must direct and regulate his conduct. And thus we, on our side, are not content with vague allusions to the authority of the Church, as a voucher for the doctrines therein taught; but believe that we have an express definition, that its authority is the rule of faith, and that all must obey and follow its guidance."—Cardinal Wiseman, *Lectures on the Doctrines of the Church*, lect. iii.

* *Com. in Gal.* c. i. Grande periculum est in Ecclesia loqui, ne forte *interpretatione perversa, de Evangelio Christi, hominis fiat evangelium ; aut quod pejus est, diaboli.* Ibid.

less sects into which Protestantism is divided which realizes its own theory. They each of them have, beside the Bible, their own little system of theology, their catechisms and their confessions—all different, and, if different, contradictory, yet all claiming to be founded upon the same infallible rule. The conclusion is plain. "If," says Sir William Hamilton, "men will go to the Bible, not to ask of it what they shall believe, but to find in it what they believe already, the standard of unity and truth becomes in human hands only a Lesbian rule."* But all experience shows, what the philosopher seems half-inclined to acknowledge, that, when men attempt to teach themselves in divine things, they do, and must, approach the Scriptures with an intellectual and moral bias, and that, unconsciously, but inevitably, they behold in the word, as in a mirror, only the reflection of their own education, their own methods, or their own tastes. Quæ volunt, sapiunt.† Protestantism has turned the Word of God into the words of men; and every shallow worldling can now throw the volume aside, with the sneer of the old Calvinist:

> Hic liber est in quo quærit sua dogmata quisque;
> Invenit et pariter dogmata quisque sua.‡

"The Reformers," writes Bossuet, "believed that they could terminate all disputes by the Scripture alone, and would have no other judge than that; and the whole world was witness, there was no end to their disputes on Scripture,

---

* *Lectures on Metaphysics*, p. 185.
† St. Hilary, *De Trinitate*, l. vii. (Cf. Demos., Βούλεται τοῦθ' ἕκαστος καὶ οἴεται: et Tac., Fingunt simul creduntque.)
‡ S. Werenfels. Quoted by Sir W. H.

even on one passage of it, than which none ought to be more clear, since it regarded a last will and testament. They exclaimed one to the other, 'All is clear, and nothing more is necessary than to open your eyes.' By this evidence of Scripture, Luther discovered that nothing was more impious and daring than to deny the literal sense, and Zuinglius found nothing more gross and absurd than to follow it.* The history of Protestantism from the days of Zuinglius and Luther has been only a continued demonstration of the fact that unaided human reason is at fault in dealing with what Protestants themselves confess to be a supernatural revelation, and a melancholy confirmation of a truth which reason itself is competent to suggest, that a divine testament needs also a divine interpreter.

And now, let us, for one brief moment, look at these questions in another and clearer light.

The Catholic believes in the Holy Catholic Church. But he does not do so *merely* as a logical inference from the words of Scripture. He does not even need the Scriptures to know that the Church is divine. There she stands; and her existence is the evidence of her origin. She speaks; and her claims are her credentials. She acts; and her work is her vindication. She points to the past; and her history is her irrefutable argument. She was in the world before the first Christian penman had begun his sacred task. She was then what she is now. She is the contemporary of all ages. Her message is the same for ever. Her office is to teach; and her commission—not what was afterward written in a book, but what was *uttered* on the day of the Ascension.

* *Variations*, etc., l. ii. § 43.

That living Voice from Heaven we hear to-day, as men have heard it 'through the ages all along,' and as we would still hear it though St. Luke had never written to Theophilus, nor the divine John to the seven Churches which were in Asia.

It pleased God, however, for the greater confirmation of the faith, to put it into the hearts of a few who from the beginning were eye-witnesses, or companions of those who were, to make a record of the chief events in the earthly life of the Church's divine Founder; and also, for the Church's edification, to preserve certain letters which, at divers times, were written by the first Apostles to their brethren and children in the Gospel. These documents, which are in their nature fragmentary and unsystematic, have nothing to do with the Church's mission to the nations. They were never intended to teach men 'the principles of the doctrine of Christ.' They were written *to those who had already been taught;* 'not to such as knew not the truth, but to such as knew it;' to those who had received 'an unction from the Holy One,' and who, through the Church, 'knew all things.'* They were written as occasion called them forth—for reference, for exhortation, for counsel, or comfort, or warning; but they are addressed always to those in whom both faith and knowledge are assumed. Never did an apostle write to convince the doubting and the unbelieving, nor even to instruct the ignorant. The charge to make disciples was fulfilled by other means than pen and parchment. That work was done as it is done now—by the authoritative voice of the teaching Church.

To whom, then, do the Scriptures belong? To the

* 1 St. John ii. 20, 21, 27.

Church of God; and to her alone. She saw them written. She took them from the hands of her own holy Fathers. She treasured and defended them. She transmits them to her children of the latest generation. She is the witness to their inspiration. She alone can give the key to their meaning. And she, to whom the complete revelation was delivered in the beginning, knows just how much of the faith committed to her keeping has been transcribed into their blessed pages.

The Scriptures are the Church's heritage; and she uses them as such. To the faithful believer she expounds them as the Word of God. When she addresses the unbelieving world, she makes no appeal to the Scriptures as inspired, for their inspiration can rest upon her authority alone; she employs them indeed, but only for their testimony to facts of history. But to the heretic, who, spurning the giver, lays rash hands upon the divine gift—to the heretic, who presumptuously invades and desecrates her fair domain, she speaks thus: "Who are you? Whence do you come? What business have you strangers with my property? By what right are you, Marcion, felling my trees? By what authority are you, Valentinus, turning the course of my streams? Under what pretence are you, Apelles, removing my landmarks? The estate is mine; I have the ancient possession of it. I have the title-deeds delivered to me by the original proprietors. I am the heir of the Apostles; they have made their will in my favor, while they have disinherited and cast you off as strangers and enemies."*

This passage from Tertullian is a very striking one; but not more so than many others which might be cited from

---

* Tertullian, *De Præscript.* c. xix.

the early Christian writers. The Protestant fallacy is an ancient one, and was very early exposed. It would be easy to fill pages with quotations—already often made*—defining in the most admirable manner the true relation of the Church to the written Word, and demonstrating the folly of an appeal to the latter against the authority of the former. A very few will suffice.

I have said that the Church is by its origin independent of the Scriptures. Thus wrote St. Irenæus: "Supposing that the Apostles had left us nothing in writing, should we not still follow the rule of doctrine which they delivered to those to whom they entrusted the churches? This rule many barbarous nations follow, who, being without ink or parchment, have the word of salvation written by the Spirit in their hearts, and guard diligently the tradition which has been delivered." †

I have said that the Scriptures were never intended to teach complete Christian doctrine. Could the truth be stated more clearly and briefly than by St. Chrysostom, when, commenting on 2 Thess. ii. 14 (v. 15, *Eng. Ver.*), he says: "Hence it is plain that the Apostles did not deliver to us everything by their epistles, but many things without writing. These are equally to be believed. Wherefore let us believe the tradition of the Church. It is tradition: seek no further—παράδοσίς ἐστι μηδὲν πλέον ζήτει "? ‡

---

* In quoting from the Fathers, I have not hesitated to avail myself of references to which I have been assisted by authors far more learned than myself, who am but a beginner in studies. Let it be kept in mind that the Catholic does not take his belief from the Fathers. He receives his faith from the Church, and quotes antiquity only to show that the Fathers did the same.

† *Advers. Hæres.* l. iii. c. 4.

‡ *Hom.* iv. in 2 Thess. Barrow, in an unguarded moment, says:

I have said that the Catholic takes the Scriptures from the Church, and that her authority is the sole warrant of their inspiration. " I would not have believed the Gospel," declares St. Augustine, " if I had not been moved thereto by the authority of the Catholic Church"—"Evangelio non crederem, nisi me Catholicæ ecclesiæ commoveret auctoritas."*

The Church, I have said, is the interpreter of the Word. " To him that believeth," writes St. Irenæus again, " all will be plain, if he read diligently the Scripture with the aid of those who are the priests in the Church, and in whose hands, as we have shown, rests the doctrine of the Apostles." † And St. Hilary: " Those who are out of the Church cannot have any understanding of the divine word." ‡ And St. Augustine : " To attain to the truth of the Scriptures, we must follow the sense of them entertained by the Universal Church, to which the Scriptures themselves bear testimony." § The *Commonitorium* of St. Vincent is a systematic statement of the necessity of adding to the written text "the authority of the Church's meaning." ||

"We have in divers of the Fathers, particularly in Tertullian, in St. Basil, in St. Jerome, catalogues of traditional *doctrines* [the emphasis is mine] and observances, which they recite to assert tradition in some cases supplemental to Scripture."—*Supremacy*, Suppos. V. i. 7. The Anglican Homilies, however, of course settle the question, when, in their courtly way, they speak of " the stinking puddles of tradition."

* *Contra Epist. Fundamenti.* (Crederem=credidissem.)
† *Adv. Hæres.* l. iv. c. 52.
‡ *In Matthæum* xiii. 1. So, speaking of heretics, the same Father says : " They all quote Scripture, but without the sense of Scripture."
§ *Contra Crescon.* l. i. c. 33. || *Common.* c. ii.

Protestants, I have ventured to say, behold in the Bible only the shadow of their own theology. The Scottish philosopher could not have put the point more neatly than the great Bishop of Hippo: "The sacred Scriptures themselves are of no use unless you understand them rightly. For all heretics, who admit them to be of authority, appear to themselves to follow them, when they rather follow their own errors; and it is not, therefore, because they contemn the Scriptures, but because they misinterpret them, that they are heretics."[*]

As for the absurdity of Scriptural quotation in the mouth of those whom the old Fathers so uncomfortably persist in calling heretics, from the very fact of their choosing their own interpretation—I despair of selecting passages from the number which are before me. St. Vincent alone furnishes page after page of satire so sharp that, if I were to make it my own, I should be accused of discourtesy.

Let us close the case with the masterly and unanswerable words of Tertullian: "Ergo non ad Scripturas provocandum est; nec in his constituendum certamen, in quibus aut nulla aut incerta victoria est, aut par incertæ. Nam etsi non ita evaderet collatio scripturarum, ut utrumque partem parem sisteret, ordo rerum desiderabat, prius proponi, quod nunc solum disputandum est: quibus competat Fides ipsa? Cujus sint Scripturæ? A quo, et per quos, et quando, et quibus sit tradita Disciplina, qua fiunt Christiani? Ubi enim apparuerit esse veritatem et disciplinæ et fidei Christianæ, illic erit veritas scripturarum et expositionum et omnium traditionum Christianarum." To the Scriptures there can be no appeal. The sole question to be settled is:

---

[*] St. Aug. *Epist.* cxx. 13.

To whom belongs the Faith itself? Whose are the Scriptures? By whom, and through whom, and when, and to whom was that authority to teach delivered by which men are made Christians? For where the true Christian discipline and doctrine are shown to be, there will be also the truth of the Scriptures, and of their Interpretation, and of all Christian Traditions.*

O Protestant! you who parade your unmeaning boast of being a Bible Christian, you who dare blindly to charge the Church of God with dishonoring and making void the Word of which she is the sole guardian and witness, will you never rouse yourself to see towards what a gulf of unbelief your Protestantism is leading? Do you not know how it is destroying the faith of men in the very Scriptures which it cunningly professes to magnify? Protestants began three centuries ago with a belief in the inspiration of Holy Writ. Where did they get that faith? From the Catholic Church. It was a divine Tradition, which Infallibility had rooted in the hearts of men. But Protestantism has torn down the bulwarks of inspiration; and everywhere men have eagerly hastened to attack it. In Protestant England, a clergyman can consistently and honorably teach that a supernatural theory of inspiration is without foundation.† In Protestant Germany, any 'theory' of inspiration at all is laughed to scorn. In Protestant America, the sacred pages have become a butt for the insults of every ribald jester. Whatever of veneration for the written Word is still to be found among Protestants is only the lingering of the old Catholic faith. It is the voice of infallibility still distantly sounding in ears which are most unconscious whence the voice proceeds.

---

* *De Præscript.* c. xix.   † *Essays and Reviews.*

Protestants little dream of the tribute which they constantly pay to the Catholic Church. Still less do they know that that Church is to-day the only power which saves the Bible from being torn in pieces by the caprice and passion of mankind, and the malice of all the powers of darkness. Thank God that against that power no assault can ever prevail. Thank God, too, that an instinctive reverence for their Mother's teaching is yet cherished by some who have long since forgotten their allegiance; that even in the hearts of her wandering children the great Church can still hold her protecting ægis over the treasure committed to her trust.

CHAPTER IV.

THE APPEAL TO ANTIQUITY.

HERE are a few Protestants who appeal from the voice of the living Church to what they consider the teaching of primitive antiquity. In doing so, they undoubtedly deny, equally with all other Protestants, that there is now in the world any tribunal to whose authority they are bound to submit their own opinions in matters of faith.

The appeal would be of the same force whether made by individuals or by a local church; I speak of it, however, as made by a party because, after a candid review, I find no evidence that any schismatical body has *as a church* attempted to justify its schism by such a rule. The English Reformers may have been as individuals diligent, if not very profound, students of the Fathers; in framing the new ecclesiastical constitution they may have followed, so far as their Royal master allowed them, what they thought the primitive model; but it is certain that, when, in the name of the Church of England, they were required to settle questions of doctrine, they made, or at least professed to make, no use of Christian antiquity whatsoever. The Thirty-nine Articles are avowedly based upon Scripture, and Scripture alone. And so long as plain English can be plainly read, what is known as the Evangelical party in the Protestant Episcopal Church may reasonably claim that they have derived their solibiblical principles from the dogmatical standards of their own communion.

There is no mistaking the intention of the Anglican Articles as to the Anglican rule of faith. Their authors did not pretend to interpret Scripture by antiquity; *on the contrary, they attempted to judge antiquity by Scripture.* They asserted the sufficiency of Holy Scripture, and took care not to say one word about the interpretation of the same by either Councils or Fathers.* Whatever doctrine they sanctioned, they sanctioned solely because they deemed it Scriptural, not only without reference to the testimony of antiquity, but with a studied and conspicuous avoidance of such reference. Even Infant Baptism they retained, not as having been the practice of the Church from the beginning, but because they themselves chose to consider it most agreeable to Christ's ordinance.† They pronounced a lofty condemnation upon the faith of all four of the great primitive Patriarchates. I say *primitive* Patriarchates; for they did not so much as notice the later patriarchal See of Constantinople.‡ They promptly disposed of any imaginary authority of General Councils, affirming their fallibility, and declaring that their dogmatical decrees are without force, except so far as they can be shown (ostendi possint) to be taken out of Holy Scripture.§ Therefore the great Catholic Creeds are to be received, not at the hands of Church or Council, but upon what is far more satisfactory, the assur-

---

* Art. VI. † Art. XXVII. ‡ Art. XIX.
§ Art. XXI. This article has been gravely omitted by the American Protestant Episcopal Church, on the ground that "it is partly of a *local* and civil nature, and is provided for, as to the remaining parts of it, in other articles." There is a touch of sly irony about this which is irresistibly droll, coming as it does in the very middle of one of the most respectable and dreary of documents.

ance of the Reformers themselves that they may be proved by warrants of Holy Writ.* And therefore the 'Romish doctrine' of Purgatory, Indulgences, Invocation, and what these honest iconoclasts are pleased to call the 'worshipping and adoration' of Images and Relics, is to be rejected, not as a corruption of the early faith, but on the word of a Protestant that it is 'grounded upon no warranty of Scripture.'† In fine, from beginning to end of the Articles, the only citation of the unfortunate 'Primitive Church' is to a point, not of doctrine, but of 'custom';‡ and even this allusion seems out of place in a confession in which, as a distinguished historian has said, "Calvin or Knox would have found scarcely a word to disapprove."

It soon became evident, however, that some better interpreter of the Word of God was needed than the worthy compilers of the Thirty-nine Articles. Men arose in the English Church, able and learned, who attempted to come to the rescue of the hasty and shallow theology of their predecessors. They could not supplement Scripture by what St. Vincent calls "the authority of the Church's meaning," for that meaning they had rejected, and against that authority they had rebelled. Therefore they ingeniously supplied the deficiency by adding their own notion of what the Church's interpretation *once was*. Without stopping to rehearse names which but recently I was wont to mention with reverence, or to quote passages over which I should linger with regretful memories, let me pass quickly on to

---

* Art. VIII.
† Art. XXII. The position of this article, immediately after that which denies the authority of General Councils, is very significant.
‡ Art. XXIV.

show, as briefly as possible, the utterly unsatisfactory character of this revised and amended Protestantism.

For a believer in a revelation to quote the Scriptures against the Church which gives him the Scriptures, and which certifies their divine origin, is irrational enough; but for a believer in a Catholic Church to appeal to the past against the present, and to attempt to judge the Church of the nineteenth century by the Church of the third, is, if possible, more irrational still. Either there is to-day in the world a Church which is the organ and mouth-piece of the Holy Ghost, and whose teachings are infallibly true; or there is not. If there is not, then there never was; and to search for it in the past may be interesting occupation, but will certainly be profitless. Put the dilemma back to the third century. Either the Church was then infallible, or it was not. If it was not, then what earthly use is there in referring to it? For without infallibility there is no certainty, and it is simply certainty that we are in quest of. If, however, it was infallible, then it could no more cease to be so than God could cease to be God. People who talk about a limited or a suspended infallibility, talk nonsense.

It may be said that it is not claimed for the Church of such and such a century that it was infallible, but merely that it was inerrant; not that it *could* not err, but that it *did* not. This is a fatal blunder. If you do not know that the Church could not err, *you do not know that it did not.* It is the impossibility of error which alone supplies the certainty of truth. The fact of infallibility, if a fact at all, is a perpetual divine fact, and rests upon the assurance of Jesus Christ; but the mere fact of inerrancy at a given time can rest upon no other assurance than your own. So it comes back to this, that you refer to antiquity because on the whole you choose to do so. Antiquity does not come to you; it does not speak to you; you go gallantly in search of it; you dress it up with just so much of authority as you see fit; and then reverently submit your private judgment to the authority which it has itself created. It is really amusing to see men fancying themselves models of obedience and docility, when the Church which they obey exists purely in their own lively imagination—(I am smiling, dear reader, at my former self)—and when the decrees which they receive with such docile faith are imposed upon them by no more inexorable legislator than their own sovereign pleasure.

"There can be ultimately no intermediate between the Divine mind declaring itself through an organ of its own creation, or the human mind judging for itself upon the evidence and contents of revelation. There is or there is not a perpetual Divine Teacher in the midst of us. The human reason must be either the disciple or the critic of revelation."* This is very plain. And yet there are those who honestly suppose that the study of Scripture and antiquity together is a process different in *kind* from the study of Scripture alone. When in addition to the writings of the Apostles they set to work to read the writings of the Fathers, they are blessed with the conviction that they have changed their whole rule of faith. They do not see that, in place of acting upon a new rule, they have only increased the difficulties of the old; that, instead of obtaining an interpreter, they have only multiplied the number of documents which they must themselves interpret or have interpreted for them; that, so far from resigning their prejudiced

---

* Archbishop Manning, *Temporal Mission*, etc., p. 85.

and fallible opinion to an authority external to themselves, they are innocently summoning before their own little tribunal the Scriptures and the Fathers and the Councils all in a row. It is a strange fallacy this—it would be incredible if it were not actual—that men should devoutly believe themselves Catholics when they are in fact resorting to what has been aptly called " the most ingenious of all Protestant contrivances for submitting to nothing and nobody."

Let us suppose, what has been shown to be insupposable, that the Church did continue for a limited season to be divinely preserved in the enunciation of the truth; let us even, by a vigorous effort, conceive that two persons have been found who will agree upon the day or the year when the Church ceased to exercise her infallible functions; how are you now infallibly to know what the Church then infallibly taught? It is a long way back to the Council of Chalcedon or the days of Photius. Through all those intervening centuries there has been no divine and therefore changeless transmission of the faith once delivered. Where is the assurance that in spite of convulsions and migrations, through floods of barbarism and storms of religious strife, the sacred tradition has come down to you unaltered? This is the point which is triumphantly made against the Catholic Church by men who have never so much as conceived what THE CHURCH really is, who do not believe the promises of Christ concerning her, nor in the mission and work of the Holy Ghost in the midst of her. It is really an unanswerable argument against those who deny the perpetual office of a supernatural Instructor, and therefore look blindly to the past for the truth which for them can have no existence in the present.

Again, men have been driven to the study of antiquity by

the conspicuous necessity of supplying some trustworthy expositor of a Book which irresponsible people were construing in a thousand different ways. But facts show, what it would have required no philosophy to foresee, that men must differ in the interpretation of antiquity as much as they do in the interpretation of Scripture. You will not find ten of these scholars who have been led *by their own study* of antiquity to the same conclusions. Take even the question of the primitive ecclesiastical constitution. "It is a question," says Lord Macaulay, "on which men of eminent parts, learning, and piety have differed, and do to this day differ very widely. It is a question on which at least a full half of the ability and erudition of Protestant Europe has, ever since the Reformation, been opposed to the Anglican pretensions."* Take the nature of the Presence in the Eucharist. Cranmer, in his *Treatise on the Sacrament*, denied any real presence whatever. Mr. Palmer maintains a real presence of some sort or other, and good-naturedly says that Cranmer " was misled . . . by certain passages from the fathers which he did not rightly understand." † Dr. Waterland writes a volume in explication of *his* view of the sound primitive and Anglican doctrine. And Dr. Pusey writes two bigger volumes still to prove that the belief both of the Fathers and of the Church of England is one which differs from Transubstantiation by a quantity so infinitesimal that, on mathematical principles, it may safely be neglected. Take the doctrine of Invocation. Dr. Newman, while still a Protestant, was convinced that "there is more of evidence in antiquity for the practice of

---

* *Review of Gladstone on Church and State.*
† *On the Church*, vol. i. p. 391.

Invocation than for certain books in the present canon of Scripture;"* while Dr. Harold Browne, of Ely, promptly suppresses any rising suspicions in the minds of the unlearned by the round assertion that "for this practice no early authority can be pleaded."† And so you might run through the whole list of disputed dogmas, and on every one you would find theologians varying as widely in their apprehensions of the teaching of the early Church as Luther and Zuinglius did on the meaning of the plainest words in all Scripture.

And after all this, the most practical difficulty, though just hinted at, remains to be stated. Whatever be the true Christian rule of faith, it is certain that it must be a universal one; that is, a rule uniform and therefore simple in its application, a rule adapted alike to the capabilities and the conditions of all men. But it is equally certain that the interpretation of Scripture by antiquity is a rule which is suited to the circumstances and capacities of very few men. The interpretation of Scripture by private fancy is a rule sufficiently easy of application—though hardly uniform in its results; and the translated text of Scripture is at least within the reach of the educated classes in civilized countries. But the ascertaining by documentary evidence of the exact faith of the early Church is a work requiring leisure, accurate learning, and most faithful research. The mass of mankind, on such a principle, must stake their faith, and therefore their salvation, upon the erudition and the honesty of a few self-constituted teachers, who are at variance among

---

* See *Apologia*, p. 231. So Bishop Montague (*Invocation of Saints*): "It is the common voice, with general concurrence, without contradiction, of reverend and learned antiquity.

† *Exposition of the Thirty-nine Articles*, p. 520.

themselves, and who can give no guarantee that they are not blind leaders of the blind. " Non in dialectica," says St. Ambrose—" non in dialectica complacuit Deo salvum facere populum suum." Neither did God ever intend to save the world by scholarship. But this antiquarian theory is a theory of 'salvation by scholarship alone.' To what recent writer we owe this masterly phrase, I do not know. It touches with the sharpest needle of truth this Anglican bubble, this most hollow of all the specious devices of man for evading the perpetual, unalterable authority of Christ's Teaching Church.

What has been written would be sufficient, brief as it is, were our object merely to force the position of those who think to oppose the great Catholic Church of to-day by intrenching themselves behind a mythical church of by-gone ages. It may be, however, that there are some who do not use antiquity to defend a cause to which they are already pledged; who would gladly recognize as divine an authority which even now overawes them; and who are only hindered from so doing by a fear, which, through the prejudice of education, they cannot rid themselves of, that there is a real discrepancy between what the Church teaches now and what it taught in the early centuries. To such, if such there be, I will offer a few suggestions—which I pray God may be of service in removing their difficulties.

Have you studied antiquity for yourself? If you have not, then do you honestly think that the opinions of a little group of Anglican theologians can fairly be weighed against the testimony of the great body of Catholic Doctors of all ages, who outweigh their opponents in vast scholarship as much as they exceed them in number?

The Appeal to Antiquity.

Have you ever reflected upon the damaging fact that the appeal to antiquity was, as I have already said in this chapter, an *afterthought* of the Reformation? You surely know enough of history to be aware that the outbreak of the sixteenth century was very far from being the result of patristic studies. The Continental Reformers flung the Fathers to the winds, together with Popes and Canons and Councils. And as for England, a brief review of the work that was done there will convince you that Macaulay is right after all, when he calls it a mere political job, sprung from brutal passion and nurtured by selfish policy. "A King whose character may be best described by saying that he was despotism itself personified, unprincipled ministers, a rapacious aristocracy, a servile Parliament, such were the instruments by which England was delivered from the yoke of Rome. The work which had been begun by Henry, the murderer of his wives, was continued by Somerset, the murderer of his brother, and completed by Elizabeth, the murderer of her guest."* There was at first no thought of altering an iota of Catholic doctrine. The adulterous Henry simply made up his mind to be 'his own Pope;' and his own Pope he

---

* *Review of Hallam.* "Of those who had any important share in bringing the Reformation about, Ridley was perhaps the only person who did not consider it as a mere political job. . . . If we consider Cranmer merely as a statesman, he will not appear a much worse man than Wolsey, Gardiner, Cromwell, or Somerset. But when an attempt is made to set him up as a saint, it is scarcely possible for any man of sense, who knows the history of the times, to preserve his gravity. . . . These four persons [Henry, Somerset, Elizabeth, and Cranmer] were the great authors of the English Reformation. Three of them had a direct interest in the extension of the royal prerogative. The fourth was the ready tool of any who could frighten him."—*Ibid.*

became. It was only after the separation had been fully and finally accomplished that the revolted Church perceived the necessity of reforming itself; and only after the 'reformation' had been effected, in good parliamentary style, that it occurred to Elizabethan scholars to justify the changes which had been made by evoking the attestation of early Catholic writers.*

And now, leaving the Reformation, come down at once to our own times, and read the meaning of a movement which has been going on under our own eyes, and which in certain aspects forms a striking antithesis to that of the sixteenth century. I refer to what is known as the movement of 1833. The Oxford leaders were men whose talents were only equalled by their devotion, men before the stainless sanctity of whose characters the tongue of calumny itself is now silenced, and whose pure affection for the Church in which they had been nurtured few who are familiar with their early writings can be base enough to doubt. They set out with an enthusiastic study of the Fathers, without knowing whither their study would lead them. Within a dozen years the flower of the English clergy were seeking admission by scores into the Church which their researches had identified with that of the first Councils and of the Catacombs. Dr. Newman, who may well be allowed to speak for the rest, repeatedly asserts that the Fathers made him a Catholic.† In the former instance, we found men begin-

---

* Jewel's *Apology* was the first systematic attempt of this sort.
† See *Letter to Dr. Pusey* (on the *Eirenicon*), p. 14; *Anglican Difficulties*, p. 289, *et seq.*; and the *Apologia, passim*. Mr. Lecky says of the Tractarians: "They were pre-eminently scholars and antiquarians, and in its intellectual aspect the movement was essentially a resuscitation of the past. Nor did the age seem at

ning by leaving the Church, and ending by a resort to antiquity; but here are men who began by reading the Fathers, and ended by returning to the Church of which the Fathers themselves were the primitive children.

Again, if we are to regard the identity of ancient and modern Catholicity, not as a matter of divine assurance, but as a question of pure historical criticism, we shall be safe in allowing most weight to the opinions of those who have no ecclesiastical theory of their own to nurse and bolster. Let us content ourselves, then, with a single admission, which to the impartial enquirer will be worth more than the asseverations of all the Anglican doctors that ever wrote, or that will continue to write until Anglicanism itself shall be no more. "A well-informed man," says Gibbon, "cannot resist the weight of historical evidence which establishes that in the whole period of the four first ages of the Church the principal points of the papistical doctrines were already admitted in theory and in practice." *

After such a judgment as this, how futile are the inconsistent reasonings and the utterly rash assertions with which we are so familiar! I say inconsistencies. We are told, for example, that the doctrine of Transubstantiation was forged at the Council of Lateran; but, when the Arian asserts that the orthodox faith in the Trinity dates from the Council of Nice, these men will turn round and say that the fact of the

---

first sight less suited for the enterprise. *In the time of the Reformers the study of evidences, and, indeed, all searching investigation into the facts of the past, were unknown.* [The emphasis is mine.] When, however, Tractarianism arose, the laws of historical criticism were developed to great perfection."—*Rationalism in Europe*, vol. i. p. 179.

* *Memoir*, vol. i. ch. i.

Church defining a doctrine is no argument that the doctrine was then invented, but an excellent evidence that it had then for the first time been denied. And I say recklessness. When Bishop Jewel stood at St. Paul's Cross, and cried out, "Let them show me one only father, one doctor, one sentence, two lines, and the field is theirs," he was guilty of a foolish piece of impudence, which has recoiled with disastrous effect upon his own cause. When you hear a preacher nowadays fluently refer to 'Jewel's challenge,' set it down at once that the speaker is either very ignorant himself, or else reasonably certain of a very ignorant audience. We are told that Peter Lombard was the first to discover that there were seven sacraments. "What need," says gentle, honest Barrow, "of cursing those who do not take the sacraments to be precisely seven, . . . seeing that before Peter Lombard none ever did mention that number?"* Peter Lombard the first to hold that confirmation, and penance, and extreme unction, and order, and matrimony are sacraments! *O seri studiorum!*

Enough of this. Let me put into your hands a single, simple argument, which will sweep away like so many cobwebs the labored dissertations and the bold affirmations of these erudite Englishmen. Look away from the noisy and shifting controversies of our Western Christianity off to the silent and stationary East. There, scattered in patches amid the fossil civilization of the Orient, you will find the remains of certain ancient churches, dead churches, which were cut off from the great living trunk long centuries before the days of Peter Lombard or the schoolmen, in some of which the names even of Ephesus and Chalcedon are as

* *Supremacy, ad fin.*

much unknown as those of Lateran and of Florence; yet existing still, preserved, as De Maistre beautifully says, " in the midst of Mahometanism as an insect is preserved in amber "—preserved by a wonderful providence, it would almost seem for the very purpose of bringing to naught the allegations of more modern heretics. Go there, and confront the present with the past. Ask them how many sacraments they hold. Ask them whether they believe that the Son of God offers himself up on their altars in unbloody sacrifice for the living and the dead. Ask them whether they invoke the prayers of the saints, and whether they honor their relics; whether they offer their own prayers, and their alms, for the souls which have not yet entered the abodes of bliss. Though each church has some antiquated heresy of its own, they will tell you, one and all—not Greeks alone, but Armenians and Nestorians, Jacobites and Georgians, Copts and Christians of St. Thomas—that the particular doctrines and rites which enterprising Protestants have discovered to be the accretions of mediæval Romanism, they received from the Apostles, and that they hold them more dear than life itself.

But perhaps you are yourself a student. If so, let me earnestly ask you *how* you have studied. In what spirit, and with what purpose, did you pursue your enquiry? As you read those ancient sentences, what was the *presumption* in your own mind with regard to the theological status of the writers? Where did that presumption come from? Were you or were you not engaged in making out a case against the Church of Rome? Were you or were you not glad when you had found a passage which you thought could be used in controversy against that Church? Did you or did you not ask yourself whether the passage would bear a Roman Catholic construction? Tell me, now, by what canon of criticism you rejected that construction. Should antiquity be interpreted against the Church wherever it is not hopelessly in her favor, or in the sense of the Church when not manifestly opposed thereto?

If you choose the former rule, then farewell. You and I have nothing in common. If, however, you adopt the latter, and if you are capable of following it understandingly, then as your fellow-student I ask you—not as a learned scholar (far from it), yet as one who has not idly passed the few years which God has given him; as your humble fellow-student, who for love of you has spent many painful hours over these poor pages, and who hopes to meet you at last where study shall bring weariness no more; by that candor which should be the student's amulet and the aureole about his brow, I ask you—can you truly say that the testimony of antiquity *is* opposed to the teaching of the Holy Roman Catholic and Apostolic Church; is there a sentence, is there a line, which, if you were a Roman Catholic, as I am, would give your honest conscience a moment's disquietude, or cause a single shade of doubt to fall across your faith?

I anticipate your difficulty. It was mine once; and I will try to meet it. You admit that the voice of the fourth century is unmistakably and overwhelmingly on the side of the Roman Church. You know that Dr. Middleton concedes only the truth, when he says that "every one may see what a resemblance the principles and practice of the fourth century, as they are described by the most eminent fathers of that age, bear to the present rites of the Popish

Church."* You acknowledge, also, that in the writings of the second and third centuries there is nothing which contradicts what the Church now teaches; and that there are even many things which, on the supposition that the faith of the Church was the same then as now, would confirm the identity. But you think you have no right to assume this; and so you stand halting before the fact that the earliest Fathers should have, on the whole, so *little* to say about what are now considered the distinguishing features, the *differentia*, of ' Romanism.'

No right to suppose that the teaching of the Church is always the same! Why! my dear friend, do you not know that the Catholic is convinced, on principles of purest reason, that if the Church be a divine institution, that is, if there be a Church at all, its doctrine *must* be the same in all generations, so that what is to you a 'supposition,' an assumption, is to him the stoutest link in all the chain? But, alas! you are one who has not yet learned to believe in the Church's divine immutability. And as such I must answer you. I might do so, and close the case at once, by simply calling your attention to the fact, which you will be too candid to deny, that the Fathers early and late, as with one voice, testify and proclaim this very immutability of which you as a student of the Fathers are not persuaded. So here is antiquity supplying its own *hiatus*. There can be no rejoinder to this which does not immediately carry the question into another court. If the Fathers were mistaken on this cardinal point, I care not what opinions they held on doctrine in detail. But, while this argument might

---

* *Free Inquiry*, Introductory Chapter, p. 45.

effectually silence you, I fear it would not so meet your difficulties as satisfactorily to account for them.

Observe, then, that the question is not whether the faith of the third century be identical with that of the nineteenth, *but whether it be identical with that of the fourth.* Is it probable, is it conceivable, that the 'papistical doctrines' which are inextricably interwoven with the whole theology of one age, which were then not only universally professed, but professed as the Catholic faith which three centuries before had been left with the Church by the Apostles, should have been comparatively unknown in the age immediately preceding? Why, then, do you say, should we hear less about them? Surely you can yourself supply the answer.

What was the fourth century? It was the golden age of Christianity; it was the age of the conquest of the Roman Empire; the age of the first Councils; the palmy age of the great Saints and Doctors—of Athanasius and Basil, of Gregory of Nazianzum and Gregory of Nyssa, of Ambrose and Jerome, of Chrysostom and Augustine. And what were the second and third centuries? They were the iron ages of persecution; the ages when the powers of darkness strove to destroy the kingdom of God ere it should spread abroad among men, and when storm after storm of savage fury broke over the infant Church; they were the days of the Catacombs and the martyrs; the bloody days of Septimius and Decius and Valerian and Diocletian. To be a bishop in those days was to be a witness unto death. Down till past the middle of the third century *every Pope save one*, twenty-four one after the other, (O glorious record!) obtained the martyr's crown. And then the tempest slackened a moment, only to gather for a fiercer outpouring. There is a medal of Diocletian still extant, struck at the beginning of the fourth century, bearing a legend which sums up in one terse phrase more than is contained in all the pages of Lactantius and Eusebius. The words are these: *Nomine Christianorum deleto.* Vain boast! Within a decade the reign of Constantine had begun; and the Church, set free at last, came forth from the very bowels of the earth. She arose and shone, because her light was come, and the glory of the Lord had risen upon her.*

Protestants are too apt to separate the study of the patristic writings from the history of Christianity itself, forgetting that the latter furnishes the key to the former. If we only keep in mind the simple facts just stated, we shall have no difficulty in understanding, not merely why the productions of the fourth century are sufficient to fill a library while the principal authors of the two preceding ages can be numbered on the fingers of one hand, but also why the range of subjects directly treated of by the earlier writers is necessarily limited. The Christians under the pagan emperors had something else to do than composing treatises for the benefit of future Protestants. So far as they were called upon to write at all, it was mainly as Christians in the midst of heathens, as the advocates of a divine revelation against Roman bigotry and Grecian incredulity. The more ancient

* How ridiculous now (for I am not going to use a harsher word) appears the conservatism of those more cautious High Churchmen who, in their references to antiquity, are very careful not to advance beyond the third century! How much do these good people *know* about the third century? It is comparatively safe to appeal to a vacuum. If we are to construct a church on paper, by all means let us have *carte blanche* to begin with, *or as nearly* '*blanche*' *as possible.*

Fathers, says the learned Dr. Waterworth, "were rather engaged in strengthening the foundations and establishing the evidences and leading mysteries of Christianity than in defending its outworks. Theirs was the task to establish the unity of God, and the divinity of Christ, and to vindicate religion against the heavy and unjust charges which were urged against it by the learned and powerful advocates of paganism; and all things considered, it is nothing less than wonderful that they have referred so often and so distinctly to so many of the doctrines and practices of the Church. As long as no one doctrine of Christianity is denied, so long have we nothing to fear from that silence which Protestants are at times disposed to make so much of."* Remember, too, that what you call the differentia of the Roman Catholic Church are only such *as heresy has made them so.* So long as any article of the faith had not been denied, there was no occasion for undertaking its defence; but the instant it was called in question, it sprang into prominence. Before Nestorius was no one who refused to the ever-blessed Virgin Mary the title Mother of God.† Before Vigilantius

---

* *England and Rome*, Pref., p. ix.

† The scholarship which finds it impossible to translate Θεοτόκος by 'Mother of God' is certainly of a most extraordinary kind. My good Heliodorus, *Græcorum longe doctissime*, are you aware that in Greek ἡ μήτηρ and ἡ τεκοῦσα mean one and the same thing? and that the Greeks themselves, in Liturgies which are older than the Council of Ephesus, use ἡ Θεοτόκος, ἡ μήτηρ τοῦ Θεοῦ, and ἡ Θεὸν τεκοῦσα *indifferently?* Take the following passage from the Liturgy of St. James:—" *Then the Priest* (ὁ ἱερεύς) *says aloud.* Especially our all-holy, immaculate (ἀχράντου), excellently laudable, glorious Lady, the Mother of God (Θεοτόκον), and ever-Virgin Mary. *Choir.* It is very meet to bless thee, the Mother of God (Θεοτόκον), the ever-blessed and all-immaculate (παναμώμητον) Mother of our God (μητέρα τοῦ Θεοῦ ἡμῶν), who art more honorable than the

there was none who had found it impious to invoke the
intercession of the saints reigning in glory.* Before the
Arian Aërius none had doubted that the great unbloody
sacrifice is efficacious for the souls of the dead.† Before
Berengarius none had dared to dispute the truth that in the

Cherubim, and incomparably (ἀσυγκρίτως, Dr. Neale, by a rare care-
lessness, translates 'infinitely') more glorious than the Seraphim;
thee who, remaining a virgin, didst bear God the Word (τὴν Θεὸν
Λόγον τεκοῦσαν), thee truly the Mother of God (Θεοτόκον) we magnify." This ascription is from the older portion of the Liturgy,
though the angelical salutation which precedes, and the beautiful
hymn which follows, beginning, "In thee, O full of grace, all
creation rejoices," were added later.

"No man," says Dr. Nevin—most candid but most consistent of Protestants—"no man whose tongue falters in pronounc-
ing Mary *Mother of God* can be orthodox at heart on the article of
Christ's person."

* The castigation which St. Jerome gave this Vigilantius ought
to interest Protestants, who are the real *Vigilantians;* for the
wretched man obtained no following in his own day. "Thou
dolt!" says the great polemic, "who at any time *adored* the martyrs? Who could fancy that a mortal was God?" And referring
to the devotion of the 'ignorant and simple' Catholics of his time,
he indignantly exclaims: "*Idolatras* appellas hujusmodi homines?"
—*Adv. Vigilant.*

† I use the adjective 'unbloody' a second time for the sake of
calling attention to the astounding argument which Bishop Bull
draws from it, in his Letter on the *Corruptions of the Church of
Rome.* "The ancient Doctors," he says, "yea, and Liturgies of the
Church, affirm the Eucharist to be *incruentum sacrificium,* a ' sacrifice without blood' [so he translates it]; *which it cannot be said to be
if the very blood of Christ were therein present and offered up to God*"!
The *ancient* Doctors! Why not the *modern* Doctors, and be done
with it? Does this Anglican Goliath know anything about the
Catholic doctrine of the Eucharist? Has he ever read the decrees
of the Council of Trent? Is he acquainted with the instruction
which the Catechism sanctioned by that Council requires every
Catholic priest to give his people?

holy mysteries the substance of bread and wine is changed into the very Body and Blood of our Lord God. Dr. Waterworth may well speak of the frequency and distinctness of early allusions to doctrines whose future denial it was impossible to foresee, as truly 'wonderful.' If you ever become a Roman Catholic (which may God grant), I am sure, my dear friend, you will find abundant confirmation of the antiquity of your faith in St. Irenæus and Tertullian and St. Cyprian, though you should never reperuse a page of St. Chrysostom or St. Augustine.

So much for what may strictly be called patristic evidence. Be it not forgotten, however, that the Catholic does not refer, in proof of the perpetual identity of the faith, only to the expressed opinions of the Fathers. There are other mute voices, other records whereby the past 'being dead yet speaketh.' And with the briefest possible reference to these I will close this already lengthy chapter.

Consider, then, attentively the nature and object of the oft-mentioned Discipline of the Secret; and be convinced by the light which it now throws upon the mysteries it was once intended to conceal. Weigh, also, carefully the character of the charges brought by unscrupulous heathens against the votaries of the new religion, and the remarkable *manner* in which those calumnies were met. Scrutinize, moreover, well the silent witness of the Catacombs. Here is testimony to which Protestants were once very fond of alluding, in easy, off-hand manner, but to which their appeals have lately been growing singularly infrequent, and all mention of which, I venture to say, will in a few years be rigorously eschewed. It is but recently that the scientific study of these subterranean antiquities was undertaken on a large scale. At first the work under the direction of the Cavaliere de Rossi was watched by many Protestants with that interest which it so well deserved. But, alas, as the enthusiastic savant pushes his investigations, and the *opus magnum* approaches its completion, it is becoming hopelessly evident, not only that (as Bishop Newton would say) " the seeds of Popery were sown even in the Apostles' times," but that already in those days they had sprung up, and borne costly fruit.

Finally, study the primitive Liturgies—of which the Roman Mass itself is a most ancient example. I speak with the greater pleasure of these venerable and precious relics, because it was whilst reading them that the last trace of my own Protestant doubt vanished for ever, like a dream. They are all the same in substance; "one drop of water," as Bossuet says of them, "is not more like another;" take, however, if you choose, only two—those of the Churches of Jerusalem and Alexandria—and strike out any passages which there is reason to suppose were added after the third century. There can be no just doubt that the general forms of these Liturgies (of St. James and St. Mark) were given by the Apostle and Evangelist whose names they bear. So careful a scholar as Dr. Neale thinks it likely that St. Paul quotes from the Liturgy of St. Mark, and more than probable that he does so from that of St. James. For myself, I think that Dr. Neale's argument for supposing that the quotation in 1 Cor. ii. 9 is made, not from Isaiah, but from the Anaphora of St. James's Liturgy, may fairly be called a demonstration. Remembering, now, that the question before us is one of variation in *faith*—tell me whether the belief which was reaffirmed by the Church at the Council of Trent has swerved by a hair's-breadth from that held *in the first century* concerning the great primary doctrine of

Sacrifice; concerning the wondrous change wrought by Almighty power in the holy symbols; concerning the adoration due to our Divine Lord then present under the sacred veils;* concerning the intercession of the blessed Saints in our behalf; concerning the effectual commemoration of those who have slept in the faith of Christ; concerning the honor which should be paid by every creature to her who, being by divine grace immaculate, was chosen to be the Mother of her Creator.

Suppose that the Church of the present day were suddenly blotted from the face of the earth, and that the only memorials left of its existence were the Apostles' Creed, the Apostolic Letters of the New Testament, and the 'Petrine' Liturgy—the Liturgy of the Mass. Given these quantities, put together the faith of the Church in the nineteenth century. Substitute, now, for the Liturgy of St. Peter that of St. James, which is its precise equivalent, and solve the same problem for the first century. What is the result?

---

* "This is the prayer of Intense Adoration, which has its place in all Oriental Liturgies, and answers to the worship paid by the Western Church to our Lord's Sacramental Body and Blood at the Elevation of the Host. An attempt has been made to prove that the East does not agree with the West in paying the worship of *latria* to that Body and that Blood, from the long interval which separates the prayer of Intense Adoration (in all Liturgies except the present one) from the Invocation of the Holy Ghost. Nothing can be more futile ; the obvious tangible reason being, that during the consecration the holy doors were closed, or, in the Armenian Church, the veil was drawn ; so that the people could hardly be called on to worship that which was not presented to their eyes, as they can be and are in the Western Church, where it is so presented. But now the holy doors are opened ; hence the reason of the position of this prayer."—Dr. Neale, *Note* on the Liturgy of St. Mark.

$a+b+c=x;$
but $c=d;$ therefore
$a+b+d=x.$

If Protestants would only study *all* the Apostolic writings, what would become of their Protestantism? If they would take, for instance, the Epistle to the Hebrews, which was addressed, of course, to the Church at Jerusalem, and read it side by side with the formal ritual which was in use in that church at that very time, what a flood of light would be thrown for them upon the meaning of the Apostle's great argument concerning the one perfect and perpetual Sacrifice of the New Law! Whether, as Dr. Neale thinks, the Apostle quotes from the Liturgy of the Church to which he was writing, or whether the liturgical compilers adopted the words of their Apostolic correspondent, is of not the slightest consequence. The doctrine of the Epistle and of the Liturgy must in either case be identical. Hear, now, the words of the Apostle: "Having therefore, brethren, boldness to enter into the Holiest by the blood of Jesus, by a new and living way which he hath consecrated for us through the veil, that is to say, his flesh; and having an high-priest over the house of God; let us draw near with a true heart, in full assurance of faith, having our hearts sprinkled from an evil conscience, and our bodies washed with pure water." Hear also the words of the Prayer of the Veil in the Liturgy: "We render thanks to thee, Lord our God, for that thou hast given us boldness to the entrance in at thy holy places, the new and living way which thou hast consecrated for us through the veil of the flesh of thy Christ. We therefore, to whom it hath been vouchsafed to enter into the place of the tabernacle of thy glory, and to be within the veil, and to behold the Holy of Holies, fall down before thy goodness: Master, have mercy upon us: since we are full of fear and dread, when about to stand before thy holy Altar, and to offer this fearful and unbloody sacrifice for our sins, and for the ignorances of the people. Send forth, O God, thy good grace, and hallow our souls, and bodies, and spirits; and change our disposition to piety, that in a pure conscience we may present to thee the mercy of peace, the sacrifice of praise."

Setting aside the whole question of the Church's divine authority and infallibility (though that is really the ONLY question to be settled), I consider this last simple argument so overwhelmingly conclusive as to decide at once the entire doctrinal controversy between Protestantism and the Church whose ancient teaching Protestantism has seen fit to revise.

NOTE.

The history of the early heresies belongs properly to a period subsequent to the third century, and, therefore, has not been noticed in these last remarks. Moreover, the point which it decides is this, that the authority exercised by the Church of the first Councils is identical with that exercised by the Church of the last Councils: whereas for the nonce I have ignored authority, and argued upon lower ground. Of course, to a mind capable of being purely logical, the question of authority, as remarked above, is the only one to be determined. It was the study of Monophysitism which first startled Dr. Newman, by forcing upon his observation the similarity between the attitude of the Church towards Protestants and towards the heretics of the fifth century. It is hardly necessary to refer to the familiar passage in which he speaks of the "awful similitude" which he discovered, the "more awful because so silent and unimpassioned, between the dead records of the past and the feverish chronicle of the present." (*Apologia*, p. 156.) How many Anglicans may have been converted by a study of the Donatist schism in Africa? Doubtless not a few. I suppose Cardinal (then Bishop) Wiseman's application of this bit of primitive history to the case of the Anglican Church did more than any other one thing to open the eyes of the more earnest Tractarians to the direction in which their principles were leading them. They suddenly found themselves hoist with their own petar; antiquity was discovered to be on the side of authority; and great was the confusion which ensued.—(See *Dublin Review*, Aug., 1839. Article: *The Anglican Claim of Apostolical Succession*.)

The following from the Epistles of St. Augustine is not among the quotations given by the great English Cardinal. I borrow the passage from the late lamented R. I. Wilberforce, upon whom it seems to have made a deep impression : " How many, as we well know, were already wishing to be Catholics, having been aroused by the obvious call of truth, but, out of respect to their friends, put off giving offence to them from day to day! How many were held, not by truth, to which you have never trusted, but by the heavy bond of obdurate custom; so that in them was fulfilled the divine statement, 'a stubborn servant will not be corrected by words; for though he understand, he will not hearken'! How many, too, thought that the party of Donatus was the true Church, because their security made them torpid, fastidious, and tardy in recognizing Catholic truth! How many ears were stopped by the tales of slanderers, who alleged that it was some strange offering that we presented on the altar of God! How many, believing that it did not matter to what body a man belonged, provided he were a Christian, remained in the party of Donatus, because they had been born there, and because no one compelled them to depart thence, and to pass over to the Catholic Church!"—*Epist* xciii. 17.

CHAPTER V.

THE NOTES OF THE CHURCH.

THE Church at the Council of Constantinople declared concerning herself that she is One, Holy, Catholic, and Apostolic. These are not only her essential qualities, but her outward and visible signs, the marks whereby she may always be infallibly recognized.

I. The Church is, first, ONE. Unity is its prime characteristic. *Whatever else* the Church may be, it is one—visibly one, unmistakably one, incontrovertibly one.

A little while ago, unity, instead of being to me a mark whereby the Church might be plainly known, was rather an article of faith to be believed as a great mystery; or at best it brought before me an apparent contradiction, which it was necessary to explain away. I reasoned thus. The Church is as a matter of fact undeniably divided. But as a matter both of reason and faith the Church is undeniably one. Here is a difficulty. But it is only a difficulty. The Church must be one in some hidden, divine sense, which is not superficially apparent. And so I set myself to work to show how the Church might be one and at the same time not one. Of course it would be obvious to remark that in affirming the Church to be actually divided, I assumed that the Church was made up of such and such religious bodies. To this I would have promptly answered that the Church is apostolic; apostolic, that is, in its foundation, its order, and its succession. All the several churches, therefore, which can legitimately trace back the succession of their bishops to the Apostles, are parts of the one universal Church.* All apostolical churches are branches of the Catholic Church, and the Catholic Church is one; and if facts do not appear to tally with this conclusion, so much the worse for the facts.

Now, without stopping to notice how much is taken for granted in the word 'legitimately,' nor to comment in detail on the absurdity of a mode of reasoning which would include in the Church almost all the heretical bodies that were ever cut off from it, let me point out at once the fallacy which at the very outset turned my feet into a snare, and which has entangled many and many a clumsy thinker beside myself. *I had read the notes of the Church backwards.* I began with the note of Apostolicity; and from that advanced to the note of Catholicity; and ended with the note of Unity. I said in effect: The Church is Apostolic, Catholic, Holy, and—if it is not One, *it ought to be*. I believe that this unwarrantable (not to say illogical) inversion of the divine method for the identification of the Church is at the bottom of almost all the confusion and perplexity with which the minds of so many Anglicans are bewildered. They have put last what should have been taken first, and

---

* I did not insist upon agreement in *doctrine*, because I found it impossible to hold that doctrines which were mutually contradictory could be equally apostolic. Take, for instance, the Articles of the Synod of Bethlehem (A.D. 1672), and those of what Mr. Palmer calls the Synod of London (A.D. 1562). No man retaining his straightforward common-sense could pretend to reconcile the one with the other. And yet, both the Greek Church and the Anglican Church were, of course, members of the Universal Apostolic Church.

so have found only a stumbling-block and a puzzle in what might have been to them a shining beacon to guide their steps into the fold of peace.

The Church, then, is FIRST One. It is one because God is one, and *as* God is one.* The Church cannot be divided; for, if it could be divided, it would cease to be one; and, if it could cease to be one, it would cease to be the Church. To refer to an 'undivided' Church in the past is to assert the existence of a divided Church in the present; and to affirm the fact of division is to admit the loss of unity; but unity is of the Church's eternal essence, and cannot be lost. There is a sense in which we may speak of the undivided Church; but it is the same in which we speak of the undivided Trinity—undivided because indivisible. Nothing can be plainer than this. And now, O reader, ask yourself whether anything can be more plain than this also which I am about to assert further. All churches *but one* acknowledge that the Church universal is divided. *There is one Church, and only one, which holds and proclaims that unity has never been and never can be severed.*

Let us go back to more than a hundred years before the time when the Church first dogmatically announced the fact of that unity with which her Lord had endowed her, and read the faith of the primitive Fathers concerning the nature of this supernatural oneness. The treatise of St. Cyprian *De Unitate Ecclesiæ* is, incidentally, a splendid dissertation upon the truth that divine unity implies indivisibility, and that the Church, being divinely one, can never suffer partition or mutilation. Members may be cut off from

---

* St. John xvii. 21.

the Church, but the Church itself remains whole and undivided. A few passages will give the tenor of the whole discourse.

"The Lord says: I and the Father are one. And, again, of the Father, and the Son, and the Holy Spirit, it is written: And these three are one. And does anybody believe that this unity, coming from the divine solidity, cohering by means of heavenly sacraments, *can possibly* be divided in the Church, and divorced by the collision of wills?" "He who holds not this unity of the Church, does he think that he holds the faith?" "He cannot have God for his Father who has not the Church for his Mother." A type of the Church's unity is found in the seamless coat, woven from the top throughout, which even the Roman soldiers did not rend. In short, "unity *cannot be severed*, nor the one body by laceration (*discidio compaginis*) be divided." Surely it is solemn trifling for a man like Mr. Palmer to come and tell us that the "meaning" of the great Father "is that the unity of the Church cannot be so divided by laceration that in *one place* there shall be several true churches."[*] I have chosen St. Cyprian merely because he was the first to write directly and formally upon this subject. It would be easy to multiply quotations indefinitely; for the eternal unity of the Church is the burden of all Christian antiquity.

I said a moment ago that I used to consider the Roman, Greek, and Anglican 'Communions' as so many branches of the Catholic Church. In other words, I was guilty of cherishing that most fantastic of all conceits by which a rational being ever jeoparded his intelligence, which is known as the 'Branch Theory.' This remarkable hypothesis has

[*] *On the Church*, v. i. p. 59.

been devised as an attempt to explain how bodies which have ceased to have any connection with each other can still be parts of one organic whole; and its unique extravagance consists in the supposition that a branch begins to exist as a branch from the time that it is severed from the trunk. It might be called the artistic theory of unity. Unity is not necessarily synchronous (ὡς ἔπος εἰπεῖν), but historical; it is not a fact, but a diagram. By losing sight of the Church as an existing organization, and regarding it as a sort of genealogical tree, we succeed in obtaining a delineation which, if it does not give us unity as a present reality, shows us, by a very pretty and symmetrical picture, how unity may at least be represented on paper. Take, for instance, the following simple "illustration of the Catholic Church." The Church is, as it were, a tree. " For eight feet above the soil its trunk stands one and entire. Somewhere along the ninth foot the trunk branches into two main limbs. We will call the Eastern the Greek limb, and the Western we will call the Latin. Six feet further out on the Latin limb, that is to say, fifteen feet from the ground, that Western limb subdivides into two vast branches. The outmost of the two we will call the Anglican branch, the other we will call the Roman. These two branches and the Greek limb run up to a height of nineteen and a half feet [sic] from the ground. There they are, the three great boughs, each with its foliage, Anglican at the West, Roman in the centre, Greek at the East."*

The exquisite *naïveté* with which, in this passage, the Greek and Anglican Churches are represented as springing into vigorous ramose existence at the precise moment of

---

* *Sermons on the Failure of Protestantism*, p. 118.

abscission was too much even for *my* Protestant simplicity. "There they are, the three great boughs." But where is the trunk? 'Oh—don't you see?—the trunk ceased to exist ten centuries ago or more; we have nothing but branches now.' But how are these branches united? 'Why, dear sir,—do you not perceive in the sixteenth century the indissoluble connection of the Anglican bough with the parent stem, and the equally firm juncture of the Greek limb in the ninth?'

It is scarcely necessary to remark that the figure of a tree has been used by Divine Wisdom, and by inspired Apostles, as well as by uninspired Fathers of the Church, to illustrate the unity of many members in one body. The unity thus typified is, however, instantaneous, and the same through every moment of time. Schism is not the partition of unity; still less is it the germination of a new branch (risum teneatis, amici); but it is the cutting off from unity of that which had been a branch before. "I am the vine," says our Blessed Lord, "ye are the branches. If a man abide not in me, he is cast forth as a branch, and is withered." "Some of the branches," says St. Paul, writing of the Jewish Church, "were broken off." "The Church," says St. Cyprian, "is one, though she be spread abroad, and multiplies with the increase of her progeny. Even as the sun has rays many, yet one light; and the tree boughs many, yet its strength is one, seated in the deep-lodged root; and as, when many streams flow down from one source, though a multiplicity of waters seem to be diffused from its broad overflowing abundance, unity is preserved in the source itself. Part a ray of the sun from its orb, and its unity forbids this division of light; break a branch from the tree, once broken it can bud no more; cut the stream from its fountain, the remnant will be dried up. Thus the Church, flooded with the light of the Lord, puts forth her rays through the whole world, yet with one light, which is spread upon all places, while its unity of body is not infringed. She stretches forth her branches in the richness of exuberance over the whole earth, and pours abroad her bountiful and onward streams; yet there is one Head, one Source, one Mother, abundant in the results of her fruitfulness." *

St. Augustine follows St. Cyprian, and uses his metaphor with excellent effect against the Donatists. " The Catholic Church, which, as Cyprian says, ' stretches her branches in the richness of exuberance over the whole earth,' endures everywhere the scandals of those who, through the fault of their grievous pride, are cut off from her, some in one place and some in another. . . . For where they fall there they remain, and in the place where they are severed there they wither away; whence the Church herself from which they are cut off is spread even through those lands where those broken branches lie each in its own region." † And again : " Wherever heretics exist there is also the Catholic Church ; but the reverse is not true, that wherever the Church exists there is also any particular heresy. Whence it is evident enough which is the tree that

---

* *De Unitate.*

† Ecclesia Catholica, quæ, sicut ait Cyprianus, ' ramos suos per universam terram copia ubertatis extendit,' ubique sustinet scandala eorum qui ab illa, vitio maximæ superbiæ, præciduntur, aliorum hic, aliorum alibi atque alibi. . . . Ubi enim cadunt ibi remanent, et ubi separantur ibi arescunt, unde ipsa de qua præciduntur etiam in eas terras extenditur ubi jacent illa in sua quæque regione fragmenta.—*Contra Crescon.* 1. iv. c. 60. Such a passage as this deserves to be committed to memory.

spreads its branches over the whole earth" (here he quotes St. Cyprian again), "and which are the broken branches, that have no vital connection with the root, but lie and wither each in its own place."* Even the rude people of Africa could have told us what was meant by the figure of the vine and the branches; for their great Bishop taught them to sing a psalm against the Donatists, one of the closing stanzas of which runs thus:

> "Come, brethren, if you wish to be ingrafted in the vine;
> We grieve to see you lie thus cut off from it.
> Number your bishops from the very Chair of Peter,
> And in that list of Fathers trace the succession.
> This is the Rock against which the proud gates of hell do not prevail." †

"Every question concerning the Church," said the Bishop of Orleans a short time since, "is reduced finally to this question, *Where is Unity?*" Alas! how many sincere and earnest men are wearing out their lives in vain attempts to

---

* Ubicumque sunt isti (hæretici) illic Catholica, sicut in Africa, ita et vos; non autem ubicumque Catholica est, aut vos estis aut hæresis quælibet illarum. Unde apparet quæ sit arbor ramos suos per universam terram extendens, et qui sint rami fracti non habentes vitam radicis, atque in suis cuique jacentes et arescentes locis.—*Ibid.* c. 61. To the same effect, and with equal force, does St. Augustine use the similitude of the body and its members: Contingit ut in corpore humano, immo de corpore aliquod præcidatur membrum, manus, digitus, pes; numquid præcisum sequitur anima? Cum in corpore esset, vivebat; præcisum amittit vitam. Sic et homo Christianus Catholicus est dum in corpore vivit, præcisus hæreticus factus est, membrum amputatum non sequitur Spiritus. Si ergo vultis vivere de Spiritu Sancto, tenete caritatem, amate veritatem, desiderate unitatem, ut perveniatis ad æternitatem.—*Sermo in Die Pent. I.*

† The Latin is given on page 79. In a somewhat ambitious lampoon which appeared lately, under the title of the *Comedy of*

answer the vain question, *How can a lost unity be restored?* I have in mind the sorrowful instance of one, about whom I fear I have already written too harshly, whose career has been a strange illustration of his own confession that the restoration of unity has been the dream of his whole life.* We have seen how this man, scholar and thinker though he was, entered the Roman Catholic Church without acknowledging her claim to be an infallible teacher. We can now see at least why he was unable to recognize this lofty prerogative in the Church of his adoption; for it is plain, from all that he has written, that he never for one moment believed the Church in communion with the Successor of St. Peter to be the ONE CHURCH of our Lord Jesus Christ. Ah! if such men, instead of fancying themselves called of God to agonize for the recovery of that which if lost is lost for ever, could learn the truth of those words of the great martyr-bishop, ONENESS CANNOT BE DIVIDED,† and would set themselves to seek each for himself this indestructible unity, which is now what it has been from the beginning, and which 'if a man does not hold he cannot hold the faith,' how quickly would their troubles be ended, with what prompt obedience would

Canonization, the 'Metropolitan of Terra Nulla' is represented as narrating a conversation that had taken place between himself and a certain Greek bishop. The schismatic broaches the wonderful Branch Theory. Whereupon, says the Metropolitan, "I laughed at all this, and said, 'You believe, then, I see, in *the Branch Theory.*' 'I believe,' he replied, 'in the very words of our Lord.' I only laughed again, and kept on saying *Branch Theory, Branch Theory*, till the poor bishop was quite confounded, and left me in possession of the field." Really, his Grace of Terra Nulla was not only a prelate of excellent humor, but a man of uncommon good sense withal. He did well to be 'merry on a merry subject.'

* *The Church's Creed*, etc., p. 19.
† Scindi unitas non potest.

they return within the inviolable circle of the Church, and how cheerfully, while laboring each in his place for the blessed consummation, would they leave it to the great Shepherd of the sheep to bring back in his own good time those who have long been wanderers from the One Fold!*

II. The Church is Holy. Holiness is of the essence of the Church. The Church, therefore, cannot cease to be holy without ceasing to exist. As the unity of the Church implies its indivisibility, so the sanctity of the Church implies its incorruptibility. But the Reformation can only be justified by the assertion that the Church had become corrupted. Protestantism, therefore, is founded upon an absurdity. It is not to be supposed that as a Protestant I failed to see this difficulty. But, said I again, it is only a difficulty. The Church in the fifteenth century must have been holy in some divine sense which is not obvious. And so I set myself to work to demonstrate, this time, that the Church could be holy and at the same time not holy. I did not perceive, any more than before, that no absurdity could be greater than to turn what should be a note of the Church into a difficulty to be explained away.

The true Church, then, is holy. It is holy because the Third Person of the Eternal Trinity, who inhabits it, guides it, and controls it, is Holy. The true Church not only has never been reformed, but cannot possibly be reformed. The Council of Trent, as Bossuet somewhere says, feared not the word reformation; but the work accomplished at Trent was

---

* Unity and infallibility are complementary ideas. No man who has once comprehended the office of the Church as a *teacher* can misunderstand the nature of the Church's unity. The Ecclesia Docens must be infallible. But infallibility implies indivisibility

a reformation, not *of* the Church, but *by* the Church. It was the same which has been done by all Councils from the beginning, for which Councils are assembled, and for which the Church itself was created. The Church is engaged in a perpetual reformation of the degenerating tendencies, the evil passions, and the erring imaginations of men. But the Church itself, in its faith, in the order of its government, and in all its means of grace, is incorruptible, and cannot be reformed. " Men may gird a dome, or reform a political society, but they can no more reform the Church of God than they can give cohesion to the earth, or control the order of the seasons or the precessions of the equinox."* The Church which Christ loved and for which he gave himself, which by a divine lustration he has sanctified and cleansed, remains for ever holy and without blemish—a glorious Church, not having spot or wrinkle, nor any such thing.

The Church is holy, and its office is to make men holy. By the communication of the merits of Christ, through supernatural channels of grace, man believing is justified. Of unjust he becomes just, receiving the justice of God within him, which the Holy Ghost distributes to every one as he wills, and according to each one's proper disposition and co-operation. By the merits of the most holy Passion, man receives both the remission of sins, and the infusion of faith, hope, and charity; for faith, unless hope and charity be added thereto, neither unites man perfectly with Christ, nor makes him a living member of his body; for which reason it is most truly said that 'Faith without works is dead' and profitless (St. James ii. 20), and, 'In Christ

* Manning.

Jesus neither circumcision availeth anything nor uncircumcision, but faith which worketh by charity' (Gal. v. 6).*
But Protestantism, having declared the Church itself corrupt, proceeded to deny the effectual operation of grace in the justification of the sinner. Not content with endeavoring to soil the stainless robe of the Spouse of Christ, the Reformers aimed a deadly blow at the principle of divine sanctity in man. With the recklessness which marked all their movements, they announced the new doctrine † that when God justifies man he does not do what the word implies that he does; that, in fact, he does nothing at all, but merely considers as done what his Almighty power does not actually accomplish. In justification man is not made just, but only accounted so.

It does not enter into the argument of this book to discuss any point of doctrine whatever. Nevertheless, at the risk of appearing to digress needlessly, I will venture a word or two of comment upon what the Protestant heresiarch made bold to call 'The Doctrine' of the Reformation,‡ hoping that I may perchance touch thereby some misconception in minds which (like my own once) have never apprehended the teaching of the Catholic Church on this most important matter.

The fundamental maxim alike of the Continental and the Anglican Reformers was that man is justified by faith only.§

---

* See *Council of Trent*, Sess. VI. chap. vii.

† The most learned as well as the most candid of the Reformers admitted the novelty of the Protestant doctrine of justification. "I am aware," writes Melancthon, "that none of the ancients treated it in this manner."—Lib. iv. ep. 126, col. 574, *ap.* Bossuet.

‡ "If *the doctrine* fall, it is all over with us."—*Table-Talk*, quoted by Moehler.

§ *Thirty-nine Articles*, Art. XI.

Surely infatuation could have gone no further than to erect a dogmatical system upon a proposition which is not only contrary to the uniform teaching of Jesus Christ and the whole tenor of Holy Scripture, but which Scripture has distinctly and formally and *totidem verbis* condemned.* That no man was ever justified without faith the Church has always held.† Moreover, the Church teaches that no man can be "justified before God by his own works, whether done through the teaching of human nature or that of the law, without the grace of God through Jesus Christ," proscribing the contrary doctrine by an anathema,‡ and declaring it "necessary to believe that sins neither are remitted, nor ever were remitted, save gratuitously by the mercy of God for Christ's sake,"§ and that "none of those things which precede justification—whether faith or works—merit the grace itself of justification; for 'if it be a grace, it is not now by works,' otherwise, as the same Apostle says, ' grace is no more grace.'" ‖ But that the grace of justification itself is only the accounting righteous of those who are not actually made such, so that, without good works wrought by the grace of God through Jesus Christ, a man is justified by faith and faith only, this is a principle inconsistent with sound reason, logically subversive of holiness, expressly refuted by Scripture, and solemnly condemned by the Church.

It is a terrible confirmation of the warning of inspiration itself that in the Epistles of St. Paul there are some things

---

* St. James ii. 24.

† " Fides, sine qua nulli unquam contigit justificatio."—*Concil. Trid.* Sess. VI. cap. vii. " Fides est humanæ salutis initium, fundamentum et radix omnis justificationis, sine qua impossibile est placare Deo, et ad filiorum ejus consortium pervenire."—*Ibid.* cap. viii.

‡ *Ibid.* Can. I. § *Ibid.* cap. ix. ‖ *Ibid.* cap. viii.

which the "unlearned and unstable wrest to their own destruction," that for three hundred years Protestants have failed to perceive the distinction, nay, the antagonism which the great Apostle to the Gentiles everywhere recognizes between the works of the law (ἔργα νόμου), wrought without faith and without grace, and good works (ἔργα ἀγαθά), which are the very gifts of grace, and meritorious solely through the satisfaction of Jesus Christ. Nowhere does St. Paul say that we are justified by faith only. God forbid. Nowhere does he say that we are justified by faith without good works. Μὴ γένοιτο. What then? That we are justified by faith without the works of the law.* And this is precisely what the Catholic Church said at the Council of Trent. The negative formula 'faith without the works of the law' finds its complement in the positive expression 'faith with the works of charity' (Gal. v. 6). So far was St. Paul from denying the merit of the works of grace that no inspired writer is more explicit in affirming that to perseverance in such works the crown of eternal life will be awarded.†

To hunt down all the Protestant misrepresentations of the Catholic doctrine of justification would be a dreary task. Nor would it be of the slightest use to notice calumnies which are still repeated hundreds of years after their miserable hollowness has been exposed. With shame and confusion I remember how I used once to hold and teach that the doctrine of the merit of good works obscured—yea, made void—the infinite satisfaction of our blessed Redeemer. O my soul, *cave in ista tam frigida, tam jejuna calum-*

---

* Romans iii. 28.
† Rom. ii. 6, 7, 10; 1 Cor. xv. 58; Gal. vi. 8, 9; Phil. ii. 12, 13. See Moehler, *Symbolism*, § xxii.

nia delitescas! How couldst thou so long have sheltered thyself behind such a 'poor and cold and hungry cavil'! The virtue of good works derogatory to the sacrifice of Jesus Christ, when it is the justice of Jesus Christ within us which alone makes those works acceptable before God! The merit of Christian charity incompatible with grace, when it is the "very gift and fruit thereof"!* Shame on you, Protestants—for I, who have reproached myself, have a right to reproach you also—shame upon you, I say, for your ignorance, your blindness, and your folly! "According to Catholic principles, Christ, by justification, stamps inwardly and outwardly his living impress on the believer, so that the latter, though a feeble and imperfect, becometh yet a real copy of the type; on the other hand, according to the Protestant doctrine, Christ casts on the believer his shadow only, under which his continued sinfulness is merely not observed by God."† Tell me, which of these two doctrines redounds most to the praise of that mighty redemption which was accomplished upon Calvary? The Church, as the theologian just quoted says elsewhere, requires us to become righteous "in our own persons"; but

---

* Bossuet, in his *Exposition* (ch. viii.), sums up the Catholic doctrine of merit in the following propositions: " First, that our sins are pardoned by an act of pure mercy, on account of Jesus Christ; secondly, that we are indebted to the operation of a gratuitous liberality for that justice which is in us by the influences of the Holy Ghost; thirdly, that whatsoever good works we do, they are, all of them, the effects of grace." The form, " not weighing our merits, but pardoning our offences," which occurs in the English Communion Office, is a thoroughly Catholic one, and is, in fact, taken from the Canon of the Mass : *non æstimator meriti, sed veniæ, quæsumus, largitor. Per Christum Dominum nostrum.* But most Protestants read it as if it were ' not weighing our *demerits.*'

† Moehler, *Symbolism*, c. iii. § xiv.

at the same time she teaches us that we can never become righteous " through ourselves." Tell me, what room is there here for vainglory and confidence in the flesh? Would you know what it is in which a Catholic delights to make his boast and glory? Listen, then, to the words of our heaven-guided Teacher, the Church herself, as she tells us that neither the justice which we receive, nor the satisfaction which we are enabled to perform, is " so our own as not to be through Jesus Christ. For we who can do nothing of ourselves, as of ourselves, can do all things he co-operating who strengthens us. Thus man has not wherein to glory, but all our glorying is in Christ: in whom we live; in whom we merit; in whom we satisfy; bringing forth fruits worthy of penance, which from him have their efficacy, by him are offered to the Father, and through him are accepted by the Father."*
" God forbid that a Christian should either trust or glory in himself, and not in the Lord, whose bounty towards all men is so great that he will have the things which are his own gifts to be their merits."† As a Catholic, I understand for the first time the 'glorying' of that exalted Saint, who while he was the least was yet the greatest of all the Apostles. " By the grace of God I am what I am; and his grace in me hath not been void; but I have labored more abundantly than they all: yet not I, but the grace of God with me." " God forbid that I should glory save in the cross of our Lord Jesus Christ."

---

* *Concil. Trid.* Sess. XIV. cap. viii.
† *Ibid.* Sess. VI. cap. xvi. " Life eternal is due to the merits of good works; but the merits unto which it is due are gratuitously given us by our Lord Jesus Christ."—St. Augustine (Bossuet, *Var.* l. iii. § 27).

But I have wandered farther even than I intended, and it is time to go back.*

The Church is holy, and she is the fruitful Mother of Saints. Far be it from me that I should ever speak slightly of men whose pure and gentle lives have been the fairest ornament of the Church of England. I would not blot a single name that shines upon her roll. Shall I ever think of that pious Bishop, the manuscript of whose prayers was found at his death " worn in pieces by his fingers and wet with his tears," whose beautiful petitions I have tried in days gone by to make my own, and over which my tears too have fallen—can I think of *him* without the silent tribute of tender and respectful emotion? Can I, who have at least endeavored to learn humility at Bishopsborne, and

---

* There is power as well as keenness in the following passage from a writer whom it is always a privilege to lay under contribution : " In studying the writings of the Reformers, the thought has often involuntarily occurred to us that they entertained the opinion that it was something extremely dangerous to be really good ; nay, that the principle of sanctity, so soon as it was on the point of acquiring complete dominion over a man, contained the germ of its own destruction, as such a man must needs become arrogant, fall into vainglory, liken himself to the Eternal, and contend with him for divine sovereignty. Hence the security of believers seemed to require that they should ever keep within themselves a good germ of evil, because in this state we are better off! Accordingly, the matter was so handled as if real goodness were incompatible with humility, and as if it were in evil only that this virtue flourished."—Mochler, *Symbolism*, ch. iii. § 18. " These were new ideas," says the Eagle of Meaux, " with which Christianity was as yet unacquainted : a justice which the Holy Ghost infuses into our hearts, by infusing charity, is a pharisaical justice, which cleanses but the exterior ; a justice infused gratuitously into our hearts, for the sake of Jesus Christ, is a justice of reason, a legal justice, a justice through works !"—*Variations*, book iii. § 45.

devoutness at Bemerton, and who was taught from Hursley my first lesson of high affection for Her

> " whose name
> All but adoring love may claim,"

recall with aught but reverence and gratitude the memory of Hooker, and Herbert, and Keble? No, dear, true, sweet souls! May you rest in peace! Requiem æternam dona eis, Domine: et lux perpetua luceat eis. Yet do I not remember how as a Protestant I ever felt that the days of the Saints had passed away? There was something incongruous, half-ludicrous, in the notion of an Anglican Saint; and as for the inner life of Catholics, I knew nothing of it as yet. I looked wistfully back to those distant ages, hazy with a far-off glory, when virtues grew colossal, and devotion burned at a white heat; I knew that there were giants in those days; their heroic forms loomed upon me through the golden mist of the past. And I thought of our dwarfishness, and of the cold, calculating, niggardly piety of the present; and the words of the heathen poet came up to my lips:

> Hos utinam inter
> Heroas natum tellus me prima tulisset!

O the rush of indescribable joy which broke over me when I first began to study the lives and the writings of the Catholic Saints of modern times! The New World rose not more fair from the sea before the eyes of the Genoese navigator than did to me these undiscovered Islands of the Blessed. Here were the delights inexhaustible of which I had only distantly dreamed. Here was the lost race of

Saints, which I had fancied long extinct. O holy Church! O bountiful Mother! who, at the very time when men called thee barren, didst have for thy children an Ignatius, a Francis Xavier, a Charles Borromeo, a Theresa, an Aloysius, a Philip Neri; who in these latter days hast nourished a Francis de Sales, and a Vincent de Paul; who almost in our own times hast given us an Alphonsus Liguori, and a Paul of the Cross!

III. The true Church is Catholic. Catholicity is the third note of the Church. I have already spoken of the error of those who make it the first or the second. No one can rightly apprehend the Church's universality who does not first understand the nature of the Church's unity. *Unitas Catholica, quæ toto orbe diffusa est*, is the canon to which St. Augustine holds the Donatists, and by which he annihilates one after another their versatile sophistries.* The formula which is to guide us in our work of identification is not, The Catholic Church is somehow or other One; but, The Church, which is one and undivided, is also Catholic. And, read thus, the mark of Catholicity is so plain that 'the wayfaring man, though a fool,' cannot err by it. For, first, there is only one Church which *claims to be* Catholic, to be the whole Church. All other churches, though absolutely isolated—though between each and all the rest a great gulf is fixed—pretend only to be portions of the universal Church. And, secondly, there is only one Church which is *in fact* spread throughout all the world (toto orbe diffusa). All churches but one are local. Ubi cadunt ibi remanent.

* *Ep.* xliii. al. clxii. cap. 1. Unitas Christi, quæ toto orbe diffunditur.—*De Bapt. cont. Petil.* c. xxiv. Christiana unitas, diffusa toto orbe terrarum.—*Cont. Lit. Petil.* l. i. c. 20, *et alibi*.

The Notes of the Church. 199

The incomparable Augustine, who says the best things on almost every subject, applies the test of Catholicity also in another manner, equally simple and equally decisive. He finds in the *popular use of the name* 'Catholic' an argument as irresistible as it is obvious. More than once, while feeling my way towards the Catholic Church, I had occasion to discuss this argument with intelligent Anglicans; but, strange to say, I never found it treated with any respect. Such a criterion might do for St. Augustine's time, but—*nous avons changé tout cela.* Pardon me, gentlemen, but do you see the point? St. Augustine's appeal is to the common sense of mankind. That is Catholic which all the world calls Catholic. All question of doctrine is by him absolutely excluded. The word Catholic, he says, was not intended to express an opinion, but a fact.* Now, there is only one body—there always has been, and there ever will be, only one—having an objective, recognizable existence, which is *known* by the name of the Catholic Church. When the word Catholic is employed otherwise than in designation of this body, it represents, not a fact, but a theory. Here are St. Augustine's words. They need no comment, and admit no evasion.

" We are to hold," he says, " the communion of *that Church* which is Catholic, and which is *called* Catholic, not only by her own children, but also by all her enemies. For, in spite of themselves, even heretics and schismatics, when speaking, *not with their own set, but with strangers*, call the Catholic Church nothing else but the Catholic Church; for they would not be understood if they did not call her by the

---

* *Cont. Lit. Petil.* l. ii. c. 91.

name by which all the world calls her."* In another place he tells us that he is himself held in the Catholic Church, not only by that true wisdom which heretics do not believe to be in her, not only by the consent of nations and peoples, not only by her miraculous and perpetual authority, not only by the succession of her bishops from the very Chair of Peter to whom the Lord committed his flock down to the present bishop, but also, and "lastly, by the very name of Catholic, which this Church alone, amid so many heresies, has, justly, so appropriated that, though *all heretics wish to be called Catholics, yet if a stranger ask them, Where is the Catholic church? not a heretic of them all will dare show you his own church.*" †

This is the argument which I ventured to use at the very beginning of this little work, when I spoke of the Catholic Church as the great spiritual organization which is for ever vexing the peace of the world. Perhaps, good reader, you accused me of starting with an assumption. Be reasonable, and you will see that I wrote accurately. I did not say that the object of *your* aversion was the Catholic Church. What *you* hate is 'Romanism' and 'Popery.' But I was talking of the world, and I spoke as the world speaks. You call yourself a Catholic. Yes, I amused myself in the same way once; and St. Augustine has just told us that heretics

---

* *De Vera Relig.* c. vii.

† *Cont. Epist. Man. q.v. Fund.* c. iv. This test is not employed by St. Augustine alone. St. Cyril of Jerusalem, in his Catechetical discourses, tells his pupils: "When you go to any city, do not ask merely for the house of God, or for 'the church' merely, for all heretics pretend to have this; but ask, Which is the Catholic church? for this title belongs to our holy Mother alone."—*Catech.* xviii.

generally have a weakness of this sort. " Every one being free to assume whatever name he pleases, Laïs herself might write over her door: ' The House of Artemisia.' The great point is to induce others to give us such and such a name, which is not quite so easy as to decorate ourselves with it by our own authority; meanwhile there is no real name except that which is recognized."* Those whom the blundering populace persists in calling Catholics you are properly scrupulous to stigmatize as Romanists. Exactly; and we know from St. Gregory of Tours that the Arians and other careful heretics of his day were distinguished by the same nice scrupulosity. "*Romanorum* nomine vocitant nostræ religionis homines."† You say that it is the Papacy which is schismatic. Well, you and I have not been the first to distinguish ourselves by urging this brilliant paradox. The Donatists once turned the tables in the same dexterous manner upon the Church which ' numbered its bishops from Peter.' And poor St. Augustine was at his wit's end to answer them. Writing to one of their bishops, Petilianus by name, he could only exclaim: " How can we be the schismatics whose communion is spread over the whole world? But just as, if you were to tell me that I am Petilianus, I would not know how to refute you, unless by laughing at you as in jest, or by pitying you as insane, I don't see but I must do the same now." ‡

IV. Finally, the Church, One, Holy, and Catholic, is also Apostolic. We shall now have no difficulty in ascertaining the sense in which Apostolicity is, and was intended to be, a note of the Church. Evidently it cannot be meant

---

* De Maistre.   † *Hist.* l. xvii. c. 25.
‡ *Cont. Lit. Petil.* l. ii. c. 91.

that the Church is to be recognized by the fact that its doctrine is apostolic. This would be saying that the true Church is that which teaches the truth—which might be called an indeterminate proposition. We cannot know what the truth is until we have first found the true Church. And to discover the true Church we must have some external and visible mark to guide us. The sign which we are seeking can conceivably be no other than that of which all the ancient Fathers speak, and by which they identified the Church of their creed. It is found in the fact of the Apostolic Succession.

Are we to understand, then, that all churches which claim to have derived their orders from the Apostles are apostolic? Most assuredly not. We are not taught to believe in two apostolic churches, but in One Apostolic Church. To interpret the note of Apostolicity in such manner as to make void the note of Unity is rank absurdity. Away, then, with the threadbare notion that a church with orders is, ipso facto, a portion of the Church Apostolic. It is our old acquaintance, the Branch Theory, in a shabbier garb than ever. Why, all the heretics and schismatics that were ever anatomized by the Fathers and anathematized by the Church, set up this self-same pretension—and on far more plausible grounds than is done nowadays; and it was in condemnation of them that the Church defined herself to be Apostolic, and against them that the Fathers triumphantly turned the note of Apostolicity. The Apostolic Succession implies not merely the transmission of orders, but also, what is equally important, the conveyance of mission and jurisdiction. But jurisdiction must flow always from a single source. What this source has always been, what by the plighted promise of

Almighty God it ever will be, no one who has read the history of the Church, except through the pages of Anglican schismatics, can for one instant fail to understand or hesitate to believe. It resides in that supreme Episcopal Chair, where first sat one who by divine election was the Chief of the Apostles, to whom a New Name was given, and upon whom the indestructible Church was builded; in that central seat, where all the offices of the Kingdom of God meet and find their expression, which from the days of PETER to the days of PIUS THE NINTH has been known and honored, in grand pre-eminence, as THE APOSTOLIC SEE.

And thus we are brought at last to the direct consideration of that aspect of the Church towards which it is evident we have been gradually tending, and upon which we have more than once indirectly trenched. Indeed, I have found it impossible to treat of many things which are of the Church's essence without some reference to that which is the crown and consummation of them all, that in which, as I have just said, concentre all the functions of the divine economy which infinite Wisdom devised and called into action for the salvation of a fallen world.

Ah me! I feel as if I had but now laid the foundation of the work which I have undertaken. Not only the true proportion of the subject, but the plan which I had actually drawn out for myself, and the material already at hand, would make what has been thus far written only the introduction to a stately volume. But the circumstances under which I write warn me that it is time to be drawing to a close. Yet let me take courage from the hope that, though the labor be hurried and the execution imperfect, there may still be enough of symmetry in the design to accomplish the effect which I so earnestly desire. It will not, perhaps, be difficult even in a few words to give some sort of completeness to what has been thus far premised. We have learned that the Church must be one; it will be easy to understand by what means its unity has been divinely secured. We have seen that the Church is holy; we shall see what provision has been made for the perpetual purity of its faith and integrity of its government. There can be no indestructible unity without a fixed and indivisible centre. There can be no incorruptible faith without a constant and infallible tribunal by which that faith may be determined. There can be no true universality without agreement, and no agreement without a standard of uniformity. There can be no apostolic order without an apostolic governor, presiding "as a head over the members." Thus the several notes of the Church will be summed up in one. We shall know and believe that the Church is One, Holy, Catholic, and Apostolic because it is also ROMAN.

PART III.

THE CHURCH CONSIDERED AS AN ORGANIZATION.

CHAPTER I.

THE PRIMACY AND CHRISTIANITY.

PREJUDICE is always obstinate, but no prejudice is so wilfully stubborn as that which is professional. It is bad enough in any case that the mind should be settled in opposition to the truth, but, when a man has made it the special business of his life to oppose and controvert that truth, his intelligence becomes so fortified by his will as to be almost inaccessible. The citadel of his heart is well-nigh impregnable. *Missis ambagibus*, I have been led by my own experience to feel that the studies of a young Protestant divine, so far from fitting him to decide with greater promptness and accuracy upon the weighty yet simple proofs by which the Church is identified, have only the effect of deadening his intellectual susceptibility. His mind is systematically warped. He is trained to reason from false premises. He becomes, perhaps by sheer habit, the champion of untruth, and repels with something like angry impulsiveness the notion that he has from the first been defending an error, if indeed such a suggestion ever comes at all.

For myself, I had proposed it as the definite object of my theological reading to collect materials with which to confute what I considered the usurpation of the Papacy. I regarded the Papal Supremacy, not only as the one great barrier to the reunion of Christendom, and the one prolific source of corruption in the faith, but as historically *the perversion of Christianity*. I was sufficiently shrewd to perceive that a consistent Anglican must be an unmitigated opponent of the claims of the Roman See; but I was too shrewd, alas, to suspect that consistent Anglicanism was unmitigated folly. I had discernment enough to know that, if the Pope' was not Christ's Vicar, he must be Antichrist. But I had not the wit—or more truly the simplicity—to see that the syllogism which I boldly used as constructive was necessarily and evidently destructive. Looking back now, I can only shudder and weep, trembling as one who by the hand of a loving Watcher has been shaken from a deadly trance; and shedding tears of gratitude, that ere my heart was wholly cased in adamant a shaft from the quiver of God's grace found an entrance and a lodgment there.

And now, in entering upon the discussion of this subject, let us leave behind us all our prepossessions. It is not an easy thing to do. We often think that we have banished our prejudices, when we have only consented, *pro forma*, to waive them. I am not so foolish as to ask you to start with a determination to be convinced; but I do ask you to begin with a true *willingness* to be convinced. And let us reason, too, not lightly, and as over our nuts and raisins, but fasting in spirit and intent with every faculty of our soul; for, as a great thinker has said, Christianity itself is at stake in this matter. * To quote again, if I may do so on such a subject, the admirable words of a pagan :

> Discite, non inter lances mensasque nitentes,
> Cum stupet insanis acies fulgoribus et cum
> Acclinis falsis animus meliora recuset,
> Verum hic *impransi* mecum disquirite.

* "Agitur de summa rei Christianæ."—Bellarmine, *Præf. de Rom. Pont.* Dr. Waterworth says, and well says : " The Supremacy is to the heretics and schismatics of the nineteenth, what the

In the chapters which follow, I shall endeavor briefly to show that the Primacy of the Roman Pontiffs is an essential feature of organic Christianity.* In the present chapter I have only to introduce the subject by a few general and cursory, but, as it seems to me, very important observations.

First, then, it is quite inconceivable that the Supremacy is a mere accident of Christianity. *It is too big a thing to be an excrescence.* Its roots are struck too deep and too closely twined in the very heart of the Church to be torn away. It has grown with the Church's growth. It has for ages pervaded with its strength and spirit the whole body of Christendom. But more than this, if the Primacy be not of the essence of Christianity, then it has not merely invaded Christianity, but absorbed it. It is not simply an irregularity, but, as I lately called it, *the perversion* of Christianity. In so far as I admitted the alternative, I judged in accordance with reason; but in the use which I made of the alternative, I acted in defiance of reason, for I accepted the consequent—I made the argument, as I said, constructive—and yet continued to believe in the divine origin of Christianity and the Godhead of Jesus Christ. Whether I could have persevered in such an inconsistency I shrink from conjecturing. Perhaps there would have come a time

ὁμοούσιον was to the Arians of the fourth century: it is the saving doctrine, the doctrine which will lead men to Christ."—*England and Rome*, p. 46.

* I, of course, use the word Primacy here as equivalent to Supremacy. With the primacy which some generous Protestants are so willing to concede—a primacy which is a barren ecclesiastical title, a mere accidental honor, and means nothing at all—we are not concerned. A Primacy *jure divino* is a primacy of jurisdiction, and means Supremacy.

to me, as it comes to men all the world over who are not afraid to be logical, when the terrible conviction would have flashed upon me that to denounce the authority of the Popes as a usurpation, and as a perversion of Christianity, is to strike at the root of faith by denying the power and therefore the fact of the Incarnation. The alternative, then, really is, submission to the Apostolic See or infidelity. Men, I say, are being constantly driven by their Protestant principles into the dreary negation—which nowadays they call rationalism. Whether I should have been so driven I cannot tell; for before the day of trial came (if indeed it would have come at all) I gave up my Protestant principles, having seen the glory of God manifested in the organization of his Church, which, as Clement of Alexandria says, is "a city upon earth which can neither be taken nor tyrannized over, being administered by the Word."*

Let us look at this point more steadily, and in a somewhat different manner. Christianity, if it be not the most magnificent delusion which has ever dazzled the mind of man, is the realization in time of God's eternal plan for the restoration of a fallen race. But God's plans must have, so to speak, a divine intelligibility. Above all, must a work devised for the salvation of a creature discover in its development such marks of unity and order, such adjustment of forces to difficulties, such omnipotent energy in the gradual accomplishment of ends, as will enable the creature to recognize and co-operate with the design of his Creator. But, upon any Protestant theory, the history of Christianity presents the amazing spectacle of a God baffled in the execution of his intention, of a God who has miscalculated,

---

* *Stromata*, iv. 26.

a God perpetually struggling and perpetually foiled by the very powers of darkness whose conquest he had attempted. What intelligent heathen would find his faith coerced by such an exhibition? What intelligent believer could retain his faith in the shadow of such a consciousness? Protestantism is thus its own refutation; its principles are mutually destructive; its negations are at war with its assertions. If it be right in condemning the Roman Supremacy, it is convicted of absurdity in maintaining the supernatural origin of the Christian Church. Need I say that the incoherence which confounds us in this Protestant view of Christianity disappears the moment we cease to regard what is called the growth of the Papacy as the action of a disturbing power? Immediately the Primacy becomes as illustrious with meaning as it is prominent in fact. The history of Christianity referred to the Holy See as its centre is luminous with consistency, and marked throughout with the evidence of an almighty purpose. Here is evolution worthy of the mind and will of Deity. The very perturbations of heresy serve now only as an index of the resistless force whose advance they can neither hinder nor divert.

The fundamental conception of Christianity is that of restoration, not the restoration of individuals merely, but, as I said just now, of a race. It is God's method of reorganizing a world which, in the mysteries of his providence, has been thrown into disorder. Sin has brought derangement; its fruit was anarchy. The pride of man was followed by his dispersion. The condition of the gentile world is one of divisions, dissensions, and hostilities; and the highest effort at unity of which mankind is capable, that is to say, nationalism (if the word may be thus used), is only a species of systematized alienation. In the midst of this discordance God has set up a kingdom, which, in all its characteristics, no less than in its origin, is not of this world, but which is the type upon earth of the sinless City of God in Heaven. The distinguishing feature of this Kingdom is unity. In it all middle walls of partition are to be broken down; in it men are strangers no longer (for there is neither Greek nor Jew, Barbarian nor Scythian, bond nor free); its subjects are fellow-citizens with the saints, and of the household of God; its dominion shall continue until, in the consummation of time, the kingdoms of this world shall be no more, for they shall have become the Kingdom of our Lord and of his Christ.

And now look back through the eighteen centuries of Christianity, and discover in one glance the unfolding hitherto of this tremendous scheme. Behold the new Jerusalem, which is built as a city that is at unity in itself. Aye! 'walk about Sion, and go round about her, and tell the towers thereof. Mark well her bulwarks; consider her palaces; that ye may tell it to another generation.' Where are the celestial battlements before which the kings of the earth have gathered and gone by together—'they saw it and marvelled, they were troubled and hasted away'? Do you not know that in all the earth there is but one such city of the Great King? I say it again—and I would say it, if I could, a thousand times over—there is no escape from Protestantism but in infidelity. If this Holy Roman Catholic and Apostolic Church be *not* the Church which God founded, whose organization he has supervised, and within which he dwells among men, then Christianity is devoid of any supernatural proof which can persuade man's understanding. *There is then a fatal inconsistency between the theory of Christianity and its history.* That history only furnishes another problem, the strangest and most insolvable of all problems, to perplex the tired intellect. It adds only another load to "the burden of the mystery"—

> "the weary and the heavy weight
> Of all this unintelligible world."

But if this Roman Church be indeed the Mother and Mistress of all churches, then the phenomenon of *Protestantism* presents no difficulty whatsoever. On the contrary, it has its place in the development of the economy of redemption, and gives its confirmation to the harmony of the vast plan. We see in it only a revival of the old pagan spirit. It is merely a fresh attempt, though a more than usually violent attempt, on the part of gentilism to invade and take possession of the Church. The Church has thrown off many such assaults; doubtless it will have many more to throw off hereafter. However men may seek to disguise the meaning of the Reformation, the real and obvious aim of the movement was to break up that unity of type which distinguishes the Church as a spiritual kingdom. This unity, being supernatural in its nature, is galling to the mind which has not become spiritualized by grace. And at the time of the Reformation many men in the Church had so far lost all spiritual instinct that they had forgotten the primary purpose of Christianity. Their conceptions of the Church had become earthly. They endeavored to reproduce within the Church those very conditions of unregenerate humanity which it is the Church's mission to supersede. 'Humanam conati sunt facere Ecclesiam.'

This attack of the sixteenth century developed itself in the assertion of two antichristian principles, namely, of man's ultimate independence of all authority in matters of faith, and, secondly, the subordination of the spiritual to the secular order in matters of jurisdiction. The first of these doctrines, which was by no means consistently carried out in the reformed systems, is the much-boasted right of private judgment. Its source is self-will; its manifestation is individualism; its end is the destruction of all organized Christianity, and the miserable denial of the existence of any Church whatsoever.* So far as this irrational tenet has been permitted to produce its effects, it has driven man back towards spiritual and moral anarchy. Its history is summed up in an exclamation:

> En quo discordia cives
> Perduxit miseros!

The second principle, which was promptly realized wherever Protestantism gained a foothold, though it has not the glaring absurdity of the first, is intrinsically quite as extravagant, and equally deadly in its results. It was hailed with greedy joy by all the infidel forces of human society. And well may it have been welcomed, for its triumph would have been the victory of the world over the Church. Erastianism is the subjection of the eternal to the temporal. It means more than this. It is the appearance in an ecclesiastical form of that pagan nationalism which can have no counterpart in the true City of God. It means the partition of the Church, as a spoil, among the thrones and principalities to whose antagonisms her unity is in heavenly antithe-

---

* I say, the Reformers never carried out their own dogma. It is logically impossible that the right of private judgment should be the basis of any *system* whatsoever. What the Reformers practically did was to substitute for the precept, Hear the Church, the exhortation, Hear *us*.

sis. It was the badge of Protestantism everywhere, but it found its most complete expression in the Anglicanism of the Establishment.

Dr. Newman calls Erastianism the 'fruitful mother of all heresies.'* It would be easy to demonstrate the truth of this, as well as to illustrate it from history. But I have been rather anxious to direct attention to the heresy of Erastianism itself, to its inherent falsity, and its incompatibility with the notion of the Church as a single theocratic organization. National Christianity is a pitiful contradiction in terms. Its advocacy could be undertaken only by men who have declined, I do not say to low views, but to utterly mundane and carnal views of the nature and office of the Church; by men whose souls are dead to the past, and who look not into the future; by men who have forgotten, or never understood, the meaning of that mighty drama which began with the Fall and will end with the Judgment, and in the midst of which stands out that awful fact whose significance is lost unless we see it against the background of eternity—the fact of the Incarnation. Yet this, *this* is the principle which was urged by men calling themselves Christian against that unity which subsisted and can only subsist under the Primacy of the Holy See. "Whereas now," says Barrow, "Christendom is split into many parcels, subject to divers civil sovereignties, it is expedient that correspondently there should be distinct ecclesiastical governments, independent of each other, which may comply with the respective civil authorities in promoting the good and peace both of church and state."† I have

---

* *Anglican Difficulties*, p. 137.

† *Supremacy*, Suppos. V. iv. 10, p. 239. "No ecclesiastical power can interpose in the management of any affairs within the territory of any prince without his concession. By the laws of

had occasion to study only too often the pages of this anti-papal champion; I have found them hot, indeed, with vituperation; I have read of 'pretences' and 'usurpations,' of 'cursings and damnings,' of 'janizaries' and 'mercenary clients,' of 'wriggling' popes and 'vixenly'* popes, of 'rakehells' and 'vessels of Satan'; but I have searched the reeking volume in vain for any plain *reason why* the Church *should not* be united under a single central government, other than this: that 'by the laws of God' the Church was meant to be 'split up into parcels,' and to be the pliant handmaid of the state.

There is generally little profit in speculating concerning the future, nor is it any sign of acuteness to say that we are on the eve of great changes, seeing that there has scarcely been a period of history when men have not reasonably said the same thing; yet in taking leave of this subject it is difficult to avoid the remark that that particular phase of Protestant heresy which was expressed in the Royal Supremacy seems to have already run its appointed course. The Established Church is even now breaking up. "The Anglicanism of the Reformation," as a far-sighted watcher said a few years ago, "is upon the rocks, like some tall ship stranded upon the shore, and going to pieces by its own weight and the steady action of the sea."† Every day is giving confirmation to the truth of these words. Nothing can save the unhappy wreck from soon crumbling into the

---

God, (!) and according to ancient practice, princes may model the bounds of ecclesiastical jurisdiction, erect bishoprics, enlarge, diminish, or transfer them as they please."—*Ibid.* p. 280. Such passages are perpetually occurring in Barrow's book.

* An epithet applied to the great St. Leo.
† Manning (in 1864).

The Primacy and Christianity. 217

impatient flood, to be driven hither and thither by the undistinguishable waves of sectarianism and unbelief.

I have spoken of the unity which marks the organization of the Church as supernatural in its character. This expression would perhaps not be formally objected to by any one professing to believe in a Church at all. We need not, however, stop again to smile at a unity which is so extremely supernatural as to be altogether invisible. The unity with which we are concerned is one which *marks* the Church, and distinguishes it *as an organization*. And the point I am driving at (to use a phrase which I believe has Locke's authority) is that the unity which holds together the Catholic Church under the Primacy of the Roman Pontiffs is supernatural, and is indirectly proved to be supernatural by the fact that no satisfactory explanation of it upon natural principles has ever been achieved. Unbelievers of all grades are quite at fault in accounting for it. It is of course very easy to talk of absolutism and of autocratic rigors; but where obedience is purely voluntary there is no room for despotism. What compulsion has held the Church of France, for instance, in its allegiance, for the last three hundred years? What the Church in Ireland? What power chained the Italian bishops to the Papal Throne when the new Kingdom of Italy started on its career of mad reform? What force has prevented a Reformation and a Royal Supremacy in every state in Europe? No—coercion will not afford us a solution. Neither shall we fare better if we run through the whole list of human motives and passions. They are all ranged not on the side of unity, but of schism. Pride, self-will, ambition, the right of private judgment, and what men by a euphemism call the spirit of independence, all these are centrifugal forces. They are natural tempers, which flourish in that state of humanity which we have called gentilism. They will account perfectly for the Greek schism, and for the rebellion which proved so contagious in the sixteenth century. But they will *not* explain the attraction which, in opposition to all carnal instincts, in disdain of every temporal allurement, in defiance of threats and persecutions, in poverty and loneliness, amid scorn and contumely, through dungeons and exile and martyrdom, has bound the hearts of millions, not in loyal submission merely, but in unselfish, unswerving, passionate fidelity, to a single defenceless old man, himself perhaps a captive, perhaps a martyr, but a tyrant never. This obedience which is more than obedience, this unquenchable devotion, can have but one adequate incentive. The fire which has burned thus steadily is lighted on the altar of faith, and kindles in the flames of hope and love. Yes, this force, by which the unity of the Church is as it were *fused*, is FAITH. But faith is the gift of God.*

One word more. The mission of the Church is not to bring itself into harmony with the world, but to bring men back from the world into unison with God. The world itself—using the word in the sense in which Jesus Christ and his Apostles used it—can never, never be won over. An evil power is in possession, who has been called with a terrible distinctness the 'prince of this world,' the 'spirit which now worketh in the children of disobedience.' Between the Christian and the world stands the Cross of Christ, whereby the world is crucified unto the Christian and he unto the world. Between the Church and the world there is waged a truceless warfare, which shall cease only when he who

---

* 'Fides est donum Dei'—words which have rung in my ears ever since the day I became a Catholic.

now sits at God's right hand shall have put the last enemy beneath his feet, and shall deliver up the kingdom to God and the Father, having abolished all authority and principality and power. The Church, as St. Augustine says, is in conflict with the spirit of the age; nor is it with the spirit of any particular age, but of every age. The long struggle is at this moment going on; and never surely was the encounter more deadly, and the issue to human sight more doubtful. At the beginning the young Church stood on one side, and over against it was the ancient 'civilization.' A Greek or a Roman would have called it the war of politics, culture, luxury, and philosophy against a rising flood of superstition, bigotry, asceticism, and fanaticism. But God chose the mean things of the world to confound the mighty, and the foolish things to confound the wise, and the ancient civilization fell. But its fall was not its destruction. Slowly but skilfully the enemy has gathered his scattered forces. His attack, never intermitted, has grown bolder. The treacherous strategy of the sixteenth century is followed up now by open assault. The old forms of Protestantism have done their work, and the great mass of Protestant Christendom is Christian only in name. With subtle craft, the 'god of this world'—the Welt-Geist—has been laboring to disassociate once more the Church and 'civilization.'* Once more the cry is raised of superstition and fanaticism, but with a new and more insidious significance; for the Church is represented now as effete, obstructive, retrogressive, while the world boasts of fresh life and exults in the heat of vigor-

---

* I have said enough elsewhere in refutation of the monstrous supposition that the Church is the antagonist either of civilization or true progress.

ous advance. Again the Church stands on one side, venerable with the toil of eighteen centuries, and over against it lower the menacing ranks of 'progress, liberalism, and modern society.'

And does not the Church quail at the onset? Not for an instant. Christ's Vicar speaks, and his words are as the words of Christ himself. Jesus Christ, in the night in which he was betrayed, said to his disciples: 'The prince of this world cometh, and in me he hath not anything.' The Head of the Church to-day answers the fierce clamor of the nations, and, with a voice that trembles not for either haste or fear, condemns the demand that the Roman Pontiff should reconcile himself and come to terms with progress, liberalism, and modern society.* Thank God, thank God for this last, this most convincing confirmation of the divine origin and the divine destiny of the Christian Church. The Church is true to her mission. She has swerved not since the days of the Apostles. Still she calls aloud to men: 'Save yourselves from this perverse generation.' Still she repeats to her children those words which once in her hearing the Eternal Son addressed to the Eternal Father: 'I have given them thy word; and the world hath hated them, because they are not of the world, as I also am not of the world.' Still she calmly faces the hate of her foes, and endures their reiterated onslaughts. The gates of hell shall not prevail against her.

O my brothers, you to whom I have been bound by ties of association so dear and tender, you whom I know to be

---

* *Syllabus*, Error LXXX. Romanus Pontifex potest ac debet cum progressu, cum liberalismo, et cum recenti civilitate sese reconciliare et componere.

honest and earnest men, I would turn back a moment, I would fling myself at your feet, and with tears and passionate entreaty implore you to collect yourselves and look about you ere it be too late. While nothing has more confirmed my faith in the Church than the spectacle of this its battle with the world, nothing has so filled my heart with terror for those whom I have known so long and well as to hear Protestants of every grade—and you, too, O my companions—joining in this wild infidel shout that the Pope has declared war upon modern civilization. The awful words sound heavily in my ears: 'The God of this world hath blinded the minds of them which believe not.' Will *you also* reject Christ in the person of his Vicar, saying: 'We will not have this man to reign over us'? Will you, too, be found fighting on the side of the world, the flesh, and the devil? You know full well that between the Church and the world there can be neither peace nor compromise. Behold the Church, behold the world! If this which you see be *not* the great conflict of the ages, *then where* is *the Church and where the world?* The world does not care a straw for your Anglicanism and your Protestantism. You may work yourself up into an illusory rage against the world, you may call it all the names you choose, and defy it to combat; but the world shrugs its shoulders and smiles at you. It knows that you are enrolled among its most efficient auxiliaries; it counts on you to do its deadliest work; for you wear a uniform which is like that of the army of the Lord. If you have any Christianity in you at all, surely this argument must frighten you. For God's sake, then, stop—before you again utter that mad battle-cry of 'progress and modern society.' 'Know you not that the friendship of the world is enmity with God? Whosoever therefore will be a friend of the world is the enemy of God. Do you think that the scripture saith in vain, The spirit that dwelleth in us lusteth to envy? But he giveth more grace. Wherefore he saith, God resisteth the proud, but giveth grace to the humble. Submit yourselves therefore to God.'

CHAPTER II.

THE PRIMACY AND PROPHECY.

THE beginnings of Christianity should be studied in the light of its subsequent history. It will not do to examine the record of our Lord's life upon earth with eyes which are industriously averted from the procession of events which forms the divine sequel to that divine introduction. Still less rational is it (on the part of those at least who acknowledge the supernatural origin of the Christian religion) to set Christianity as it were in opposition to itself, and to seek in effect to demonstrate that things have not fallen out as Christ designed that they should. This nevertheless is what Protestants attempt to do. They would persuade us that words which Christ uttered with a really innocent intention have been so wrested by the perversity of man as to be made the foundation of the most consolidated system of error and oppression which the world has ever known. Protestants either do not believe what they profess, or do not understand what they profess to believe. I mean that they either have no faith or a most unintelligent faith in the divinity of Jesus Christ. They have no 'real apprehension' of our Lord's omniscience. They do not truly understand that what he did during his brief earthly ministry he did with the future all before him, as it had been before him from all eternity; that every word which fell from his human lips had been predetermined in the counsels of the Trinity, and was uttered with the most absolute foreknowledge of its consequences. Neither do they comprehend his omnipotence. They are not conscious that whatsoever he promised he has himself performed. To them it is as if Christ gave men a religion, and then left it to push its own way to conquest, or rather left it in the hands of men, to be debated over, and misunderstood, and tampered with, and perverted. They know not that he who laid the first stone has superintended the whole construction; that the Church has been built up, as it was founded, by the power of God.

Prophecy is God's method of giving men an intimation of what he intends to do. Men are sometimes so foolish as to interpret the prophecy according to their own ideas of the fitness of things. They would cheerfully instruct the Almighty as to the proper meaning of the words which he has vouchsafed them. But God, for all that, accomplishes his predictions after his own manner. The ancient people of Israel were forewarned of the coming of the Anointed One; when Messias came he did not answer their expectations; such was not the fulfilment which in the exercise of their private judgment they had an undoubted right to anticipate; and on the day that their King was brought forth to them, they cried out, 'Away with him.' The Jews were mistaken; they had *not* a right to interpret God's words for him; and Jerusalem is trodden under foot of the Gentiles until the times of the Gentiles be fulfilled.

But while it is one thing for men to say how a prophecy *ought or ought not* to be brought to pass, it is quite another thing that they should recognize the accomplishment which God himself has made good. It is not difficult to perceive that God has kept his word. Otherwise prophecy is altogether useless and absurd, and the Christian Church has stultified itself by repeating through all these centuries those words of Philip to Nathanael: 'We have found him of whom Moses in the law, and the prophets, did write, Jesus of Nazareth.' No! It is easy, as St. Cyprian says, to offer proofs to a faithful mind.* Even in Jerusalem there were a few elect souls who were waiting for the consolation of Israel, and who knew it when it was come.

The Primacy of the See of St. Peter is the most prominent fact in the history of Christianity. And it is a fact which is inseparably associated with a distinct prophecy. Moreover, the Primacy is not only professedly grounded upon the prophecy in question, but is actually so grounded. I do not speak yet of any divine correlation between the prediction and the event, but merely of such connection as is a matter of historical certainty. I mean that the words of Christ are so substantially the foundation of the Papal power that the latter could never have existed without the former. No intelligent student will think of denying this. Indeed, without looking into the past at all, it is perfectly plain that, if it were not for the divine sentences so often quoted, the Pontifical claims would be wholly without sanction, and the Papacy would fall to pieces in an hour. Such being the case, I affirm that the admission of Christ's divinity compels also the admission that the connection between the prediction and the event is of divine intention, and exhibits the most literal illustration of the saying of the Apostle that the Son of God upholdeth all things by the word of his power. The fact must be either the fulfilment of the prophecy or its misinterpretation. But the latter supposition is an absurdity. Facts are never misinterpretations of God's promises. Men may misinterpret a prophecy in their own minds, but God never misinterprets himself in

* *De Unitate Ecclesiæ*, 3.

history. It is no answer to this whatsoever to say that men may be mistaken in supposing that there is any essential relation between the words of our Lord and the fact of the Supremacy; for I have already shown that the association cannot be a mere subjective misapprehension, since it is an objective reality. It would be, indeed, sufficiently incredible that God should have uttered a promise which he eternally foresaw would be misunderstood by the great body of Christians in all ages; but that God should have so ordered events in the development of his Church as to make his own words the very prop and corner-stone of a system which opposes itself to his gracious purposes and perverts the truth which he has revealed, this is inconceivable. Be candid, O my friend, and confess that this argument is unanswerable.

We have been reasoning in general from the fulfilment to the prediction. It may be worth our while for a moment to review the prophecy itself, and see how plain it is. Barrow indeed says: "Such a power [as that of the Roman See], being of so great importance, it was needful that a commission from God, its founder, should be granted in downright and perspicuous terms; that no man concerned in duty grounded thereon might have any doubt of it, or excuse for boggling at it."* But what Barrow boggled at was not so much the granting of the commission as that exercise of it which did not suit his notions of national Christianity. Mr. Palmer, too, is very courageous. "Power," he says, "in order to be *developed*, must first be *instituted*; and it is exactly this *institution* which we do not see in the case of the pretended supremacy. Let the divine *institution* of this

* *Supremacy*, Suppos. I. iv. 1.

power be demonstrated, and we will not offer any objection to its development."* Ah, Mr. Palmer, how is it that the words of the old proverb did not steal into your recollection: 'None are so blind as those who *won't* see'? Alas! it becomes me not to speak lightly of such visual incapacity. It is but a few short months ago that I also was as one who saw not; and it is no thanks to my faithless heart that a compassionate finger was laid upon my dull eyelids. I did not even cry out: O son of David, have mercy on me. "Jesus passed by, and saw a man which was blind from his birth. . . . And he anointed the eyes of the blind man, and said unto him, Go, wash in the pool of Siloam (which is by interpretation, Sent). He went therefore, and washed, and came seeing."

To proceed, then. What Jesus did during the three years of his public ministry was done (I repeat) in preparation for the ages which were to come. He was silently engaged in laying the foundations of the new Kingdom of God. Every act of his had a meaning which runs through all time. I speak of his operations, moreover, as in a manner silent. His purposes were veiled by the majestic reserve of Deity. He did not need to explain what he either said or did; for his words would work their own accomplishment, and his actions would discover in due time their own significance. Thus much he implied when, on a certain occasion, he told one of his disciples: "What I do thou knowest not now, but thou shalt know hereafter." Jesus, so far as we are allowed to know, had very little to say concerning the *future constitution* of his Kingdom. He trained his chosen apostles rather to have a simple faith in himself, and prepared them

* *On the Church*, part vii. ch. viii. append.

by a divine discipline to receive his parting assurance: "All power is given unto me in heaven and in earth. Behold, I am with you all days, even unto the consummation of the world." Once, however, he saw fit to break this august reticence in a more marked manner than at any other time. *Once and once only* he used the words MY CHURCH, and made a distinct affirmation of his far-reaching intentions in regard to that Church. What he then said must have been of the gravest possible import. All the world knows that dialogue by heart; alas, that we should need to repeat it here!

Jesus had asked his disciples of the opinions of men concerning him; and they had replied indiscriminately. He then put them the direct question: "But whom do you say that I am?" And Simon Peter answered: "Thou art Christ, the Son of the living God." It was the first *confession* of the Incarnation. "And Jesus answering said to him: Blessed art thou, Simon Bar-jona; because flesh and blood hath not revealed it to thee, but my Father who is in heaven." God the Father had elected Simon, and made known to him before all others a mystery which no one could acknowledge but by the Holy Ghost.* "And *I* say to *thee*, that THOU ART PETER." See how the one declaration corresponds to the other. Simon had said: "Thou art Christ." Jesus answered: "Thou art Peter." The one was the most sublime confession that man could make to God; the other was the most momentous announcement which God could make to man. He had called him Simon just before; now he gives him his new name. When Simon had first been brought to Jesus by his brother Andrew,

---

* 1 Cor. xii. 3.

Jesus had looked upon him, and said: "*Thou art* Simon Bar-jona; thou *shalt be* called Cephas, which is interpreted, Peter"—a Rock. As God, having set apart a chosen race in preparation for Christ's coming, gave new names to Abram and Jacob, the ancestors of that long royal line, so Christ, having come, singles out Simon the son of Jona, and tells him that his name also shall be changed. And now the new title is both conferred and explained. "Thou art Cepha; and upon this Cepha"—the words in the language which our Lord spoke are identical:—"THOU ART A ROCK; AND UPON THIS ROCK I WILL BUILD MY CHURCH; AND THE GATES OF HELL SHALL NOT PREVAIL AGAINST IT." Stupendous prophecy! Where among all the words of God shall its mate be found?*

Upon Peter, then, Christ would build his Church. In what manner he would build it, he did not say; that would

---

* It is too late in the day to 'boggle' at the difference in gender between Πέτρος and Πέτρα. As Dr. Hammond says, "the word Πέτρος in the masculine is exactly all one with Πέτρα in the feminine, it being in the Syriac, 'Thou art Kipha, and on this Kipha.'" No one will think of quoting St. Augustine's criticism on this point who has read St. Augustine's ingenuous confession of his literary antipathies. With perhaps the greatest intellect that ever adorned a Christian soul, it is quite clear that his forte was not etymology; nor is it, I trust, irreverence towards the chief of the Fathers to speak of his linguistic acquirements as small Greek and *less Syriac*—even if one happens to know about as little Syriac as the great St. Augustine. The criticism in the *Retractations* (1. xxi. 1) is a verbal one. St. Augustine was "*held in the Catholic Church by the succession of its Bishops from Peter*" (*Cont. Epist. Fund.* c. iv.)—Peter, who "by reason of the Primacy of his Apostolate represented the person of the Church" (*In Johan.* cxxiv. 5), Peter, whom "Christ made one with himself, committing his sheep to him as to another self" (*Serm.* xlvi. 30). But I must not anticipate.

be 'known hereafter.' It was enough that against the Church *as built upon Peter* the gates of hell should *never prevail.*

It would be sufficient for our argument if we stopped here. I have shown that, if Christ be God, the Papal Supremacy must be the fulfilment of the prophecy upon which it is grounded. I might now turn the proof round, and say that, if Christ be God, the prophecy which we have glanced at can find an adequate fulfilment only in the Papal Supremacy. It needed such a fact to satisfy the terms of such a promise. And I might say, moreover, that Christ is proved to be God by the awful correspondence of the event to the prediction. But, though the argument is complete, let us not think our time misspent if we comment briefly upon what Jesus chose to say still farther, upon this and two other memorable occasions.

"And I will give to thee the keys of the kingdom of heaven." It was God who spoke, and the words were "not idle and inoperative words." * What mortal man will dare to circumscribe the bounds of the power here conceded? To Peter and to Peter alone the words were addressed. To Peter was promised supreme jurisdiction in the Church which was to be built upon him. "And whatsoever thou shalt bind upon earth, it shall be bound also in heaven; and whatsoever thou shalt loose upon earth, it shall be loosed also in heaven." Here we come at last to a grant which was afterwards extended to the other Apostles also. But that God chose to make it to Peter first *means something.* To Peter *singly* was given in promise what was subsequently so bestowed upon the rest *collectively*

---

* St. Jerome.

and with him. It is one thing to exercise authority in a house, and a very different thing to hold the keys thereof.

Passing on now to the night of our Lord's betrayal—the hour of his enemies, and the power of darkness—we are arrested by another sentence, which might well be deemed a continuation of the words of prophecy and promise already rehearsed. At any rate, it is by the bright light of the earlier revelation that the deep significance of the later assurance is disclosed. " Simon, Simon, behold, Satan hath desired to have you "—ὑμᾶς, *all of you*, you my chosen Apostles—" that he may sift you as wheat; but I have prayed for thee "—σοῦ, *thee in particular*—" that *thy faith fail not;* and thou being once converted, *confirm thy brethren*." To Peter the true faith had been first revealed; for Peter's faith alone God gave a guarantee that it should be indefectible. And because his faith was thus divinely secured, it was to be Peter's office, after he had once passed his trial, to be the strengthener of his brethren.*

Finally, when the humiliation of that trial was over, Jesus, having fulfilled his infinite agony and risen for ever

---

* Notice that Jesus this time calls his disciple ' Simon.' It was his habitual mode of addressing him (St. Matt. xvi. 17; xvii. 25; St. Mark xiv. 37; St. Luke xxii. 31; St. John xxi. 15-17). Though Jesus had promised him the name of Peter, he himself (so far as we know) used the name only twice: once, *when he formally conferred it* (' Thou art Peter,' etc.); and again immediately after the declaration above quoted, that his disciple's faith should never fail: "And he (Simon) said to him: Lord, I am ready to go with thee both into prison and to death. And he said: I say to thee, *Peter*, the cock shall not crow," etc. As if he would say: ' I tell thee that though thou art the Rock upon which I have promised that I will build my Church, thou shalt first deny me.' The evangelists almost always use the name Peter. See St. Mark xiv. 37.

impassible from the grave, spoke to Peter yet once more The work of redemption was accomplished; the ascension was at hand; and all things were now ready for the action of the Church to commence. And this time Christ gave neither a prophecy nor a promise, but a commission. Why recite the words of that triple charge? If we are determined to see in it nothing but an admonition and a reinstatement, we shall doubtless be allowed to succeed in our determination. Yet it is impossible to conceive language which shall express more positively a delegation of authority over the universal fold of God. No limitation is hinted at. The entire flock is committed to Peter's care. Moreover, as if to emphasize the completeness of the investiture, the words of the terse triplet are varied each time: Βόσκε τὰ ἀρνία μου: Ποίμαινε τὰ πρόβατά μου: Βόσκε τὰ πρόβατά μου.* No language even distantly resembling this was ever addressed to any other Apostle. It seems as though Christ were as it were anxious

---

* That Christ meant nothing by committing *the sheep as well as the lambs* to Peter's charge, they may maintain who dare. Observe, also, that ποιμαίνειν is a wider word than βόσκειν. It is not merely *pascere*, but *regere, docere, tueri*. Every one knows the Homeric ποιμὴν λαῶν as a kingly appellation. What is much more to the point, Christ had called *himself* ὁ ποιμὴν τῶν προβάτων (St. John x.) Now he makes Peter *his Vicar*—as St. Ambrose has beautifully said: "Peter is grieved because he is asked the third time, 'Lovest thou me?' For he is questioned who is doubted. But the Lord does not doubt; and he enquires, not to learn, but to teach, now that he is about to be raised to heaven, whom he was leaving unto us as it were the Vicar of his own love. For thus have you it: 'Simon, son of John, lovest thou me? Yea, Lord, thou knowest that I love thee. Jesus saith to him, Feed my sheep.'"—*In Luc.* l. xv. 175. Compare St. Augustine: "It was the will of Christ to make Peter, to whom he commended his sheep as to another self, one with himself, that so he might commend his sheep to him."—*Serm.* xlvi. 30.

to call our attention to this circumstance; for before he laid upon Peter the burden of such a pastorate, he took pains to elicit the fact that Peter loved him more than all the rest. Ah, my friend, what means that '*more than these*'?

It is easy now to understand the acknowledgment of St. Peter's primacy which appears on almost every page of the inspired narratives. Peter's name is always at the head, whether in the formal lists of the Apostles, or when only two or three are mentioned incidentally. St. Matthew expressly calls him "the first;" and St. Luke, in his second catalogue, distinguishes his name by the article. The other Apostles are often in a manner included in Peter, by such a form as this: "Peter and they that were with him." Even the Angels recognized his singular eminence, and set his name apart from all the rest: "Go, tell his disciples and Peter"—was the message of the shining watcher at the sepulchre to the women whose sweet spices were no longer needed. It is easy also to interpret the personal prominence of St. Peter in all the scenes in which he bore a part while our Lord was yet visibly present with his disciples. Peter it is who acts for the rest; Peter, who speaks in behalf of all. It is easy finally to anticipate the reason that from the day of the ascension, without debate, without election, without a formal organization of the apostolic college, St. Peter assumed the lead in all things. In the brief chronicle of the apostolic Church which has been left us in twelve chapters of the Book of Acts, St. Peter's figure is not only in the foreground, but so conspicuous that his position might almost be compared to that which Christ himself had so recently occupied towards his disciples.* In a word, from

---

* R. I. Wilberforce.

the beginning to the end of his history St. Peter is what the evangelist calls him, The First—" the first to confess the faith ; the first in the obligation to exercise love ; the first of all the Apostles who saw Jesus Christ risen, as he was to be the first witness of it before all the people ; the first when the number of the Apostles was to be filled up ; the first who confirmed the faith by a miracle; the first to convert the Jews; the first to receive the Gentiles; the first everywhere." *

Thus simple is the task of discovering that divine institution of the Primacy which Mr. Palmer finds it so difficult to 'see.' If St. Peter obtained and exercised a primacy, then a primacy was '*instituted.*' And that he did enjoy a primacy *of some sort* even Mr. Palmer cannot but acknowledge ! The straits to which controversialists are reduced if they attempt to prove that the primacy was not transmissible are as ludicrous as they are lamentable. Hear what the doughty Barrow has to urge on this head : " If some privileges of St. Peter were derived to popes, why were not

---

* Bossuet, *Sermon on Unity*, part i. "Is the Church likened unto a house ? It is placed on the foundation of a rock, which is Peter. Will you represent it under the figure of a family? You behold our Redeemer paying the tribute as its Master, and after him comes Peter as his representative. Is the Church a bark ? Peter is its Pilot ; and it is our Redeemer who instructs him. Is the doctrine by which we are drawn from the gulf of sin represented by a fisher's net ? It is Peter who casts it ; it is Peter who draws it ; the other disciples lend their aid ; but it is Peter that presents the fishes to our Redeemer. Is the Church represented by an embassy? St. Peter is at its head. Do you prefer the figure of a kingdom? St. Peter carries its keys. In fine, you will have it shadowed under the symbol of a flock and a fold? St. Peter is the shepherd and universal pastor under Jesus Christ." —St. Francis de Sales.

all? Why was not Pope Alexander VI. as holy as St. Peter? Why was not Pope Honorius as sound in his private judgment? Why is not every pope inspired? Why is not every papal epistle to be reputed canonical? Why are not all popes endowed with power of doing miracles? Why doth not the pope by a sermon convert thousands? (Why indeed do popes never preach?) Why doth not he cure men by his shadow? (he is, say they, himself his shadow.) What ground is there of distinguishing the privileges, so that he shall have some, not others? Where is the ground to be found?"* Is it speaking too ungently —is it, in short, too *Barrowish*—to call this argument contemptible? What does the author of the *Supremacy* mean by "distinguishing the privileges"? None of the articles which he enumerates with such a strange relish were "privileges of St. Peter." If the primacy was not intended to continue, it is sufficient (as Mr. Palmer has admitted) to ask, *why was it instituted?* When we receive even a plausible answer to this question, it will be time to fall back on the prophecy: "Upon this rock I will build my Church, and the gates of hell shall not prevail against it."

It is with a feeling almost of shame that I have gone over the familiar ground which has been traversed in controversy so many thousand times. The pre-eminence of St. Peter is one of those truths which are so plain that no comment can make them plainer; and the inability of some Protestants to perceive the fact, and of all Protestants to apprehend its significance, is one of the most marvellous instances of the power of prejudice and education to hood-

---

* *Supremacy*, Suppos. II. 5.

wink the intelligence.* The moment a man is willing to become a Catholic, the proof which before was disguised and unnoticed, springs out into unimagined and vivid prominence.

No less striking becomes the unanimity with which the early Fathers of the Church, in their expositions of holy Scripture, combined to recognize and celebrate the superlative honor which our Lord conferred upon his chief Apostle. And here I am brought to a stand. I have been spending a day in looking over a few of the almost innumerable paragraphs in which the Fathers refer, directly or indirectly, to St. Peter's headship; and instead of having made the selection which I at first intended, I have put aside the precious texts, literally dizzy with the effort of choosing from such a multitude. I do not like to confine myself to a few, for fear those who do not take the trouble to read for themselves should suspect the paucity of my examples. Nor, by giving many, do I care to incur the charge of parading a cheap erudition which is now within the reach of everybody. Besides, I have a much more important reason for not quoting largely from the Fathers: *I do not wish to divert attention from the main argument of this chapter*, which has very little to do with what the Fathers had to say. And yet it is hard to pass by altogether testimony which is very dear to a Catholic, and which he marvels to find less convincing to others. Perhaps the best thing I can do, in order to illustrate the wealth of

---

* It has often been noticed that the two points upon which the New Testament speaks with a more direct simplicity, if possible, than any other, namely, the Primacy and the Real Presence, were those singled out for attack by men who professed to draw all their religion from the Bible.

patristic comment on this subject, will be to bring together some of the many apposite passages which occur in the writings of a single Father.

I choose St. Chrysostom for several reasons. First (and it is no idle motive), this is St. Chrysostom's day upon which I write. Second, because he was an Eastern. Third, because special anxiety has been manifested to obscure the meaning of his expressions. And lastly, because St. Chrysostom is one of those fathers who, in discoursing upon the well-known words in St. Matthew's Gospel, speak of the Church as built upon the faith confessed by St. Peter.

Nothing more clearly shows the shifts to which Protestants are driven than the fact that they have seized upon this last circumstance as an argument against the Catholic interpretation of our Lord's promise. So far is the Roman Church from ignoring or fearing this construction of Christ's words that she makes it her own, and grounds her loftiest claims upon it. It was not a disembodied dogma, nor yet was it Peter apart from his confession, but Peter as proclaiming the truth which the Eternal Father had revealed to him, Peter as endowed with a faith which should never fail, who was made the rock upon which the Church should stand secure for ever. The perpetuity of the faith is the security of the Church; but the permanence of the faith is signally identified with Peter. Therefore the Eighth General Council, in the profession which it transmitted to the Roman Pontiff, says that the words of Christ find their fulfilment in the fact that "in the Apostolic See the Catholic religion has ever been kept immaculate, and holy doctrine celebrated there."* And the Fathers of Trent hesitated not to call the

* Mansi, xvi 27.

faith which the holy Roman Church makes use of "that firm and alone foundation against which the gates of hell shall not prevail." * So we shall see that St. Chrysostom was as far as possible from intending to separate the faith of Peter from Peter himself. Indeed, he speaks indifferently of the Church as founded upon the Apostle and upon his confession—as, for example, in the following passage: Christ on the night of his betrayal prayed for Peter that his faith might not fail; "as he is going to suffer, he speaks humbly, to show that he was man; for he who built the Church on the confession of Peter, and so strengthened her that no danger nor death itself can vanquish her, he who gave to him the keys of the kingdom of heaven and entrusted him with so great power, without at all needing to pray for this purpose, how much less should he need it in this circumstance? For he did not say, I have prayed, but he spoke with authority: I will build my Church on THEE, and give to thee the keys of the kingdom of heaven." †

Observe the argument of this extract. A shallow Arian cavil, drawn from the incident of our Lord's prayer for Peter, is answered by the recital of the promise previously given, the utterance of which implied divinity. Now this reasoning is of twofold interest to us. It shows, in the first place, how great the power conferred upon Peter was, since it proved the Godhead of the bestower. And also, it explains the emphasis with which St. Chrysostom and other writers of his age sometimes speak of St. Peter's *faith* as the rock upon which the Church immovably rested. Before the rise

---

* Sess. III. *Decree touching the Symbol of Faith.*
† *Hom.* lxxxii. in Matt.

of the Arian heresy, the Fathers always represented St. Peter himself as the foundation, without direct reference to his confession. It was the denial of our Lord's eternal Sonship which developed the later and, may we not say, more adequate interpretation of the divine promise. See how admirably the argument agianst the Arians is handled in the following passage, and how distinctly at the same time the sublime prerogatives of St. Peter are recognized: " How does Peter act, the Mouth of all the Apostles, the summit of the whole college? All were interrogated; he alone answers. What then does Christ say: 'Thou art Simon, the son of Jonas; thou shalt be called Cephas; for since thou hast proclaimed my Father, I also mention him who begot thee.' But since he had said, 'Thou art the Son of God,' in order to show that he was the Son of God, as he was the son of Jona, namely, of the same substance with his Father, he added, 'and I say to thee that thou art Peter, and upon this rock I will build my Church;' that is, upon the faith which thou hast confessed. . . . He foretold that the number of believers would be great, and he elevates the thoughts of Peter, and makes him the pastor. . . . Then he adds another prerogative: 'And to thee I will give the keys of the kingdom of heaven.' What means, 'I will give to thee'? As the Father has given to thee the knowledge of me, so *I* will give to thee. And he did not say, I will ask the Father to give thee; but, though the power was great, and the greatness of the gift ineffable, nevertheless he says, 'I will give thee.' What, I pray, dost thou give? 'The keys,' he says, 'of the kingdom of heaven.' . . . You perceive how he leads Peter to a sublime idea of himself, and reveals and shows himself to be the Son of God by these two promises. For what God alone can grant, namely, the power to remit sins, and that the Church should remain immovable amidst the swelling surges, and that a fisherman should be stronger than any rock, whilst the whole world wars against him, he promises that he will grant. Thus the Father also said to Jeremiah: 'I have made thee a pillar of iron and a wall of brass.' But the Father set him (Jeremiah) over one nation; he (the Son) placed this man over the entire world. Wherefore, I would willingly ask those who say that the dignity of the Son is less than that of the Father, which gifts appear to them greater, those which the Father, or those which the Son granted to Peter? The Father made to him the revelation of his Son; but the Son spread everywhere throughout the world the revelation both of the Father and of the Son, and to a mortal man gave the power of all things in heaven, giving him the keys. He spread the Church throughout the entire world, and showed that it is stronger than the firmament; for 'heaven and earth shall pass away, but my words shall not pass away.' How is he inferior who granted all these things, who accomplished all these things? I do not speak thus as if I would separate the works of the Father from those of the Son; for 'all things were made by him, and without him was made nothing'; but I speak with a view to silence the shameless tongues of those who utter such things. See in all things how great is his power. 'I say to thee, Thou art Peter; I will build my Church; I will give to thee the keys of the kingdom of heaven.'"*

St. Chrysostom's object in this masterly passage was not to prove that St. Peter was set over the whole Church, but

---

* *Hom.* lv. in Matt. I take Abp. Kenrick's translation, to whose learning I am indebted for many of my citations.

The Primacy and Prophecy. 241

that the Son was equal to the Father. The former truth had not yet been disputed, the latter had. If the same eloquence had been employed in defence of St. Peter which overflowed in the cause of his Master, we might have had a more telling quotation; at the same time, the vindication of the primacy which the passage really contains is heightened in value by the fact that it is incidental—a remark which is of force in regard to what the Fathers in general say concerning St. Peter's prerogatives.

Such titles as those used at the beginning of this long extract are over and over again applied to St. Peter by the Saint whose testimony we are hurriedly reviewing. He calls him the "foundation of the confession," the "leader of the choir of the Apostles," the "buttress of the faith," etc. Even more sweeping is that other class of expressions, represented above by the words: "He set this man over the entire world." St. Peter is the "fisherman of the universe"; he is "set over the whole habitable globe"; "to him is entrusted the doing and supporting of all things"; "into his hand Christ put the government of the universal Church."* St. Peter, he says moreover, not only was the leader of his fellow-Apostles, but presided over them: "Why does Christ address Peter concerning the sheep, passing by the others? He was the chief of the Apostles, and mouth of the disciples, and head of that body; on which account Paul also went up to see him in preference to the others. Showing him at the same time that he must have confidence hereafter, He cancels the guilt of his denial, and gives him the presidency over his brethren. . . . And he says: 'Because

---

* Τὴν ἐπιστασίαν τῆς οἰκουμενικῆς ἐκκλησίας ἐνεχείρεσε.

thou lovest me, preside over the brethren.'"* Mr. Palmer tries to turn this passage into the mere recital of an "admonition," and translates προίστασο "*protect*."† Barrow is at least more straightforward; for he renders προστασίαν τῶν ἀδελφῶν "charge, or presidency, over his brethren," though he says that, if we are obliged to refer the phrase to the Apostles, "it must not signify authority over them, but at most a primacy of order among them."‡ There can, I think, be no doubt what St. Chrysostom really meant. In another place he remarks incidentally that Christ gave St. Peter "special authority far surpassing the other Apostles, for he says: 'Peter, dost thou love me more than all these?'"§

The Abbé Guettée is at pains to show that St. Chrysostom uses the most exalted language when speaking of *St. Paul*, and that he sometimes couples his name with that of St. Peter in terms of equality. Granted, *secundum quid*, to use a handy scholastic phrase. Here is another passage, which the Abbé does not quote, but which might have rejoiced his heart, for it is more *Pauline* than anything that he has given us: St. Paul went up to Jerusalem to see St. Peter; "after so many illustrious actions, though he stood in no need of Peter, nor of his teaching, but being equal with him in dignity, for I will say no more here, he yet goes up to him as to a superior and elder; and the cause of his journey thither

---

* *Hom.* lxxxviii. in Johan. προστασίαν τῶν ἀδελφῶν; προίστασο τῶν ἀδελφῶν. The phrase occurs several times.
† *On the Church*, part vii. ch. i.
‡ *Supremacy*, Suppos. I.
§ *De Sacerdotio*, l. ii. "Why did Christ shed his blood? Certainly that he might purchase the sheep, the care of which he committed to St. Peter and to his successors."—*Ibid*.

is solely to see Peter."* The Roman Church, on the Feast of St. Paul's Conversion, says that God "taught the whole world" by his mouth;† which is very much what St. Chrysostom says. When the Church celebrates a festival of either Apostle, she adds a commemoration of the other; and on the twenty-ninth day of June—nay, whenever a mass is said, or a confession made—she unites their glorious names without a word of comment. Every time a Papal bull is signed, the same names are brought into impartial and majestic conjunction. And as for private sentiment, what Catholic has not written in the most unreserved terms of the great Apostle to the nations? I have myself elsewhere ventured to call St. Paul the greatest as well as the least of the Apostles; and have I thereby implicitly denied the supremacy of St. Peter? And yet the Abbé Guettée gravely announces that "it is most important to observe that St. Chrysostom attributes an equal dignity to these two Apostles when he mentions both of them together."‡ Ah, M. l'Abbé, would it not be much more important if you could astonish the 'schismatical Papacy' by a string of sentences in which the Constantinopolitan bishop should tell us that Jesus Christ put into the hands of St. Paul the government of the universal Church, and gave him the presidency over his brother Apostles?

As we have spoken of St. Paul, let us stop a moment to appreciate the critical nicety with which St. Chrysostom notices the significant order in which St. Peter's name is mentioned so many times in the first Epistle to the Corin-

---

* In Gal. i. 18.

† Deus, qui universum mundum beati Pauli apostoli prædicatione docuisti, *et seq.*

‡ *The Papacy Schismatic,* c. iv.

thians. "'I am of Paul, and I of Apollos, and I of Cephas, and I of Christ.' It was not to prefer himself before Peter that he set Peter's name last, but as preferring Peter greatly before himself; for he speaks in the ascending scale."* "'Have we not power to lead about a woman, a sister, as well as the other Apostles, and as the brethren of the Lord, and Cephas?' Observe his wisdom; he has put the chief last; for that is the place for putting one's strongest points." †

In commenting upon the Apostolic Council at Jerusalem, St. Chrysostom bids us " observe how Peter first allows the question to be moved in the Church, and then himself speaks." ‡ "See how Paul speaks after Peter, and no one restrains; James waits and starts not up; for he (Peter) it was to whom had been committed the primacy ($ἀρχή$)."§ In the first of these passages he seems to praise St. Peter's moderation and condescension. At any rate, there can be no doubt that such is his meaning in the following notable commentary upon St. Peter's conduct in the matter of the election of St. Matthias: " Being fervent, and entrusted by Christ with the care of the flock, and being the leader of

---

* *Hom.* iii. in 1 Cor.
† *Hom.* xxi. in 1 Cor.
‡ *Hom.* xxxii. in Act.
§ *Hom.* xxxiii. in Act. The Abbé Guettée refers the last clause not to St. Peter, but St. James. If this reading be the correct one, the evident reference is not, as the Abbé has the hardihood to intimate, to any superiority of St. James over St. Peter, but to his local dignity, as bishop of the city in which the Council was held. In the Homily on St. John from which we have already quoted (lxxxviii.), after saying that Christ gave St. Peter the "presidency," he asks: " Why then did James receive the chair at Jerusalem?" The reply is, that Peter was "appointed teacher not of the chair, but of the world."

the band, he is always the first to speak. Why did he not himself alone beseech Christ to give him some one in the place of Judas? Why do not the brethren of themselves undertake the election? See how he does all things with the general consent, nothing arbitrarily, nothing imperiously. Brethren, he says. Since the Lord called his disciples brethren, still more should he style them such. Wherefore he addressed them, all being present. Behold the dignity of the Church, and its angelic state. Why does he confer with them on this matter? Lest it become a subject of dispute, and they fall into dissensions. He leaves the choice to the judgment of the multitude, thus securing their regard for the objects of their choice, and freeing himself from jealousy. Could not Peter himself have chosen the individual? By all means. But he abstains from doing it, lest he should appear to indulge partiality. He is the first to proceed in this affair, because all have been delivered over into his hands; for to him Christ said: 'Thou being once converted confirm thy brethren.'"*

And now farewell, O Saint of the Golden Mouth. I have well spent thy holiday. Cease not, strong advocate, to hasten by thy intercession the approach of that millennial morning when, as in thy own happy times, the East and the West shall meet together to share the solicitude of him whom Christ has made the Vicar of his love and the shepherd of his blood-bought flock.

Let me say once more, before closing this chapter, that it has not been my intention to turn aside into the field of patristic controversy. I am tired and sick of this intermi-

---

* *Hom.* iii. in Act. I have followed St. Chrysostom's hint about the proper place for putting one's strongest things.

nable wrangling over the Fathers. The more a man loves the Fathers, the less he feels like fighting over them, especially with those who too often care little enough for what the Fathers really thought or taught. And mark my words, O Anglicans, the day has gone by when you can satisfy the minds of men by your dissertations upon the meaning of this or that early doctor. You have something more important to explain away than a text of St. Cyprian or St. Optatus; and that is, THE FACT OF THE SUPREMACY. Know that you are called on to face, not an ancient interpretation of a prophecy, but the present fulfilment of a prophecy. The Eighth General Council, in the profession from which we have already quoted, declares: " The sentence of our Lord Jesus Christ cannot be passed by, who says : ' Thou art Peter, and upon this rock I will build my Church ;' THESE WORDS ARE PROVED BY THE REAL EFFECT WHICH HAS FOLLOWED."* Exactly a thousand years have passed on since this memorable testimony was sent to Rome; and each year of the thousand is vocal with the attestation: GOD'S WORDS ARE PROVED BY THEIR RESULTS. This, this is the argument which thunders in your ears, O ye of little faith. There is the promise, as terribly distinct as Divinity itself could make it ; and there is the accomplishment, written by the finger of Omnipotence in the history of eighteen centuries. The Jews rejected the Messias whom their prophets had foretold ; will you resist the Church whose triumphs the Messias himself predicted ? God in-

---

* Hæc quæ dicta sunt rerum probantur effectibus.—*Act.* I. Syn. The sentence is much older than the Eighth General Council, being taken from the Profession of Faith of Pope Hormisdas (A.D. 517), a document which is said to have been signed by 2,500 bishops.

terprets his own prophecies. It is God, not man, who has made the Church what it is. Will you carry on a controversy with *him?* Will you, O foolish children, still further prove the meaning of the assurance that against the Church which is built upon the rock of Peter the gates of hell shall not prevail?

CHAPTER III.

THE PRIMACY AND ANTIQUITY.

HE only historical fact which is of any real importance in establishing the connection between the promise of Christ to St. Peter and its fulfilment in the Primacy of the Roman Pontiffs is that St. Peter fixed his Episcopal Chair in the city of Rome. This fact is at the same time essential and sufficient. If it be *not* ' a fact,' then the Supremacy (and Christianity itself, for that matter) is indeed a baseless fabric, and the long glory of the Papacy is but an insubstantial pageant. But if on the other hand the succession of the Roman Bishops from St. Peter is a matter which cannot reasonably be disputed, then the argument of the last chapter is clinched; there can then be no 'excuse for boggling' at the construction which God has put upon his own sentence.

Why do I speak of St. Peter's Roman Episcopate as if it were something which could be called in question ? Because it has been called in question. By whom has it been denied ? By Protestants. Why have Protestants raised a controversy on this point ? Out of hatred towards the Roman Catholic Church. Have Protestants no other motive for their scepticism ? No other conceivable motive. The late Mr. Wilberforce says: " It is difficult to understand how such a question can have been seriously raised, since there is scarcely an ancient (Christian) writer who does not either assert or allude to his (St. Peter's) residence in that city (Rome)."* But it is by no means difficult to understand *why* the question has been raised. Protestants, with an almost universal instinct, have felt the necessity of severing at all hazards the connection between St. Peter and the See which bears his name; and they have stuck at nothing in order to effect the separation. If fact—history—common-sense stood in the way, then perish facts, perish history, perish common-sense. Such heroic disregard of consequences, while it indicates the importance of the point assailed, betrays also the unprecedented character of the cause in which it is itself displayed. Protestants have been impelled by the extraordinary falsity of their principles into an extraordinary blunder, in which it will be fatal to persist, and from which it will be equally fatal to withdraw. Since the world began, there has been but one system, religious, social, or political, whose existence has been felt to depend upon the denial, not of a dogma, not of a principle, not of a theory, but of a simple fact of history.

Of course the question is one which must be decided with perfect indifference to the theological interests involved. And having been led to look at the subject in a purely critical manner, I affirm without hesitation that there is no more reason to doubt that St. Peter went to Rome, that he was for twenty-five years identified with the government of the Church in that city, that he ordained bishops there, and died there, than for doubting that Epaminondas broke the Spartan supremacy, or that Hannibal wintered at Capua. It is not necessary to go over the testimony in the one case any more than in the others. I shall not swell my pages with well-worn quotations, and transcriptions of

* *Principles of Church Authority*, ch. ix.

ancient lists and mural catalogues. The truth will stand, until it shall have dawned upon the mind of the last Protestant that it is very unprofitable to argue against the stone wall of indubitable certainty. I have only one or two observations to make upon the character of the evidence by which this certainty is established.

That St. Peter was Bishop of Rome was so notorious a matter that for thirteen centuries it never occurred to any heretic or schismatic to deny it. One Marsilius of Padua was the first who conceived the idea of opposing a Pope by thus disputing the legitimacy of his succession. And Martin Luther was the hero who took up the ingenious conception, and showed how, by a little fervent effrontery, it could be turned to good account. In the olden times men fought with more old-fashioned weapons. Zenobia would as soon have thought of resisting Aurelian by questioning his succession from the first of the Cæsars. The Donatists did not venture on such a line of defence, even though they were challenged to do so. "You dare not deny," said St. Optatus, addressing them, "that Peter established at Rome an episcopal chair, which he was the first to occupy, in order that through this one chair all might preserve unity."* The Greeks did not dream of such a justification of their schism.

* *De Schism. Donatist.* l. ii. n. 2. I give this solitary passage from the Fathers because it comes nearer than any I have seen to suggesting the possibility of denying the fact we are treating of. But even this suggestion is only apparent; for what St. Optatus called upon the Donatists to deny was not that St. Peter established his chair in Rome—which was too simple a matter—but that he did so in order to create a centre of unity, "and that the other Apostles (so the passage continues) might not assert for himself each his individual chair; but that he might be a schismatic and a sinner who against this peculiar chair set up another."

They lived too near the days of the Apostles by some half a dozen centuries.

Moreover, there have been not a few even among Protestants whose learning and prudence have recoiled from the rash pyrrhonism into which nothing but the insanity of hatred could have driven their fellow-religionists. The candor of individuals has exposed the suicidal error to which the system was obliged (if I may speak in a paradox) to commit itself. Thus Cave: "That St. Peter was at Rome, and for some time had his seat there, we affirm without hesitation, with the whole body of the ancients."* And the greatest of all Protestants, the correspondent of Bossuet, accepts without question what "the ancients unanimously attest," namely, "that the Apostle Peter governed the Church, suffered martyrdom, and appointed his successor, in the city of Rome, the capital of the world."†

---

* *Hist. Lit.* t. i. c. i.

† The passage in which Leibnitz thus disposes of a popular folly, though hardly in place here, deserves to be given entire. It occurs in the *Systema Theologicum*. "As from the impossibility of the bishops frequently leaving the people over whom they are placed, it is not possible to hold a council continuously, or even frequently, while at the same time the person of the Church must always live and subsist, in order that its will may be ascertained, it was a necessary consequence, by the divine law itself, insinuated in Christ's most memorable words to Peter (when he committed to him specially the keys of the kingdom of heaven, as well as when he thrice emphatically commanded him to feed his sheep), and uniformly believed in the Church, that one among the Apostles, and the successor of this one among the bishops, was invested with pre-eminent power; in order that by him, as the visible centre of unity, the body of the Church might be bound together; the common necessities be provided for; a council, if necessary, be convoked, and, when convoked, directed; and that in the interval between councils provision might be made lest the commonwealth

It is in the mouth of those who make a boast of drawing their 'churchmanship' from antiquity that the absurdity of Protestant unbelief on this head becomes most exquisitely apparent. This is appealing to antiquity with a vengeance. It is like appealing to the Bible for proof that Jesus Christ was a mere man. No less amusing is the effort of these scrupulous antiquarians to divert attention from the positive testimony which is so uncomfortably abundant, by constructing an imaginary negative proof on the other side out of the *absence* of testimony in certain of St. Paul's epistles.* As though the evidence on which we receive the authenticity of these very epistles was not identical with that which their silence is supposed capable of overthrowing!

Finally, nothing can be more nugatory than to argue that, because St. Peter certainly did not remain in Rome for twenty-five years, therefore the period which history assigns to his Episcopate is a pure fiction. No one ever imagined

---

of the faithful sustain any injury. And as the ancients unanimously attest that the Apostle Peter governed the Church, suffered martyrdom, and appointed his successor in the city of Rome, the capital of the world; and as no other bishop has ever been recognized under this relation, we justly acknowledge the Bishops of Rome to be chief of all the rest."—Dr. Russell's trans. *apud* Kenrick. Whiston says: "That St. Peter was at Rome is so clear in Christian antiquity that it is a shame for a Protestant to confess that any Protestant ever denied it." And Gieseler: "Nothing but the polemics of faction have induced some Protestants . . . to deny that Peter ever was at Rome." And Berthold: "There is, perhaps, no event in ancient (ecclesiastical) history so clearly placed beyond doubt by the consenting testimony of ancient Christian writers as that of Peter having been at Rome." Similar sentences might be taken from Pearson, Dodwell, Young, Blondel, and Lardner.

* See, *e.g.*, Harold Browne, *Exposition*, etc. Art. XXXVII. sec ii. 2.

that he did or could tarry in the city so long. What history, however, undoubtedly does say is that in the second year of Claudius he went to the metropolis, and that twenty-five years after he suffered martyrdom there. "There is an interval of exactly twenty-five years from the second year of the reign of Claudius, to which is assigned the first arrival of St. Peter at Rome, to the death of St. Peter. As for a continuous residence of twenty-five years' duration at Rome, that was never maintained by any person whatever."*

We have thus made it clear that the succession of the Roman Pontiffs from St. Peter is a matter which cannot reasonably be disputed. Protestants can give no other reason for wishing to contradict history than their desire to upset the claims of the Roman Pontiffs, which is immeasurably worse than no reason at all. Therefore the connection between the promise of Christ to St. Peter and its fulfilment in the supremacy of St. Peter's See is made good. And therefore, to a mind which believes and knows what it

---

* Döllinger, *Beginnings of Christianity*. "No Catholic ever pretended that St. Peter always remained in Rome after the establishment of his Episcopal see in the Imperial city. All suppose that he did not remain there. And if they still allow that he was the Bishop of Rome for upwards of twenty-five years, notwithstanding years of absence, they maintain this precisely on the same grounds as they ascribe twenty-three years of spiritual sovereignty to Pius VI., and twenty-three also to Pius VII."—Waterworth. The Bishop of Ely (*ubi sup.*), after twice endeavoring to fasten upon St. Jerome the assertion that St. Peter "*resided* twenty-five years at Rome," contentedly says that the statement is "simply impossible." This is 'simply' an outrage upon one of the most accomplished of critics. ·St. Jerome's words are: *cathedram episcopalem tenuit*. Bishop Browne implies that St. Jerome is the first to mention the twenty-five years. On this point see Waterworth, *England and Rome*, c. ii.

is to believe in the divinity of Jesus Christ, it is evident that the Papal Supremacy must be an essential characteristic of Christ's Holy Catholic Church. Which is what we set out to prove. I know very well that I have not handled the proof in the orderly manner and with the satisfactory fulness with which it has been often treated before. I have been content to give the demonstration in the form in which it first brought conviction to my own mind. Nevertheless, I am quite certain that, however ill-arranged and truncated my argument may be, it is one which no Protestant can meet by a satisfactory answer.

Henceforward what we have to say will not be written in the hope of winning the acquiescence of faith. If, dear reader, you are not, by the grace of God, already a believer, I have little expectation that any further discussion of which I am capable will be made the occasion of your conversion. With the fond confidence, however, that the grace which was solicited when you began to read these pages has not been ineffectual in your behalf, I am willing to labor on a little longer, trusting that some things which I may perchance have it in my power to say may be serviceable, if not in wholly removing such difficulties as remain in your mind, at least in convincing you that they are capable of removal.

Protestants contend that the supremacy of the Holy See is a power which *grew* upon the Church; that from small beginnings it advanced, by a gradual and almost imperceptible process, to the attainment of gigantic proportions. Granting the mere fact of development, we ask, does it follow that this evolution was not in accordance with a divine purpose? Growth and development are universal laws of organic creation. All human societies are organic. And the Church, though it be divine as well as human, is also a society; and *it* has followed the laws of organical increase. From a very small germ it has expanded into a vast and complex system. "The Kingdom of Heaven is like to a grain of mustard-seed, which a man took and sowed in his field; which indeed is the least of all seeds, but when it is grown it is the greatest among herbs, and becometh a tree, so that the birds of the air come and lodge in the branches thereof." We have shown unanswerably that the Papacy is not (to speak loosely) a development out of *nothing*. It had its germ in the Primacy which our Lord saw fit to institute in the person of his Apostle Peter, and in the association of that Primacy with the Roman See by the act of the Apostle himself. Why then should the Primacy not grow with the Church's growth? It is absurd to suppose that its history could be anything but a development. "Never did any important institution result from a [written and anterior] law, and the greater the institution, the less is it written. It is formed of itself by the concurrence of a thousand agents, who are almost always ignorant of what they are doing; so that they often appear not to perceive the right which they themselves are establishing. The institution vegetates thus insensibly in the course of ages. *Crescit occulto velut arbor ævo* is the never-failing device of every great political or religious creation." *

But we emphatically deny that the Papacy is a development *in the sense* in which Protestants affirm it to be such. I deny, that is to say, the oft-repeated assertion—which until recently I had not the wit to challenge—that during the three first ages of the Church the primacy of the Bishop of

* De Maistre.

Rome was unrecognized, and that only after the triumph of Christianity, in the fourth age, the Church in the Imperial City rose into eminence with the decline of the Empire. When it had once occurred to me that, instead of endeavoring to accommodate facts to what I had used as a postulate, I ought to test the truth of the proposition by the facts, it took but little time to discover that I had been an unreasoning promoter of a plausible Protestant theory, as destitute of foundation in actual events as it was of honor and candor in its uses. When I came to question history calmly, without a desire of reading it in accordance with a traditional and cherished hypothesis, I found that it furnished no materials out of which I could honestly construct such a theory for myself, but rather afforded me abundant reason for believing that the Primacy of the See of St. Peter was both exercised and acknowledged from the very first.

I have spoken elsewhere with sufficient emphasis of the great difference that there is between the documentary evidence we possess of the faith held by the Church during the first ages and that which was taught in the fourth and succeeding centuries, as well as of the obvious causes of that difference. The same remarks are equally in place with reference to our knowledge of events in the Church's history. The early Church, as an English ecclesiastic has said, "was working its way, in the literal sense of the word, 'under ground,' under camp and palace, under senate and forum."* Afterwards it became a city set upon a hill, which could not be hid. This is the primary point to be kept in mind in an attempt to construe fairly the records of Christian antiquity. The conclusions to which, I am confident, such an attempt,

---

* Dean Stanley.

faithfully carried out, will lead are these. First, that from the time when our information concerning the constitution and working of the Church becomes full and minute, the operation of the Papal power is everywhere distinctly manifest. The writings and events of the fourth and fifth centuries are a continual witness that the relation of the Primacy to the Church was then essentially what it is now; indeed it is no extravagance to say that there is no epoch of ecclesiastical history in which the Popes appear more prominently as governors and guardians of the universal Church than the age of the third and fourth General Councils.* This fact, in all truthfulness, establishes a presumption that the functions of the Papacy had been the same during the period of which our knowledge is more meagre and confused, when moreover it had been impossible as well as unnecessary that its legitimate powers should be called into full exercise. This presumption is vastly strengthened, and turned into a powerful argument, by the fact that everything in the later action of the Papacy *supposes* that it had always possessed the prerogatives whose use was continually developed with the gradual organization of the Church. That is to say, the Popes constantly professed to act by an authority which was inherent in their office, as having been transmitted to them by their predecessors from the Apostle to whom Christ gave the keys and committed the flock; and the whole Church, aye, and all the world, knew that they acted and had always acted by virtue of such authority. Such being

---

* Barrow says of St. Leo that " no pope could well exceed (him) in zeal to maintain the privileges and advance the eminence of his See." (Suppos. VI.) It was St. Leo who discovered for Dr. Newman the weakness of the Anglican appeal to antiquity. (*Apologia*, parts v., vi.)

the first result of our studies, we go back and carefully review all that has come to our knowledge concerning the polity of the Church during the antecedent ages of persecution. And our scrutiny discovers nothing which tends to overthrow the presumption whose force we have considered; on the contrary, we meet with many things which, *taken by themselves*, indeed, might not *prove* the existence of a *primitive Supremacy*, but which admit of no satisfactory explanation except on the supposition of an extraordinary authority resident in the Roman Episcopate, and which, therefore, give a full and final confirmation to the retrospective testimony of later times, and convert what was for us already a sufficient probability into a certainty.*

Such, most assuredly, is the true interpretation of antiquity in the matter of the Papal Supremacy. After having exercised a little manly criticism on this subject, the ordinary Protestant argument—that we hear little about the power of the Popes in the second century; in the third century, not much more; in the fourth century, we hear a great deal; and in the fifth century, we hear of hardly anything else; *ergo*, the Papacy is a usurpation and a development out of nothing—such reasoning, I say, appears very juvenile. Did I not know how many men there are who never think of overhauling the axioms of their childhood, I should be tempted to say that a controvertist who could draw such an inference from such premises must be destitute either of brains, or of scholarship—or of principle.

I shall not attempt any formal review of evidence which

---

* I of course use the word 'certainty' here in a historical, not a theological, sense. Faith is not grounded upon probabilities, nor even upon historical certainties. Faith rests upon authority.

is too voluminous to be treated in detail. Following my usual plan, I shall content myself with a few comments and references.

Probably no one will be reckless enough to dispute the statement that after the beginning of the conciliar period the Primacy of the Holy See was universally recognized. It is a conceded point. " If anything," says the President of Marshall College—" if anything in the world can be said to be historically clear, it is the fact that, with the close of the fourth century and the coming in of the fifth, the Primacy of the Roman See was admitted and acknowledged in all parts of the Christian world. This is granted by Barrow himself, in his great work on the *Supremacy;* though he tries to set aside the force of the fact by resolving it into motives and reasons to suit his own cause." * Now, the consideration which I wish to urge—and it is one of the utmost importance—is, that the Primacy was confessed by the Church in its œcumenical and provincial *Councils. The Primacy was never canonically instituted;* it was never conferred and proclaimed by synodal decree; it was, as Dr. Nevin says, *acknowledged.*† Barrow has made a woful

---

* *Mercersburg Review,* " Early Christianity."

† And this from the first. *Council of Nice,* Canons VI., VII. Whether the words " The Roman Church always had the Primacy " were included in the original draught of the sixth canon is a matter of no great importance, as was shown by the discussions at Chalcedon. Again, and more notably, at the Council of Sardica, in Thrace, a synod which followed that of Nice by an interval of only twenty-two years. It is not to be wondered at that Anglicans have contended that this Council *granted* the right of appealing to the Roman See (Canons III., IV., V.) But such appeals had been made before ; and the Council only formally recognized a method of proceeding for which Divine forethought had made provision, and which the necessities of the Church had already

mistake in calling attention to this fact. "It is more wonderful," he says, "that this point (of the Supremacy) should never be defined, in downright and full terms, by any ancient synod."* Sooth, good Barrow, it is indeed more wonderful than your insular theology could attain unto. To you the Church was the creature of kings and emperors; and the laws which governed it of old were in your sight only the enactments of ecclesiastical parliaments, for "General Councils might not be gathered together without the will and commandment of princes."† Had your soul

made available. The all-important point, which Anglicans studiously overlook, is that reference was to be made to the supreme jurisdiction of the Pope, *as being the successor of St. Peter, and the Head of the Church*. The canons find their best interpretation in the words of the synodical epistle which was sent to Pope Julius: "For it shall seem best and most proper if the bishops of the Lord from all the provinces refer themselves *to the Head, that is, to the See of the Apostle Peter*." The Sardican decrees were often confounded with those of Nice. The later Council, which had been called in behalf of St. Athanasius, and was presided over by the already celebrated Hosius, seems to have been regarded as a sort of supplement of the earlier. Barrow thinks it probable (as many others have done) that the acts of the two Councils were sometimes bound together, and admits that the mistake of Pope Zosimus in citing the Sardican canons as Nicene was an innocent one. (*Account of the Synod and Canons of Sardica*, printed for the first time, as Appendix to the *Supremacy*, in the edition of the S.P.C.K., London, 1851, p. 538.) An excellent indication of the force of these Sardican canons is the undisguisable anguish with which Anglicans set about explaining them away. Barrow calls them "the most unhappy that were ever made to the Church." (*Supremacy*, Suppos. VI.) And Bishop Harold Browne takes up the lamentation: "In an unhappy moment the Synod of Sardica," etc.

* *Supremacy*, Suppos. V. What Barrow meant by 'defined' will appear presently.
† Thirty-nine Articles, Art. XXI. This sentence from the

been capable of rising above courts and cabinets, you might have seen that this wonderful acquiescence of ancient synods in an authority which they had never dared to bestow is a magnificent confession that "this point" had been "defined in downright and full terms" by the Lord Jesus Christ.

But since the author of the *Supremacy* has appealed to Councils, let a Council answer him, and explain to him and to us why the Church accepted what it had not granted. The Roman Council which was convened under Pope Gelasius, in the year 494, says: "Though all the Catholic churches throughout the world be but *one* bridal chamber of Christ, yet *the Holy Roman Catholic and Apostolic Church has been preferred to the rest by no decrees of a Council, but has obtained the Primacy by the voice in the Gospel of our Lord and Saviour himself, saying:* 'Thou art Peter,' etc. . . . First, *therefore*, is the Roman Church, the See of Peter the Apostle, 'not having spot or wrinkle, nor any such thing.' "*

This *acknowledgment* of the Primacy by the first Councils is rendered the more conspicuous by the fact that the Fathers did attempt by synodical enactment to "*confer*" (ἀπονέμειν), not indeed another Primacy, but "like privileges" upon "the most holy throne of New Rome," the Church of Constantinople.† But the great Leo cancelled their edict,

---

Articles is of itself sufficient to blacken Anglicanism for ever in the eyes of one who believes the word of Christ : "My kingdom is not of this world."

* Labbe, iv. 1261 ; Mansi, viii. 149 ; Harduin, ii. 938.

† See the decree which sometimes follows the twenty-seventh canon of the Council of Chalcedon. This decree, which was drawn up in the interests of the Emperor, was an attempt to expand the third canon of Constantinople, a council, by the way,

in what Barrow calls " these blunt words " : " But the agreement of the bishops (touching the privileges of the Constantinopolitan See), being repugnant to the holy canons made at Nice, your faith and piety joining with us, we make void, and by the authority of the blessed Apostle St. Peter, by a general determination we disannul."*

And this leads us to a second and no less important observation, namely, that the authority which was recognized by Councils as having always resided in the Apostolic See was a *supreme* authority. It would be easy to show this by taking up the history of some particular Council, say that of Ephesus, or of Chalcedon; for it is quite plain—I speak deliberately—that St. Celestine was to the former synod, and St. Leo to the latter, all that Paul III. and Pius IV. were to the Fathers of Trent. After having many times reviewed the evidence, and having read all that can be pleaded by the bitterest enemy of the Holy See, I cannot help expressing my belief that the study of the Council of Chalcedon must make a Roman Catholic of any Anglican who honestly intends that his Anglicanism shall stand or fall by the testimony of the four first Councils. At Chalcedon, " Peter spoke by Leo." There Dioscorus was condemned because he had " even extended his madness so far as to assault him to whom the care of the vineyard had been committed by our

---

which was really only a local synod, and became œcumenical by the ratification of its *dogmatic* definitions, when Pope Damasus accepted its creed as the symbol of the universal Church. It is not too much to say that the third Constantinopolitan canon is the little root out of which grew the great Eastern schism.

* *Epist*. lv. In another epistle St. Leo says : " The City of Constantinople has its privileges, but these are only secular ; it is a royal, but it cannot become an Apostolic See." Golden words, but the Greeks soon forgot them.

Saviour," having "opened his mouth against the Apostolic See itself." There, from first to last, the Pope of Rome "presided, as a head over the members, through those who occupied his place."* It will be more in keeping, however, with these brief discussions if I rather insist upon one or two general facts, which will be as conclusive as they are undeniable.

First, no council, intended to be œcumenical, was ever held without the authority of the Supreme Pontiff. A single proof will suffice on this point. The Patriarch of Alexandria was degraded from his seat in the Council of Chalcedon, and took his place as an accused criminal, because, in the words of the legate Lucentius, he had "presumed and dared to hold a synod without the authority of the Apostolic See, *a thing which never had been done, and never could be done lawfully.*" † Secondly, no council was ever accepted by the Church as œcumenical except it had received the Pontifl's ratification. The Nicene Fathers in their synodal letter to Pope Sylvester asked that their decisions might be confirmed by his agreement. ‡ The confirmation was given; and from that day to this all councils whose decrees have a like validity have obtained it through a similar endorsement.

---

* *I.e.*, through his Legates (*Synodical Epistle* to Pope Leo). Allies and Wilberforce have both given good proof of all that I have said about this great Council.

† Labbe, iv. 93; Mansi, vi. 582; Harduin, ii. 67. Dioscorus had presided two years before (449) at the Ephesian synod, known in ecclesiastical history as the Latrocinium. It is worth noticing that this synod had been regularly called, but, having assembled, its acts were opposed by the papal legates, and its sessions continued in spite of their protest.

‡ Quidquid autem constituimus in Concilio Nicæno precamur vestri oris consortio confirmetur.

Some have for this cause been accounted general which were in their design and constitution only local;* while others from which the papal approbation was withheld have failed to establish their claim to universality.† Thirdly, in the very words of a Pope, "in universal Councils no act, as you know, is valid, or to be received, but what the See of St. Peter has approved; and on the other hand, whatever she alone has rejected, that only is rejected."‡ Witness St. Leo and the Council of Chalcedon. And now for a specimen of Anglican logic on these premises. "Seeing," says Barrow, "in none of the first general synods any such canon was framed in favor of that Bishop (of Rome), what ground of right could the Pope have to prescribe unto them, or thwart their proceedings?"§ O altitudo sapientiæ! If the

---

* *E.g.*, the Second, Fifth, and Seventh.

† *E.g.*, that of Ariminum (359), and the second of Ephesus. "We never read of any synod that was valid unless it were confirmed by the Apostolic authority."—Pope Pelagius II. "We trust that no true Christian is ignorant that the appointment of every Council which the assent of the universal Church has approved ought to be executed by no other See but the first, which both confirms every council by its authority, and maintains them by its continued government, in virtue, that is, of its headship, *which St. Peter received indeed from the Lord's voice, but the Church, no less following that voice, hath ever held and holds.*"—Pope Gelasius I. Barrow, who quotes this passage, omits the clause which I have put in italics, substituting an " etc." (Suppos. VI. iii.)

‡ Denique ut in universalibus synodis, quid ratum, vel quid prorsus acceptum, nisi quod Sedes Beati Petri probavit (ut ipsi scitis) habetur; sicut e contrario quod ipsa sola reprobavit, hoc solummodo consistat hactenus reprobatum.—Pope Nicholas I. Barrow quotes this; we shall see immediately what was the best answer he could make.

§ *Supremacy*, Suppos. VI. iii. 4. Now we begin to understand what Barrow meant by ' defining ' the Primacy.

Bishop of Rome *had* derived his authority from a canon of a general synod, tell me *then*, great Barrow, what ground of right a Pope could have had to prescribe unto a Council, or to thwart its proceedings.

We have glanced at the testimony of General Councils. We might add thereto that of councils national and provincial, which from the first were accustomed to consult 'the Head" in matters not only of faith, but sometimes, even of discipline.* We might sketch the history of the early heresies, and show that in every case the lesson of their progress, arrest, and decay is a witness to the power which emanated from the chair of him whose faith could not fail and who was appointed to confirm his brethren. We might fairly jade ourselves with copying multitudinous quotations from the Fathers of the East and West, each bearing his tribute of allegiance and devotion to the one central See where St. Peter ever presided in the person of his successor. †

---

* "Consultations or references to the Bishop of Rome, in difficult cases of faith or discipline, had been common in early ages, and were even made by provincial and national councils."—Hallam, *Middle Ages*, c. vii. note.

† The evidence afforded by provincial synods, condemned heresies, and individual Fathers, is very happily combined in the instance of Pelagius, St. Augustine, and the African Councils. Pelagius had been condemned at the Councils of Carthage and Numidia, and the decrees, which were framed by St. Augustine, are sent to Innocent I. for approval. St. Augustine writes at the same time, "wishing it to be decided whether their little streamlet flowed from the same source whence came the abundance of the head." Innocent replies to both Councils, commending them for "following the prescription of the ancient rule, *which, you know* (he says) *as well as I, has ever been preserved in the whole world.*" " Especially," he continues, " as often as a matter of faith is under discussion, I conceive that all my brethren and fellow-bishops *can*

And then, perhaps, we might refresh ourselves by marking how Dr. Barrow declines to hold himself "accountable for every hyperbolical flash or flourish occurring in the Fathers;" * or by admiring the Bœotian placidity of Mr. Palmer, when he quotes such a sentence as that, for example, which St. Peter Chrysologus addressed to the heretic Eutyches—"We exhort thee to attend with obedience to all things written to thee by the most blessed Pope of the city of Rome, since St. Peter, *who lives and presides in his own See*, affords the true faith to all who enquire of him" —and calmly puts it aside with the comment: "This is to

---

only refer to Peter, that is, the source of their own name and honor." And then, "at the reference of a double synod," he "severs the offenders by his sentence from ecclesiastical communion." And St. Augustine afterwards sums up the history of Pelagianism in the memorable words: "Two Councils on this matter have been sent to the Apostolic See; whence also the replies have come. The cause is ended; may the error soon terminate also."—*Serm.* cxxxi. I am much tempted to devote some space to St. Augustine's testimony to the Supremacy, as I have elsewhere to that of St. Chrysostom to the personal Primacy of St. Peter; but *cui bono?* Mr. Allies has already brought together a good many of St. Augustine's strong sentences (*See of Peter*, sec. v. 3); and Dr. Ives adds others (*Trials of a Mind*, etc., c. xviii.). I have previously given his appeal to the Donatists (Numerate sacerdotes, *et seq.*), and his reply to the Manichæan: "I AM HELD IN THE CATHOLIC CHURCH by the succession of Bishops from the very See of Peter the Apostle, to whom the Lord after his resurrection committed his flock to be fed, down to the present Bishop." As for the Fathers in general, it would be impossible to collect from Catholic authors of modern times a list of titles more lavishly expressive of the pre-eminence of the Apostolic Throne than has been culled by St. Francis de Sales from the writings of antiquity. De Maistre gives this list (*Du Pape*, l. i. c. 10). Waterworth makes another of his own, equally ample (*England and Rome*, c. iii.)
* Suppos. I. vi.

be understood as a compliment to the virtues and piety of the Pope at that time."* But what would or could we say when, after noting that almost every testimony which we might cite (as well as those which we have cited) explicitly attributes the authority of the Roman Bishop to his occupancy of St. Peter's Chair, we should turn again to the pages of the immortal *Treatise of the Pope's Supremacy*, and there learn that the "*ground*" of that Bishop's eminence was not the fact that his See was Apostolic, but that it was metropolitan? "The Church of Rome was indeed allowed to be 'the principal Church.'" "But why? Was it preferred by divine institution? No, surely; Christianity did not make laws of that nature, or constitute difference of places. Was it in regard to the succession of St. Peter? *No; that was a slim, upstart device.*" † At such bold, hard words as these we could only stand aghast.

But I must pass quickly by all this to another point, which has already been incidentally developed, and needs only to be stated argumentatively; and that is that the Popes themselves, during the period which we are reviewing, believed that their authority was supreme, and that their supremacy had descended to them from St. Peter, who received it from Christ. I do not know that any respectable writer has denied that the Popes at least *claimed* this—unless it be Dr. Wordsworth, in his *Theophilus Anglicanus;* and Dr. Ives has disposed of this denial by the abundant evidence which

---

* *On the Church*, Pt. VII. Ch. III. ii. 3. See, *in loc.*, a long string of similar ponderous observations. This virtuous and pious Pope was, of course, none other than Barrow's 'vixenly' St. Leo.
† Suppos. V. ix.

he has collected from the papal epistles of the fourth and fifth centuries.* Barrow and Palmer, whom I have selected as the weightiest representatives of Anglicanism, early and late, both admit the fact of the claim.† But they certainly do not see, or do not choose to see, its consequences. For it was the government exercised by the Popes, and *as exercised by the Popes*, which was accepted by the universal Church. It is inconceivable that the Popes should have claimed one thing, and the Church should have acknowledged another. When St. Damasus, in 378, called his fellow-bishops his "most honorable children,"‡ saying that they rendered "due reverence to the Apostolic Chair, . . . wherein the Holy Apostle sitting taught in what way it beseems us to manage the helm which has been put into our hands;" and when those same bishops declared in council that the Bishop of Rome " surpasses all others by the prerogative of the Apostolic See;" their conceptions of the Apostolic prerogative were one and the same. So that, even if we had not all the other proofs to which cursory reference has been made, this single consideration would determine for us what was the belief of the Church in the fourth century concerning the nature of the Primacy.

The importance which Anglican controversialists, in spite of themselves, attach to this argument is betrayed by the

---

* *Trials of a Mind*, pp. 202–214. Remember that the genuine decretals of the previous centuries have perished.

† *Supremacy*, Suppos. VI. iii., iv. *On the Church*, Pt. VII. c. III. ii. 5.

‡ Pope Pius IX. calls those who are his equals *as bishops*, "Venerable Brethren."

avidity with which they all (with one noticeable exception) have seized upon a solitary instance where, as they suppose, a Pope denied his own supremacy. Who has not heard how St. Gregory the Great rebuked John of Constantinople for assuming the title of 'Universal Bishop,' telling him that such pride was befitting the precursor of Antichrist? Who does not know how this shining example of papal humility is for ever on the tongues of those who would rebuke the 'Luciferian arrogance' of the Papacy itself?* Just as if there ever was a Pope who better understood, and more faithfully maintained, and more gloriously employed his papal prerogatives than GREGORY THE FIRST! As if it were not this same Gregory who is assailed by his *quondam* eulogists for 'usurping' jurisdiction over the 'autocephalous' church of Britain! As if it were not Gregory who said: "If any fault be found with bishops, I know not what bishop is not subject to the Apostolic See"! As though it were not in the very exercise of this Apostolic authority that he rebuked the ambitious Eastern Patriarch! As though in his letters he had not written: "Concerning the Church of Constantinople, who doubts that it is subject to the Apostolic See?" and, "To all who know the Gospel it is evident that the care of the whole Church was committed by the voice of the Lord to the holy Apostle Peter, chief of all the Apostles. For to him is said, etc. Lo, he has received the keys of the kingdom of heaven, the power of binding and loosing is given to him, the care of the whole

---

* The writer who calls St. Leo a vixen lavishes blandishments upon his successor. "Good Pope Gregory," he calls him—"that great Pope." Great and good he was, and a good and great *Pope*, too.

Church and the Primacy is committed to him, and yet he is not called Universal Apostle."*

Another indication of the real antiquity of the papal claim to supremacy is the frantic assertion that the Papacy has attempted to antedate its assumptions by the use of forgeries. I can hardly help treating contemptuously this unscholarly talk about the pseudo-decretals, being weak enough to take satisfaction in remembering that I so far suspected its trivial character as never to indulge in it myself. Let it suffice, then, to remark: 1. That the Isidorian collection of canons was certainly not made at Rome, wherever else it may have had its origin; and that it was not compiled in the interest of the Popes, but, as Guizot says, "to serve the bishops against the metropolitans and temporal sovereigns." 2. That the materials used in its composition were not new, but old, being mostly taken from early papal rescripts, and synodal decrees, and the writings of the Fathers. In an uncritical age the counterfeits escaped detection, and came into gradual use, as being in accordance with a long established and recognized system. In a word, the imposture grew out of the Supremacy, not the Supremacy out of the imposture. 3. That the pious fraud was exposed and reprobated centuries ago. All the

---

* Waterworth has an admirable note on St. Gregory, which is too long to copy here. See *England and Rome*, pp. 167-8. The exception alluded to above is Mr. Palmer, who, in reply to Bossuet's exposure, thinks he "may safely allow" that the argument from Pope Gregory "may not be convincing," in fact, may be "unsound."—*On the Church*, part ii. c. ii. 2. After such a concession we may hope to hear no more of this theme in controversy, however it may continue to do good service as an *argumentum ad ignorantiam*.

world knows, or ought to know, that a Catholic would no more think of grounding the Papal Supremacy on the compilation of Mercator than would a Scotchman of vindicating his national literature by appealing to the Ossianic poems, or the good merchants of Bristol of proving the ancient respectability of their city from the contents of 'Canyng's coffre.' The forged decretals may be matter for curious and learned investigation, but they are certainly ruled out of the debate between Catholics and Protestants, as has been often shown.* If Protestants expect ever to capture the citadel of the Papacy, it is time for them to stop playing Chinese antics before an old mound, which was never used for military purposes, and which nobody dreams of defending.

I begin to be aware that the task of perpetually exposing bold paralogisms is not having any perceptible mellowing influence upon my crude style. I am sorry for it; but I have not time to do my work over again. My sincere and single desire is not to irritate, but to win. In truth, I am not only unused to controversy, but do not enjoy it. Be-

---

* *E.g.*, Moehler, *Fragmente aus und über Pseudo-Isidor, u.s.w.* Mr. Ffoulkes, by the way, makes a remarkable confession of his qualms on this subject. Having said in his work on *Christendom's Divisions* that he regarded the Church of England as guilty of wilful schism, he proceeds to modify his opinion: "I expressed this unhesitatingly *three years back* (the emphasis is not Mr. Ffoulkes's) in the first part of my book, and am far from intending to retract *all* that I said then; but having since discovered the general system of Church government in which England, in common with all other Western nations, had up to that time acquiesced, to have been based upon forgeries, and opposed to the genuine code of the Church," etc.—*The Church's Creed*, etc., p. 75. It is needless to say that of this last assertion he gives not the ghost of a proof. But, under the circumstances, what *can* Mr. Ffoulkes mean by "*having since discovered*"?

sides, I cannot yet rid my mind of an uncomfortable *aggrieved* feeling, as though I had been personally victimized by principles which had well-nigh led me into intellectual as well as spiritual captivity; so that I turn upon them—my old principles—with a sort of righteous vindictiveness. But—*vorwärts*.

We need no further evidence, no greater proof is possible, that from the period of the first General Council, from the time, that is, when ecclesiastical history may be fairly said to begin, the Bishop of Rome was recognized as occupying the position which he holds to-day, as the visible Head of the Catholic Church. The Papacy was then in existence, not in embryo, but already well developed and in vigorous action. It was a glorious era, and faith loves to linger in contemplating it—the age of triumph! The time had arrived for the Church to rise and take possession of a world which could persecute and keep her down no longer; and she came beautifully forth to conquest, not in disorder, not a tumultuous host, spreading itself without concert and without a leader, but 'terrible as an army set in array,' divinely furnished with all the yet untried means of success, moving with a precision which only discipline can give, with that compactness of organization which alone can secure discipline, and with that unity of government without which organization is impossible. And it would be a glorious undertaking to follow the centuries downward; to show how the history of the Primacy is the history of the universal Church; how under the Primacy the Church extended her domain, and perfected her polity; how Christianity owed its very existence to the force which radiated from its centre, deriving thence both its conservative and recuperative energies, surviving the crash of the Empire, and building, out of the wreck and chaos which followed, a new and better civilization. But our faces must be turned backward and not forward; and our task will be brief and simple.

We are not in strict reason called upon for any further proof of an ante-Nicene Primacy. The *onus probandi* lies with those who assail what was in the fourth century, as it is now, an existing institution. They are bound to show that the Primacy of St. Damasus and St. Innocent was a *usurpation*. And it is not only impossible for them to do this, but to produce in support of their cause even a single argument which needs refutation. If they urge the comparative silence of the first centuries, that silence has been perfectly accounted for, and can prove nothing. And if they venture to allege that the papal authority was denied from the first, it merely follows that it was *from the first asserted*. "Tell me," says Archbishop Manning, "that the waves have beaten upon the shore, and I will tell you that the shore was there for the waves to beat upon." * So the most prudent

---

* *Grounds of Faith*, lect. iii. "Tell me that St. Irenæus pleaded with St. Victor, that he would not excommunicate the Asiatic Churches, and I will tell you that St. Irenæus thereby recognized the authority of St. Victor to excommunicate. Tell me that Tertullian mocked at the 'Potifex Maximus,' 'the Bishop of Bishops,' and I tell you he saw before him a reality that bare these titles. Tell me that St. Cyprian withstood St. Stephen in a point not yet defined by the Church, and I tell you that, nevertheless, in St. Stephen's See St. Cyprian recognized the chair of Peter, in unity with which he died a martyr. . . . What truth is there that has not been disputed? Let us apply the argument. Has not the doctrine of the Holy Trinity been denied? Has not the Incarnation been denied? Is there any doctrine that has not been denied? But what is our answer to the Arian and Socinian? Because from the beginning these truths have been denied, *therefore* from the beginning they have been both held and taught."— *Ibid.*

thing which Protestants can do is to be illogical, and incessantly declaim that the burden of proof lies on the other side. We are to show, then, that St. Leo was *not* a usurper, and that too when there is not the faintest excuse for supposing that he *was !*

What we *have* made plain is, 1. That Christ built his Church upon Peter; 2. That St. Peter was Bishop of Rome; 3. That St. Leo acted as St. Peter's successor; and, 4. That the whole Church acknowledged his supremacy. We have also remarked that during the period of persecution, before the Church was free to put forth all her wonderful energies, there was neither occasion nor possibility for any conspicuous display of the governmental functions with which the Church had been endowed.* It only remains to say that in reality there is abundant evidence in the scanty records of the first ages both of a consciousness of their headship on the part of the Popes, and of a recognition of that primacy on the part of the Church. It would take a long chapter fairly to review this evidence.† From the time when St. Clement wrote his papal epistle to the divided church of Corinth, while the last Apostle yet tarried till his Lord should come, and when the disciple of that same Apostle, on his way to martyrdom, sent letters before him to the "Apostolic Foun-

---

* Remember that for three centuries nearly all the Popes were martyrs. Victor and Stephen are both numbered in that *candidatus exercitus*. Says Ranke: "During the persecutions, the Bishops of Rome had exhibited extraordinary firmness and courage; their succession had often been rather to martyrdom and death than to office."—*History of the Popes*, l. i. c. i.

† Such a chapter would not come within the scope of this book. Any reader who may not be familiar with facts and quotations can consider them for himself by referring to such works as Water-

tain," "the Church which presides* in the country of the Romans," there is an increasing succession of acts on the one hand which tacitly indicate supremacy, and of incidental expressions on the other which imply subordination and homage, whose cumulative force it is impossible to withstand, unless, alas, our heart be hardened, and our ears heavy, and our eyes closed, lest we should see, and hear, and understand—and be converted. I have allowed more to the silence of the second and third centuries than was at all required, only because I am well assured that, though the history of those centuries were an *absolute blank* touching this matter of the Papal power, even such a total intermission of testimony as to any actual exercise of authority would not in any degree affect the prospective and retrospective proofs of a divinely established Primacy, nor disturb for a moment the foundation upon which faith securely reposes.

worth's *England and Rome*, Abp. Kenrick's *Primacy of the Apostolic See*, and Wilberforce's *Principles of Church Authority*.

* Προκάθηται, Προκαθημένη. In all his epistles to other churches St. Ignatius writes Τῇ οὔσῃ, or Τῇ παροικούσῃ.

CHAPTER IV.

THE PRIMACY AND UNITY.

E have seen in an earlier portion of this work that the Church of God is one, and that because it is essentially one it cannot possibly be divided. We are now prepared to appreciate the nature of the divine provision by which the unity of the Church has been secured. We have learned to believe in the Church's unity; we are ready now to understand it.

The only conceivable *means* by which an organization can be so a unit that division shall be impossible is by having a visible, and at the same time indivisible, centre. A government cannot be conceived of without a governor. A visible body must have a visible head. The eternal and invisible Head of the Church is he who founded and upholds it. But *how* has he founded it, and by what agency does he sustain and direct it? God uses means for the accomplishment of his ends. And, I say, reason is competent to suggest that he must have so established and so organized his Church, as to create in it a *visible centre* and appoint over it a *visible head*. Now, as a matter of fact, we have seen that Jesus Christ built his Church upon an individual; to one man he gave the keys of the kingdom; for one man's faith he prayed that it might not fail; to one shepherd he entrusted the feeding of his flock.

It seems scarcely necessary to remark that the expedient of Councils furnishes no security whatever for the unity of the Church. A General Council is a manifestation of the

Church's unity; but it affords no guarantee of its perpetuity. A Council is merely an assembly of the united Church; but the Church must be united before it can be assembled. There may be, and there have been, councils against councils, schismatical councils, heretical councils. There must be an authority apart from Councils to determine with certitude whether a council is or is not a representation of the œcumenical Church. Moreover, it is evident that Councils cannot constitute the system of government by which the Church is directed. For, first, a Council is, as I have said, only the Church assembled in one place; and the Church assembled has no functions which are not inherent in the Church diffused.* The body itself cannot be the head; and if the Church at large requires a visible head and governor, so also does the Church convened. Secondly, the government of the Church must be perennial, as well as indefectible. But Councils, even if their recurrence were a matter of certainty, cannot be perpetual. In the words of a Protestant, " it is not possible to hold a council continuously, or even frequently, while at the same time *the person of the Church* must always live and subsist, in order that its will may be ascertained." † In the words of a Catholic, " a periodical or intermittent sovereignty is a contradiction in terms." ‡ And, thirdly, Councils cannot convoke themselves. There must be an authority competent, whenever exigency require, to call the chief pastors of the Church together for deliberation and extraordinary legislation; and this authority is evidently identical with that central, perpetual, and supreme headship by which

---

* *Unitas Catholica quæ toto orbe diffusa est.*—St. Augustine.
† Leibnitz, *Systema Theologicum.*
‡ De Maistre, *Du Pape.*

alone the Church dispersed throughout the world can be held together, watched over, and ruled. In a word, Councils are only a part of the machinery by which the action of the Church is regulated *under its divinely established government.* To quote again the weighty clauses of one who was not far from the kingdom of God—"It was necessary . . . that one among the Apostles, and the successor of this one among the bishops, should be invested with pre-eminent power; in order that by him, as the visible centre of unity, the body of the Church might be bound together; the common necessities be provided for; a council, if necessary, be convoked, and, when convoked, directed; and that, in the interval between councils, provision might be made lest the commonwealth of the faithful sustain any injury."

It is worthy of notice that the schismatical Greeks have always tacitly, if not formally, admitted the impossibility of holding a General Council except under the presidency of the Bishop of Rome. However illogical they may be in denying the reality of the Supremacy, they have never denied that it is so far a necessity as to be requisite for the convening of an œcumenical synod. During two lucid intervals of their history, they came to the Councils of Lyons and Florence; but, discovering that they had committed themselves to too wide-awake a statement of the truth, they repudiated their professions and fell back into their ancient lethargy, and are still dreaming their languid oriental dream that for a thousand years and more there has been no true Council of the Church. As for Anglicans, whose notions about Councils are as nebulous as about some other things, they have never got so far as to propose, or to be aware of the expediency of proposing, a theory by which a Council of the universal Church could on Anglican principles conceivably be brought together. When the compilers of the Thirty-nine Articles found it necessary to say something or other about Councils, they eased their loyal English consciences by the negative declaration that " General Councils may not be gathered together without the commandment and will of Princes"—a proposition which, I venture to say, is as purely antichristian as any which the fecund ingenuity of heresy has ever succeeded in producing.

Once more, then, the only means by which, so far as we can apprehend, absolute unity in the Church could be attained is that means which God has in fact made use of, and by which he now gives to the world a proof and a similitude of his own ineffable oneness. Under the economy which he has created a division of the Church is *impossible.* The head of the Church is an individual; and an individual is something which cannot be divided. Whoever is in communion with the successor of St. Peter is within the visible Church; whosoever follows not the appointed shepherd is without the fold. The Primacy of the Holy See is " the personified reflection of the unity of the whole Church." *

The language of the last paragraph is only a repetition of that employed over and over again by the early Fathers, so soon as they began to discuss, and to appreciate, the doctrine of ecclesiastical unity. † In a previous chapter I quoted St. Cyprian, who was the first to speak explicitly on this great topic, as asserting—what I have endeavored to make very plain—that unity in a divine sense means indi-

---

* Moehler, *Einheit der Kirche.*

† For the use of the word *appreciate* I have St. Augustine's authority. See the note on pages 130, 131.

visibility.* I contented myself with giving the bare proposition, in St. Cyprian's words; for our argument at the stage to which we had then advanced neither required nor allowed anything more. But it is time now to state that St. Cyprian, in the treatise from which I quoted, does not merely insist upon the truth that unity is inviolable, but points out by what means the wisdom of God has so planned and constructed his Church as to render its discerption a thing practically as well as theologically impossible. The passages which were cited should be read in their connection if their cogency is to be fairly understood. " The Lord saith unto Peter, Thou art Peter, etc. Upon him being one he builds his Church." " In order to manifest unity, he has, by his own authority, so placed the source of the same unity as to begin from one." " He who holds not *this* unity of the Church, does he think that he holds the faith?" " As when many streams flow down from one source, etc., . . . unity is preserved in the source itself; cut the stream from its fountain, the remnant will be dried up." The Church " pours abroad her bountiful streams, etc.; yet there is one Head, one Source, one Mother, abundant in the results of her fruitfulness." These sentences give the drift of one connected argument. It is in the middle of this argument that those words occur which some Episcopalians are fond of quoting, evidently without being aware of their context—" Episcopatus est unus, cujus pars a singulis in solidum tenetur." St. Cyprian is showing *how* the Episcopate is one, and how each bishop can hold a part "*without division of the whole*,"† the unity being in the

* Part ii. ch. v. sec. 1.

† This rendering of the nervous phrase *in solidum* is the best I have seen. It is due, I believe, to Mr. Allies.

Head. In his epistles St. Cyprian constantly uses expressions which agree with the doctrine of the *De Unitate*. The Roman Church, the Chair of Peter, is "the principal Church, from which the unity of the priesthood took its rise."* It is "the root and womb (radix et matrix) of the Catholic Church."† "There is one God, and one Christ, and one Church, and one Chair founded upon the rock (super Petram) by the voice of the Lord."‡

I spoke of St. Augustine as following St. Cyprian. He follows him, be it now added, in his explanation of the Church's unity as he does in his declaration of the fact of that unity. St. Peter "represented the universality and unity of the Church."§ "One stood for all, because unity is in all."‖ "By the Primacy of his Apostolate, he represented the person of the Church, and was a type of its universality."¶ "It was the will of Christ to make Peter, to whom he commended his sheep as to another self, one with himself, that so he might commend his sheep to him; that He might be Head, and the other bear the figure of the body, that is, the Church, and that like man and wife they might be two in one flesh."** Similar passages might be taken from St. Optatus and St. Jerome. But there is no need of further quotation. Let the sentiments of the

---

* *Epist.* lv.

† *Epist.* xlv.

‡ *Epist.* xl. Hallam says: "Irenæus rather vaguely, and Cyprian more positively, admit, or rather assert, the primacy of the Church of Rome, which the latter seems to have regarded as a kind of centre of Catholic unity."—*Middle Ages*, ch. vii.

§ *Serm.* ccxcv. 2.

‖ *In Johan.* cxviii. 4.

¶ *In Johan.* cxxiv. 5; also *Enarr. in Ps.* cviii.

** *Serm.* xlvi. 30.

Fathers be summed up in the grandly laconic words of St. Ambrose: "To Peter Christ said, Thou art Peter, and upon this rock I will build my Church. Therefore, where Peter is, there is the Church—UBI PETRUS, IBI ECCLESIA."*

I cannot resist the temptation to pay another greeting, as we pass, to our old friends, Dr. Isaac Barrow and Mr. William Palmer. But I will try to be very gentle this time. Mr. Palmer calls the argument that "the primacy of St. Peter was to be a permanent office in the Church because the reason for which it was instituted was *to preserve unity*," a "*Romish* argument"; and says that "St. Jerome, and perhaps one or two others, may support the views of the Romanists!"† (Understand the exclamation to be a very prolonged one.) Barrow, in his gruff way, is far more— artless. "St. Cyprian," he says, "hath a reason for it [the institution of the Primacy] somewhat more subtle and mystical, supposing our Lord did confer on him [St. Peter] a preference of this kind to his brethren (who otherwise in power and authority were equal to him), that he might intimate and recommend unity to us; and the other African doctors (Optatus and St. Austin) do commonly harp on the same notion." ‡

We have said enough, I think, upon the general truth that the Primacy which our Divine Lord instituted is the means, and the only conceivable means, by which the unity of the Church is both represented and preserved. Let us now look a little more closely at the *modes* in which—to use the words of one of the harping African doctors—St. Peter personates the Church and is the type of its universality.

* *In Ps.* xl.
† *On the Church*, part vii. ch. ii.
‡ *Supremacy*, Suppos. I. iii.

The Council of Florence gave the following definition of the Primacy of the Roman Pontiffs—a definition, by the way, which was not only heartily concurred in by the whole of Western Christendom, including of course the Church of England, but which was signed by the Greeks themselves, in one of those brief seasons of returning animation to which I have referred: "We define that the holy Apostolical See and the Roman Pontiff hold a Primacy over the whole world; and that the Roman Pontiff himself is successor of blessed Peter, prince of the Apostles, and true Vicar of Christ, and Head of the whole Church, and that he is the Father and Doctor of all Christians; and that to him, in the person of blessed Peter, full power was delivered by our Lord Jesus Christ to feed, to rule, and to govern the uni versal Church, as also is contained in the acts of Œcumenical Councils, and in the sacred canons."* Let me take this definition as the text for the remainder of my lay sermon on unity. The Council evidently declares that primacy, or headship, is related to the oneness of the Church in two distinct ways. The Roman Pontiff, as the Head of the Church, is, 1, the father and teacher of all Christians; and, 2, he has full power from God to rule and govern the uni-

---

* Mansi, xxxi. 1031. Item definimus, sanctam apostolicam Sedem et Romanum Pontificem in universum orbem tenere primatum, et ipsum Pontificem Romanum successorem esse beati Petri principis Apostolorum, et verum Christi vicarium, totiusque Ecclesiæ caput, et omnium Christianorum patrem et doctorem existere; et ipsi in beato Petro pascendi, regendi, et gubernandi universalem Ecclesiam a Domino Nostro Jesu Christo plenam potestatem traditam esse, quemadmodum etiam in gestis œcumenicorum conciliorum et in sacris canonibus continetur.

versal Church. I shall find it convenient to speak of the latter relation first. And as I may find it hard to be very concise upon such important topics, it will be as well to mark off our present chapter here, and let it serve as a brief introduction to the two divisions which follow.

CHAPTER V.

THE PRIMACY AND AUTHORITY.

HE Church is a spiritual kingdom, all of whose citizens are in one sense "kings and priests to God." * " As living stones " they are "built up, a spiritual house, a holy priesthood, to offer up spiritual sacrifices acceptable to God by Jesus Christ." † But in order that there may be always and everywhere a Church into which men may be received, and in which as living stones they may be built up, a visible Priesthood has been created, and is continually invested with power to offer sacrifice—the one Adorable Sacrifice of the Christian Law—in behalf of all the people, and to administer those sacraments whereby, as supernatural means, spiritual life is implanted and nourished in the soul, as well as to make known and interpret the words of truth which have been revealed and committed to the Church. The peculiar functions of this external Priesthood are always the same. The Order of Priesthood is essentially one. ‡

But a kingdom implies government. And for the due administration of a kingdom which is universal there must of necessity be many degrees of dignity and authority. In a word, the Church requires not only a Priesthood, but

---

* Apoc. i. 5, 6.
† 1 Pet. ii. 5. Concerning this internal priesthood of all believers, see the *Catechism of the Council of Trent,* on the Sacrament of Orders.
‡ *Catechism of Council of Trent, ibid.*

a Hierarchy. Thus a distinction is immediately apparent between Order, which is invariable, and Jurisdiction, which has many gradations. Now, without stopping needlessly to discuss the form of the ecclesiastical hierarchy, let us come at once to the point at which we are aiming. It is only a repetition of the remark which I made a good while ago, in anticipation of our present discourse, that, in a government which is indivisible as well as universal, jurisdiction, or the right to exercise authority, must flow from a single source. The proposition is in itself so plain as to be axiomatic; and it is no less plain when illustrated in the constitution and history of the Christian Church. The contradictory of this proposition is not only paradoxical, but unintelligible; and its historical contradiction has resulted not only in division, but in anarchy.

The Priesthood, then, throughout the world derives its right to exercise the powers with which it is invested from the Head of the Church, to whom in the person of Blessed Peter Christ has given the keys of the kingdom of heaven. Through Peter the power of the keys is transmitted to the universal Church.

I have been careful to bring out (however briefly) the very simple distinction between Order and Jurisdiction because I know that a disregard of it has betrayed Anglican controversialists into almost incredible blunders. How is it not amazing, for instance, that for centuries they should have gone on quoting St. Jerome as affirming that the Bishop of Rome is in no respect superior to the Bishop of Gubbio;* when they ought to know, and doubtless do know, that not one of the Fathers is more emphatic in

---

* See, *e.g.*, Barrow, *Supremacy*, Suppos. V. ii. 3.

his appeals to the authority of the Chair of Peter than this very Papal Secretary? St. Jerome, wishing to rebuke a disrespect which had been shown by certain Roman deacons to priests and bishops of other churches, uses the following language: "Wherever a bishop may be, whether at Rome or at Eugubium, at Constantinople or Rhegium, at Alexandria or Thanæ, he is *of the same merit and of the same priesthood* (ejusdem meriti ejusdem et sacerdotii)." *
And yet the writer of this sentence could address the Bishop of Rome himself in such magnificent words as these: "As the East, vexed with internal discord, with all the habitual frenzy of that people, is tearing into shreds the seamless garment of the Lord, and the foxes lay waste Christ's vineyard, so that among the broken cisterns that hold no water it is difficult to understand where is the sealed-up fountain, and that enclosed garden; therefore have I thought that I ought to consult the Chair of Peter. . . . Wherefore, although your greatness deter, yet does your mildness invite me. From a priest a victim asks safety; from a shepherd a sheep seeks protection. Envy avaunt; away with 'the pride of the topmost dignity of Rome.' I speak with the fisherman's successor, and the disciple of the Cross. Following no chief but Christ, I am joined in communion with your Holiness; that is, with the Chair of Peter. Upon that rock I know that the Church is built. Whosoever eats the lamb out of this house is profane. If any be not in the ark of Noah, he will perish whilst the deluge prevails. . . . I know not Vitalis; I repudiate Miletius; I am a stranger to Paulinus. Whosoever gathereth not with thee, scattereth —that is, whosoever is not of Christ is of Antichrist." † Can

---

* *Epist.* lxxxv. Ad Evagr.
† *Epist.* xv. Ad Dam. "The Church here is rent into three

anything be more uncritical (let us use a gentle word) than to interpret an isolated expression of an author in a sense which does violence to his reiterated and notorious principles? Read this second passage again, my good Anglican brother, and then (if you can conceive of an 'ordinary Protestant' quoting the Fathers), imagine your Puritan neighbor producing St. Jerome as his champion against prelacy as well as popery, since he had the courage—and the logic —to write to the representative of both, and tell him flatly, without fear or compromise: "Away with the pride of Rome! I follow *no* chief but Christ. Whosoever is not of Christ is of Antichrist."

<blockquote>Mutato nomine de te
Fabula narratur.</blockquote>

St. Jerome's doctrine is of course that of the Catholic Church. By virtue of his Order, the Bishop of Rome *is* the equal of the Bishop of Eugubium or of Thanæ; but by the authority of the Chair in which he sits, he is the Head of the universal Church. In the year 378, a council of Bishops said of the very Pope Damasus whom St. Jerome consulted, knowing that upon that rock the Church is built: "He is equal in

---

parts, each of which is eager to drag me to itself. . . . Meanwhile I cry aloud, 'If any one is united to the Chair of Peter, he is mine.' Miletius, Vitalis, and Paulinus, all assert that they adhere to thee; I might assent if only one of them declared this; as it is, either two or all of them are liars. Wherefore I beseech your Holiness by the Cross of the Lord—that as you follow the Apostles in honor, you may follow them also in merit—you would by your letter make known to me with whom I ought to hold communion in Syria." *Epist.* xvi. Ad eund. "For this reason one of the twelve is selected, that by the appointment of a Head the occasion of schism may be taken away"—*Adv. Jovin.*

office to the other bishops, and surpasses them by the prerogative of the Apostolic See."* The Catechism of the Council of Trent, after declaring that the Order of Priesthood is "essentially one," goes on to enumerate its "different degrees of dignity and power," ascending from simple Priests, through Bishops, Archbishops, and Patriarchs, up to the Sovereign Pontiff, who was called in the Council of Ephesus "the Archbishop of all the habitable world,"† and in whom, as the successor of St. Peter, the Catholic Church recognizes "the full amplitude of jurisdiction, a jurisdiction not based upon synodal or other human constitutions, but emanating from no less an authority than God himself."‡

It is no doubt true that the whole question of derivative authority is one of those which by long discussion have come to be better, or at least more generally, understood now than in early days.§ The familiar use of the words 'mission' and 'jurisdiction' is, I think, fair evidence of this. At most, however, this is only saying that our knowledge has become more definite. God's laws are in operation before man finds a formula for them. The power of the sun's attraction kept this little system of ours in poise before Newton had expressed the force of gravity in an equation. And the Primacy of the Holy See had held the Church together a good while before men began to call that See the Source of Jurisdiction. In saying this, and in using the imperfect simile which suggested itself, I may have given somebody a

---

* *Constant.* i. col. 528 (*apud* Kenrick).
† St. Cyril of Alex. *Encom. in S. M. Deip.*
‡ On the Sacrament of Orders.
§ Understood, I mean, by Catholics. Protestants in general (and, I am almost tempted to say, Anglicans in particular) have the crudest possible notions on this subject.

chance to misunderstand me. After all that I have written, however, it would hardly be reasonable to suppose that I believe anything less than that St. Peter, in the person of his successor, has *always* been recognized as the head of the Church, the rock of the Church, the shepherd of the flock, the holder of the keys of the kingdom of heaven. In reality, I am convinced that in the early Church not only the subordination of all authority to the head, but the derivation of all authority from the head was more clearly apprehended than we are apt to imagine. And it may be worth our while to notice a few of the considerations upon which this conviction is grounded.

The expressions used by individual writers when speaking of the power of the keys have a force which cannot easily be misinterpreted. Tertullian, for example, says: "Remember that the Lord left the keys with Peter, and through him to the Church."* St. Cyprian quotes the words of Christ to Peter, and adds: "From this source flow the ordination of bishops and the order of the churches."† St. Optatus is equally explicit: "For the sake of unity, Blessed Peter . . . was preferred to the other Apostles, and alone received the keys of the kingdom of heaven that he might communicate them to the rest."‡ St. Gregory of Nyssa uses the same words: "Through Peter Christ has given to the bishops the keys of the kingdom of heaven."§ And not to be further tedious, St. Innocent, in his correspondence with St. Augustine and the African Councils which has

---

* *Scorpiac.* c. x.
† *Epist.* xxxiii.
‡ *Cont. Parmen.* l. vii. c. 3 : claves regni cœlorum communicandas cæteris solus accepit.
§ *De Castigat.*

been mentioned elsewhere, refers to the prerogatives of the Apostolic See as coming from the Apostle "from whom the Episcopate itself and the whole authority of that title has its origin."*

Even more significant, to my mind, is the distinct recognition of the fact that the great Patriarchal Sees received their primitive mission and consequent jurisdiction from St. Peter. The declaration of the Council under Pope Gelasius asserts this in the plainest and most precise terms. After confessing, as already quoted,† that "the Holy Roman Catholic and Apostolic Church has been preferred to the rest by no decrees of a council, but has obtained the Primacy by the evangelic voice of our Lord and Saviour himself," the decree goes on to affirm: "First, therefore, is the Roman Church, the See of Peter the Apostle, 'not having spot or wrinkle, nor any such thing.' But second is the See consecrated at Alexandria, in the name of blessed Peter, by Mark, his disciple and Evangelist, who was sent by Peter the Apostle into Egypt, taught the word of truth, and consummated a glorious martyrdom. And third is the See held in honor at Antioch in the name of the same most blessed Apostle Peter, because that he dwelt there before he came to Rome, and there first the name of the new people of the Christians arose."

But the most satisfactory proofs are to be found in the official acts of the Popes, so soon as in the good providence of God they were really free to exercise their office, in the acceptance of those acts by the Church at large, and, if I may so express myself, in the use which was made of the Primacy

---

* *Epist.* xxix. Ad. Conc. Carth.
† Part III. c. iii.

by the universal Episcopate. And without going to Catholic sources at all, I venture to hope that I can collect enough material to justify this assertion out of the pages of the *Treatise of the Pope's Supremacy*.

Touching the appointment of Vicars Apostolic, Barrow makes the following admissions: "The Popes, indeed, in the fourth century, began to practise a fine trick, very serviceable to the enlargement of their power; which was to confer on certain bishops, as occasion served, or for continuance, the title of their vicar or lieutenant, thereby pretending to impart authority to them; whereby they were enabled for performance of divers things, which otherwise by their own episcopal or metropolitical power they could not perform. . . . Thus did Pope Celestine constitute Cyril in his room. Pope Leo appointed Anatolius of Constantinople. Pope Felix, Acacius of Constantinople. Pope Hormisdas, Epiphanius of Constantinople. Pope Simplicius, to Zeno, bishop of Seville—'We thought it convenient that you should be held up by the vicariate authority of our See.' So did Siricius and his successors constitute the bishops of Thessalonica to be their vicars in the diocese of Illyricum, wherein being then a member of the western empire they had caught a special jurisdiction; to which Pope Leo did refer in those words, which sometimes are impertinently alleged with reference to all bishops, but concern only Anastasius, bishop of Thessalonica : 'We have intrusted thy charity to be in our stead, so that thou art called into part of the solicitude, not into plenitude of the authority.' So did Pope Zosimus bestow a like pretence of vicarious power upon the bishop of Arles, which city was the seat of the temporal exarch in Gaul. So to the bishop of Justiniana Prima in Bulgaria (or Dardania Europæa) the like privilege was granted [by procurement of the Emperor Justinian, native of that place]. Afterwards temporary or occasional vicars were appointed (such as Austin in England, Boniface in Germany)," etc.*

A similar list will furnish us with all the evidence we need upon the apostolic confirmation given by Popes to the election of bishops and metropolitans: "Pope Leo I. saith that Anatolius did 'by the favor of his assent obtain the bishoprick of Constantinople.' The same Pope is alleged as having confirmed Maximus of Antioch. The same did write to the bishop of Thessalonica (his vicar) that he should 'confirm the elections of bishops by his authority.' He also confirmed Donatus, an African bishop: 'We will that Donatus preside over the Lord's flock, upon condition that he remember to send us an account of his faith.' Also Gregory I. doth complain of it, as of an inordinate act, that a bishop of Salonæ was 'ordained without his knowledge.' Pope Damasus did confirm the ordination of Peter Alexandrinus: 'The Alexandrians' (saith Sozomen) 'did render the churches to Peter, being returned from Rome with the letters of Damasus, which confirmed both the Nicene decrees and his ordination.'" †

On the appellate jurisdiction of the Popes I have already said somewhat, in a note on the Council of Sardica. Appeals to the Head, as the ultimate source of authority, had

---

* Suppos. VI. x.

† Suppos. VI. vi. Barrow concludes his paragraph by bravely asking: "But what, I pray, doth confirmation here signify but approbation? For did he otherwise confirm the Nicene decrees? Did they need other confirmation?" To which masterly interrogations I find that I have endeavored to add emphasis, in my copy of the *Supremacy*, by *straightening* the three little crooked notes with a rather blunt lead-pencil.

begun to be frequent even before the pressure of the pagan empire had ceased to hold the Church in constraint, as the following enumeration will sufficiently show: "Thus did Marcion go to Rome, and sue for admission to communion there. So Fortunatus and Felicissimus in St. Cyprian, being condemned in Afric, did fly to Rome for shelter; of which absurdity St. Cyprian doth so complain. So likewise Martianus and Basilides, in St. Cyprian, being outed of their sees for having lapsed from the Christian profession, did fly to Stephen for succor, to be restored. So Maximus (the Cynic) went to Rome, to get a confirmation of his election at Constantinople. So Marcellus, being rejected for heterodoxy, went thither to get attestation of his orthodoxy (of which St. Basil complaineth). So Apiarius, being condemned in Afric for his crimes, did appeal to Rome. And on the other side, Athanasius being with great partiality condemned by the synod of Tyre; Paulus and other bishops being extruded from their sees for orthodoxy; St. Chrysostom being condemned and expelled by Theophilus and his accomplices; Flavianus being deposed by Dioscorus and the Ephesine synod; Theodoret being condemned by the same—did cry out for help to Rome. Chelidonius, bishop of Resanon, being deposed by Hilarius of Arles (for crimes), did fly to Pope Leo. Ignatius, patriarch of Constantinople, being extruded from his see by Photius, did complain to the Pope." *

In two of these extracts Barrow quotes from a letter of St. Leo to Anastasius of Thessalonica. † It is probably no rash opinion that ecclesiastical literature might be ransacked in vain for a more succinct and lucid judgment upon the

* Suppos. V. x. † *Epist.* lxxxiv.

relation of headship to jurisdiction and unity than is to be found in this same Apostolic Brief. Let us see whether the Anglican doctor has any apology for the easy assurance with which he tells us that its words 'concern only Anastasius, bishop of Thessalonica,' and 'are impertinently alleged with reference to all bishops.' The Pope shall plead his own cause : " As my predecessors," he writes, " to your predecessors, so have I, following the example of those gone before, committed to your affection my charge of government; that you, imitating our gentleness, might relieve the care which we, in virtue of our headship, by divine institution, owe to all churches, and might in some degree discharge our personal visitation to provinces far distant from us. . . . For we have intrusted your affection to represent us, so that you are called to a part of our solicitude, but not to the fulness of our power. . . . But if, in a matter which you believe fit to be considered and decided on with your brethren, their sentence differs from yours, let everything be referred to us on the authority of the Acts, that all doubtfulness may be removed, and we may decree what pleaseth God. . . . For the compactness of our unity cannot remain firm, unless the bond of charity weld us into an inseparable whole; because, 'as we have many members in one body, and all members have not the same office, so we, being many, are one Body in Christ, and every one members one of another.' For it is the connection of the whole body which makes one soundness and one beauty; and this connection, as it requires unanimity in the whole body, so especially demands concord among bishops. For, though these have a like dignity, yet have they not an equal jurisdiction; since even among the most blessed Apostles, as there was a likeness of honor, so was there a certain distinction of power; and, the election of all being equal, pre-eminence over the rest was given to one. From which type the distinction also between bishops has arisen, and it was provided by a great ordering that all should not claim to themselves all things, but that in every province there should be one whose sentence should be considered the first among his brethren; and others again, seated in the greater cities, should undertake a larger care, through whom the direction of the Universal Church should converge to the one See of Peter, and nothing anywhere disagree with its Head."* So spoke Leo 'the majestic,' of whom the Fathers of the Fourth General Council declared that he presided over them as a head over the members. As for his modern traducer, he has served our purpose long enough; his name shall vex these pages no more.

As Leo the Great, in the fifth century, committed to Anastasius his 'charge of government' to 'provinces far distant,' so Gregory the Great, in the sixth, gave mission to

---

* *Apud* Allies, sect. iv. Compare the following passage from the epistle to the metropolitan bishops of Illyricum (*Epist.* v.): " Since our solicitude extends to all the churches, as the Lord requires of us, who intrusted to the most blessed Apostle Peter the primacy of the apostolic dignity, as a reward of his faith, establishing the universal Church in the solidity of the foundation itself, we communicate this necessary solicitude to those who are united with us by the affection of (Episcopal) brotherhood. Following, therefore, the example of those whose memory we venerate, we have constituted our brother and fellow-bishop, Anastasius, our Vicar, and enjoined on him to see, from his watch-tower, that nothing unlawful be attempted by any one; and we admonish you, beloved, to obey him in all that regards ecclesiastical discipline; for your obedience will not be rendered to him, but to us, who are known to have intrusted him with this office in those provinces, in consequence of our solicitude."

the holy Augustine to build up again the ruins of the Church in the yet more remote region of Britain. The British Church had been organized as early as the second century, by Pope Eleutherius.* For more than two centuries it had flourished in peace, and in full communion with the See of St. Peter. British prelates had sat at the Council of Arles, in 314, and had joined in the letter which the Fathers of that Council sent to the Roman Pontiff, together with the canons they had framed, an epistle in which they " salute the most religious Pope with deserved reverence, being joined in the common bond of charity and with the tie of unity of our holy Mother the Church," declaring that in the Roman See "the Apostles continued daily to sit," and desiring that their decrees "might be made known to all by him who holds the chief diocese."† A generation later, bishops from Britain had assisted at the Council of Sardica, and had borne their part in the superb tribute which was there rendered to the supremacy of " the Head, the See of Peter the Apostle." With the beginning of the fifth century came the great heresy of the West; and when Pelagianism, choked in Africa by St. Augustine and twice condemned by the Holy See,‡ turned northward and invaded the island which had given birth to its author—Pelagius was a native

---

* Lingard, *Hist. and Antiq. of the Ang. Sax. Church;* Waterworth, *England and Rome.* Of any organization of Christianity in the British Isles, before the mission of Pope Eleutherius to King Lucius (A.D. 179) there is no evidence whatever, despite the hypotheses of some imaginative Anglicans.

† By the first of the canons it is ordered "that Easter shall be observed everywhere on the same day, and that the time of its observance shall be announced by the Bishop of Rome, according to custom."

‡ By Innocent I. (416) and Zosimus (418).

of Britain—then "Pope Celestine sent in his own stead Germanus, bishop of Auxerre, that he might drive out the heretics, and guide the Britons to the Catholic faith."* And when the pestilence of error, arrested for a season, had broken out again in the pontificate of Leo, Germanus had once more crossed the channel and won a second conquest for the truth.† Then came days of darkness. From the time of Leo to the time of Gregory, an interval of more than a century, Picts and Scots, and still more barbarous because treacherous Saxons, had ravaged the land, and, as Gildas tells us, had "destroyed as far as possible every vestige of Christianity." The Church in the afflicted island had long been cut off from intercourse with the main Body and with the Head, and had almost ceased to exist at all, when St. Gregory, moved with compassion for those to whom he had himself desired to be sent,‡ chose out a humble monk from his own monastery of St. Andrew, and laid upon him the burden of triple duty, as missionary, mediator, and metropolitan, giving him jurisdiction in the memorable words: "We commit to you, brother, the care of all the bishops of Britain, that the unlearned may be instructed, the weak strengthened by persuasion, and the perverse corrected by authority."§

Alas! the few remaining British bishops, blinded by

* St. Prosper, *In Chronico ad ann.* 429.
† A.D. 447.
‡ When a priest, Gregory had entreated Benedict I. to send him to the nation of the English. (Ven. Bede, l. ii. c. 1.)
§ *Epist.* lxiv. Ven. Bede, l. i. c. 27. "We give you no authority over the bishops of Gaul, because from the ancient times of my predecessors the Bishop of Arles received the pallium, whom we must not deprive of the authority with which he is invested."—*Ibid.*

hatred of their Saxon invaders,* and fearing what they imagined to be the imperious temper of the new envoy,† refused to co-operate in the work of restoration which had been begun. They drew apart; and, after lingering for a while in sullen isolation, their succession died out utterly. In the glory of England's second conversion to the faith they had no share. ‡

* Bede, l. i. c. 22 ; l. ii. c. 20. " In one thing the Britons were very reprehensible, and that one thing was the *mortal hatred* which even to this day they bear to the English nation, by whom they were driven from their ancient territories ; which hatred is so irreconcilable that they would rather communicate with dogs than with the English."—Matthew of Westminster, *apud* Waterworth.

† Bede, l. ii. c. 2.

‡ I had intended making something of a digression by way of riddling the witless theory of an autocephalous, or independent, British Church, with which, like most modern Anglicans, I used to prop my singular notions of Christianity—I say modern Anglicans, for the Reformers, with all their bold follies, never weakened their cause by any such display of feeble ingenuity. But there is really no need of wasting powder on a house of cards. It is evident, even from the few facts mentioned in the text, that the British Church was *not* independent. And if the British bishops had imagined themselves independent (we have no proof that they did), they would only have been very silly Britons. And whether they cherished any fancies or not, their dreams perished with them ; the church of the Plantagenets and the Tudors had absolutely no connection with the defunct church of Lleuver Mawr. Whether the British usage was the 'Quartodeciman' or not is a matter of excessive indifference ; though it certainly was *not* the Quartodeciman, for the British Bishops, as has been said, helped to draw up the first canon of Arles, and the question of Easter had been settled once for all at Nice ; the Britons had merely lost their reckoning, " by reason," as Bede says, " of their living so far away from the rest of the world" (l. iii. c. 4). As for Dinooth's wonderful speech about the Pope and the Bishop of Caerleon, nothing can exceed my disgust at discovering it to be a stale and very clumsy forgery, suspected by old Thomas Fuller almost as soon as

It is no portion of our present task to trace those fruitful labors by which, under the direction and solicitous ministration of the successors of St. Peter, a new Christian Church

Spelman produced it, and exposed by scholars of later times over and over again. Yet Protestant bishops and doctors, with a magnanimous disregard of criticism, go on quoting it to this very day. The use which Bishop Bull makes of this speech, in his Letter in answer to Bossuet, makes an honest man stagger. He ushers it in as though it rested on "the unanimous testimony of our historians," and follows it up with the sentence : " And that this was indeed the sense not only of Dinothus, but of all the whole body of our British clergy at that time, all our historians tell us, witnessing the absolute and unanimous resolution of the British clergy, both bishops and priests, synodically met together, not to subject themselves to the jurisdiction of the Bishop of Rome ; " and, not content with this, he adds a note : " Vide Spel. Com. Gual. Mon. ii. 13, *Bedam omnesque alios*"—italics and all. Who the *omnes alii* were, poor·Bossuet could hardly be expected to divine. As for Bede, who is the only authority we possess concerning the meeting of Augustine and Dinooth, he says not one word about any rejection of the supremacy of the Pope, nor of any pretensions to independence (l. ii. c. 2). There is, I say, something confounding in all this. Nor does it revive our confidence in 'the learned Dr. Bull,' to turn the next page of his letter and read his apology for the submission of England to 'the jurisdiction which Pope Gregory challenged to himself by his legate, Austin.' " We did, indeed," he says, "yield ourselves to the Roman usurpation "—(pray, who are the ' *we* ' who thus ' *yielded* ' ?) —" but it was because we could not help it ; we were at first forced, awed, and affrighted into this submission. For who hath not heard of the barbarous massacre of the poor innocent monks of Bangor, to the number of twelve hundred, for refusing Austin's proposal, and asserting the ancient rights and privileges of the Britannic churches ? " Who hath not heard, to be sure ! And what schoolboy (as Macaulay would say) doth not know that this execrable butchery had nothing under the heavens to do with the mission of England's great apostle, whose body had turned to dust before the Saxon Ethelfred ever turned his merciless sword against the Britons, and for whose soul many a mass had been offered before

was established and built up in the island of Great Britain. Even Protestant revisers of history have been unable to obscure the splendor of those nine eventful centuries, during which the growth of Anglo-Saxon civilization made the Catholic Church of England the pride and boast of Christendom. Whatever of greatness the English nation has achieved, whatever there is that is broad and noble and enduring in the inheritance which it has received from the past, it owes to the Catholic Christianity which first reclaimed it from barbarism, and then educated it to all that is beautiful and honorable, which taught it the lessons of justice and liberty—aye! the forgotten lessons of generosity and mercy —to that grand old Church which, as poor Cobbett says, erected every edifice now remaining in the country worth the trouble of walking a hundred yards to see, and created every seminary of learning, and caused to be enacted every law, and to be framed every institution, of which England has a right to be proud. With reluctant steps, let us pass on to the day of England's calamity, when unlawful passion ministering to unhallowed pride tempted a King to lay sacrilegious hands upon the things of God, and to grasp at a jurisdiction which could be exercised only by him who held the keys of the kingdom of heaven. We have something still to do if we would elicit the full meaning of that Reformation which exchanged Catholic unity for insular

---

the fifty survivors at Bangor chanted their requiem—it was a *bona-fide mass*, by the way—for the repose of their murdered companions? Bishop Bull was once the hero of my youthful studies, my beau ideal of a solid scholar and a sturdy churchman. Alas, great Dagon, thy niche is empty.

independence, and replaced the Church of Christ by a Royal Establishment.

It has already been noted that the changes in matters of dogma which were effected under Henry, Edward, and Elizabeth were never even distantly contemplated by those who initiated the English Reformation. Heresy in England was not the cause but the consequence of schism. It has been observed further, in another place, that the Established Church was, and still continues to be, an attempt to realize the falsehood that in matters of jurisdiction the spiritual order is subordinate to the secular. It only remains to record in precise terms what that doctrine was by which King Henry and his ecclesiastical advisers justified the first fatal act of separation, and under which they were able to disguise, even from many good men, a principle which in its naked statement is simply antichristian. The postulate, then, of these reformers, the point of departure and the ultimate resolution of this national Christianity, its badge and token, sum and substance, is this: that the Head of the State is also, by God's appointment, the Head of the Church, and therefore the source of all jurisdiction, both spiritual and temporal. The Royal Supremacy meant nothing more and nothing less than the Supremacy of the Pope expressed in the person of the King.

It would be an imposition upon the patience of my readers if I were to attempt any lengthy proof of a proposition which affirms a familiar fact of history. I will only so far presume upon their indulgence as to quote a single passage, of a page or two, in which an English historian has summed up the proceedings of half a century, and into which he has condensed the evidence of unnumbered state papers, royal edicts, and acts of parliament. * Lord Macaulay, in the first chapter of his *History of England*, says:

"What Henry and his favorite counsellors meant by the supremacy was certainly nothing less than the whole power of the keys. The king was to be the pope of his kingdom, the vicar of God, the expositor of Catholic verity, the channel of sacramental graces. † He arrogated to himself the right of deciding dogmatically what was orthodox doctrine and what was heresy, of drawing up and imposing confessions of faith, and of giving religious instruction to his people. He proclaimed that all jurisdiction, spiritual as

---

* There will be no pedantry, I hope, in supplying a few marginal notes.

† The King is "the only Supreme Head in earth of the Church of England."—25 Henry VIII. 21, s. 2 ; 37 Henry VIII. 17, s. 3. To him, as the Head, appertain "all pre-eminences, jurisdictions, privileges, authorities to the said dignity belonging, and especially full power to repress, correct, and amend all heresies and abuses which by any manner of spiritual authority, or jurisdiction, ought to be repressed, corrected, or amended."—25 Henry VIII. 1. Mr. Palmer is weak enough to argue that the papal power was not transferred to the king ; it was merely suppressed ; and the royal supremacy was something distinct in its nature from the papal jurisdiction.—*On the Church*, part ii. c. iii. 2. Richard Hooker, however, is very straightforward : "There is required an universal power, which reacheth over all, importing supreme authority of government over all courts, all judges, all causes ; the operation of which power is as well to strengthen, maintain, and uphold particular jurisdictions, which haply might else be of small effect, as also to remedy that which they are not able to help, and to redress that wherein they at any time do otherwise than they ought to do. This power being some time in the Bishop of Rome, who by sinister practices had drawn it into his hands, was for just considerations by public consent annexed unto the King's royal seat and crown."—*Ecclesiastical Polity*, book viii. c. viii. 4. Bramhall also says very plainly : "Whatsoever power our laws did divest the

well as temporal, was derived from him alone,* and that it was in his power to confer the episcopal character and to take it away. He actually ordered his seal to be put to commissions by which bishops were appointed, who were to exercise their functions during his royal pleasure.† According to this system, as expounded by Cranmer, the king was the spiritual as well as the temporal chief of the nation. In both capacities his highness must have lieutenants. ‡ As

Pope of, they invested the King with it."—*Schism Guarded*, p. 340. Palmer himself acknowledges, subsequently, that "the parliament passed acts for abolishing the papal jurisdiction and establishing the regal supremacy, with an oath to that effect ;" and that by act of Parliament "all jurisdiction, spiritual and temporal," was declared to "emanate from the king."

* "Archbishops, bishops, archdeacons, and other ecclesiastical persons have no manner of jurisdiction ecclesiastical, but by, under, and from your Royal Majesty."—37 Henry VIII. 17. The new pope adopted a tone which he evidently thought was very pontifical. He was certainly successful in copying a few phrases from papal briefs ; but the words have lost their fragrance of solicitude and holy charity, and are heavy with the arrogance of rebellious self-will. Compare, *e.g.*, the following with the letter of St. Leo to Anastasius of Thessalonica : "Ceterum quia et singula hujus regni nostri loca pro præmissis exequendis nos ipsi personaliter obire non valemus, alios quorum vicaria fide freti munus hujusmodi veluti per ministros exequamur, qui quum vices nostras in ea parte supplcant, in partem solicitudinis adstitimus et vocamus."—Wilkins, *Concil.* iii. 784.

† "We name, make, create, constitute, and declare, N. bishop of N., to have and to hold to himself the said bishopric during the time of his natural life, if for so long a time he behave himself well therein ; and we empower him to confer orders, to institute to livings, to exercise all manner of ecclesiastical jurisdiction, and to do all that appertains to the episcopal or pastoral office, over and above the things known to have been committed to him by God in the Scriptures, in place of us, in our name, and by our royal authority."—Wilkins, *Concil.* iv. 10, 27, 28, 30.

‡ "All Christian Princes have committed unto them immedi-

he appointed civil officers to keep his seal, to collect his revenues, and to dispense justice in his name, so he appointed divines of various ranks to preach the Gospel, and to administer the sacraments. It was unnecessary that there should be any imposition of hands. The king—such was the opinion of Cranmer given in the plainest words—might, in virtue of authority derived from God, make a priest; and the priest so made needed no ordination whatever.

ately of God the whole cure of all their subjects, as well concerning the administration of God's word, for the cure of souls, as concerning the ministration of things political and civil governance; and in both these ministrations they must have sundry ministers under them, to supply that which is appointed to their several offices; as, for example, the Lord Chancellor, Lord Treasurer, Lord Great Master, and the Sheriffs, for civil ministers; and the Bishops, Parsons, Vicars, and such other Priests as be appointed by his Highness, in the ministration of the word; as, for example, the Bishop of Winchester, the Parson of Winwick, etc. All the said officers and ministers, as well of that sort as the other, must be appointed, assigned, and elected, and in every place, by the laws and orders of Kings and Princes, with divers solemnities, which be not of necessity, but only for good order and seemly fashion; for if such offices and ministrations were committed without such solemnity, they were nevertheless truly committed; and there is no more promise of God that grace is given in the committing of the ecclesiastical office, than it is in the committing of the civil office."—Cranmer's words. Burnet, *Records* (Append. to *Hist. of Refor.*), pt. i. bk. iii. n. 21. Thomas Cromwell, a layman, was the King's vicar-general, "with full power to exercise and execute all and every that authority and jurisdiction appertaining to himself (the King) as Head of the Church, and to appoint others his delegates and commissaries to execute the same under him; authorizing them to visit all dioceses and churches, to summon before them all ecclesiastical persons, even bishops and archbishops, to enquire into their manners and lives, to punish with spiritual censures, to issue injunctions, and to exercise all the functions of the ecclesiastical courts."—Wilkins, iii. 784.

These opinions Cranmer followed out to their legitimate consequences. He held that his own spiritual functions, like the secular functions of the chancellor and treasurer, were at once determined by a demise of the crown. When Henry died, therefore, the Archbishop and his suffragans took out fresh commissions, empowering them to ordain and to perform other spiritual functions till the new sovereign should think fit to order otherwise.* When it was objected that a power to bind and to loose, altogether distinct from temporal power, had been given by our Lord to his Apostles, the theologians of this school replied that the power to bind and to loose had descended, not to the clergy, but to the whole body of Christian men, and ought to be exercised by the chief magistrate, as the representative of the society. When it was objected that St. Paul had spoken of certain persons whom the Holy Ghost had made overseers and shepherds of the faithful, it was answered that King Henry was the very overseer, the very shepherd, whom the Holy Ghost had appointed, and to whom the expressions of St. Paul applied.

"These high pretensions gave scandal to Protestants as well as to Catholics; and the scandal was greatly increased when the supremacy, which Mary had resigned back to the

---

* The new sovereign was a docile child, and readily accepted the supremacy which was put into his hands. The parliament was as obsequious as before. "Authority of jurisdiction, spiritual and temporal, is derived and deducted from the King's Majesty, as Supreme Head of these churches and realms of England and Ireland, and so justly acknowledged by the clergy of the said realms, that all courts ecclesiastical within the said two realms be kept by no other power or authority, either foreign or within this realm, but by the authority of his most excellent Majesty."—1 Edward VI. 3.

Pope, was again annexed to the crown, on the accession of Elizabeth. It seemed monstrous that a woman should be the chief bishop of a church in which an apostle had forbidden her even to let her voice be heard. The queen, therefore, found it necessary expressly to disclaim that sacerdotal character which her father had assumed, and which, according to Cranmer, had been inseparably joined, by divine ordinance, to the regal function. When the Anglican confession of faith was revised in her reign, the supremacy was explained in a manner somewhat different from that which had been fashionable at the court of Henry. Cranmer had declared, in emphatic terms, that God had immediately committed to Christian princes the whole cure of all their subjects, as well concerning the administration of God's word for the cure of souls, as concerning the ministration of things political. The thirty-seventh article of religion, framed under Elizabeth, declares, in terms as emphatic, that the ministering of God's word does not belong to princes. The queen, however, still had over the Church a visitatorial power of vast and undefined extent.* She was intrusted by parliament with the office of restraining and punishing heresy and every sort of ecclesiastical abuse,

---

* "Such jurisdictions, privileges, superiorities, and pre-eminences, spiritual and ecclesiastical, as by any spiritual or ecclesiastical power or authority hath heretofore been, or may lawfully be, exercised or used for the visitation of the ecclesiastical state and persons, and for reformation, order, and correction of the same, and all manner of errors, heresies, schisms, abuses, offences, contempts, and enormities, shall for ever, by authority of this present parliament, be united and annexed to the imperial crown of this realm."—1 Eliz. 1. The title of "Supreme Head of the Church of England" still belongs, by act of parliament, to the British sovereigns.

and was permitted to delegate her authority to commissioners. The bishops were little more than her ministers. Rather than grant to the civil magistrate the absolute power of nominating spiritual pastors, the Church of Rome, in the eleventh century, set all Europe on fire. Rather than grant to the civil magistrate the absolute power of nominating spiritual pastors, the ministers of the Church of Scotland, in our own time, resigned their livings by hundreds. The Church of England had no such scruples. By the royal authority alone her prelates were appointed.* By

* Witness the consecration of Archbishop Parker. The Queen in her commission for the confirmation of his election inserted the following clause: "Supplentes nihilominus, suprema auctoritate nostra regia, ex mero motu ac certa scientia nostris, si quid aut in his, quæ juxta mandatum nostrum prædictum per vos fient, aut in vobis aut vestrum aliquo, conditione, statu, facultate vestris ad præmissa perficienda desit aut deerit eorum, quæ per statuta hujus regni, aut per leges ecclesiasticas in hac parte requiruntur, aut necessaria sunt, temporis ratione et rerum necessitate id postulante." When Barlow, Coverdale, and the rest (not one of whom was in actual possession of any see at the time) proceeded to carry out the Queen's injunctions, they quoted her commission as their authority: The election of "the venerable man, Mr. Matthew Parker, we confirm, by the supreme authority of the said most serene lady, our Queen, committed unto us in this behalf; supplying by the supreme royal authority, of the Queen's mere motion and certain knowledge, delegated to us, all defects in this election, as well in those things done by us, and proceeded with according to the commandment given us, or that are or shall be in ourselves, or in the condition, state, or capacity of any one of us for this performance."—Lewis, *Notes on the Royal Supremacy*, p. 71. Finally, to make the whole transaction secure, an act of parliament (that *catholicon* of princes) was passed, declaring "that all acts and things heretofore had, made, or done by any person or persons in or about any consecration, confirmation, or investing of any person or persons elected to the office or dignity of any archbishop or bishop within this realm, or within any other the Queen's Majes-

the royal authority alone her convocations were summoned, regulated, prorogued, and dissolved. Without the royal sanction her canons had no force. One of the articles of her faith was, that without the royal consent no ecclesiastical council could lawfully assemble. From all her judicatures an appeal lay, in the last resort, to the sovereign, even when the question was, whether an opinion ought to be accounted heretical, or whether the administration of a sacrament had been valid."*

The plain doctrine, then, of Anglicanism concerning jurisdiction, the doctrine upon which the Church of England was founded, and by virtue of which it continues to exist, is that all ecclesiastical authority emanates from the Head of the—STATE. There is no disguising this. If any of my

ty's dominions or countries, by virtue of the Queen's Majesty's letters patent or commission, since the beginning of her Majesty's reign, be, and shall be by authority of this present parliament, declared, judged, and deemed, at and from every of the several times of the doing thereof, good and perfect to all respects and purposes; any matter or thing that can or may be objected to the contrary thereof in any wise notwithstanding."—8 Eliz. 2. Whether Parker received any episcopal character or not is a question of no importance in the controversy with Anglicanism. The great question, which has been a thousand times asked and never honestly answered, is this: By what authority did Barlow and his fellows undertake to lay episcopal hands on Mr. Matthew Parker; and by what authority did the said Parker undertake to exercise the office of Primate of all England? And here is the honest answer: By the authority of a woman.

* The King's Court of Chancery was appointed to hear ecclesiastical causes as early as 1533. To this Court it was declared lawful to appeal from any of the archiepiscopal courts of the realm, "and that upon every such appeal a commission shall be directed under the Great Seal to such persons as shall be named by the King's Highness, his heirs or successors, *like as in case of appeal from the Admiral's Court*, to hear and definitely determine

readers really believes that the Head of the State is by God's appointment the Head of the Church, he shall not be further disturbed in his most Christian faith by any argument of mine.

As for any opinions which may be entertained on this subject of jurisdiction by members of the Protestant Episcopal Church in the United States, they require no notice at our hands. *Quod ab initio nullum est, tractu temporis non convalescit.* The truth is, however, that American Episcopalians have, so far as I have been able to discover, no theory of jurisdiction whatever. The axiom of Hooker, that "there is required an universal power, which reacheth over all, importing supreme authority of government over all courts, all judges, all causes,"[*] is something which their ecclesiastical intelligence has not yet attained unto. The English Reformation represented an *idea*, however false that idea may have been in itself, and however incoherent may be the results to which it has led. But Protestant Episcopacy in America represents nothing intelligible.

I am sorry to have to refer to the American Episcopal Church at all; and my old friends (I assume that I have a few left, 'unbeknown to myself') will please take note that I have made the reference as brief as possible. I have tried all along to fight the enemy at a distance; and for the

---

such appeals, and the causes concerning the same."—25 Henry VIII. 19. Under William IV., the Court of Privy Council succeeded to this Court of Delegates, the new tribunal reproducing the character and inheriting the powers of the old. Laymen and unbelievers may sit in judgment not only upon matters of ecclesiastical discipline, but upon the faith once delivered to the saints; and their decisions, 'like as in case of appeal from the Admiral's Court,' are final.

[*] See the quotation given in a previous note (page 303).

double reason that I considered such a method of warfare both more agreeable and more effective.

And yet this business of controversy has been a desperately painful one at the best. It might appear strange to some that throughout the anxious investigations which, by God's unspeakable mercy, ended in my submission to the Catholic Church, I thought very little indeed about the religious body with which I was immediately connected. Many, doubtless, for whom I write will know that there was nothing unnatural in this. And perhaps there are a few who will be able not only to understand the logic of my case, but to enter into its sympathies. As a Protestant Episcopalian my heart was over the sea. My eyes were ever turning to my Mother Church, the dear old Church of England. There was more than fascination in her very name. Her theologians stood to me in place of all the saints. Her traditions, as I cherished them, had for me an indescribable attraction. They were comely with the beauty of holiness, and ambrosial with the flavor of antiquity, and sweet-scented with the aroma of scholarship. Oxford, though I had never seen even "its spires, as they are seen from the railway," was the spot above all spots on earth where my imagination—I had almost said my memory—found a home.

Even now, as a Catholic, I think of the parent church as I cannot possibly do of its republican offspring. The Protestant Episcopal Church is only a new sect, very respectable, to be sure, and conservative—though undeniably very piebald; but after all only a new sect in a new land. But England was once Catholic. And like one of her ruined abbeys, she is majestic still with intimations of a glory that has been. The sepulchres of the prophets are there—alas, not even coldly garnished by the hands of Scribes and Pharisees—yet still there, and precious with the dust of the saints. And the stately minsters, though silent now and bare, mark out, from north to south, the ancient high places of the Church of God. And Oxford—ah! do I not know *now* why most of all I loved thee? Thy very stones are Catholic. Since the day when a generation wise in its own conceit invaded thy sacred seclusion, thy twenty colleges have stood and pleaded, with a most mute appeal, against the calumnies of three shallow centuries. Until these our very times not one school, not one single hall has arisen bearing the title or endowed with the revenues of heresy. If any strange name could have been fitly added to thy hallowed catalogue, it would have been that of him who, in thy

—" Shades endear'd of yore
By tread of holy feet,"

grew saintly with the graces which he inspired with the very air he breathed. Yet even Keble College does not feel itself at home in Oxford.

England was once a fruitful bough. But now, O Church of England, thou art but one of those broken branches of which St. Augustine speaks so sadly, which lie and wither each in its own place. Ubi cecidisti ibi remanes, et ubi separata es ibi arescis.

Turn us again, thou God of hosts: show the light of thy countenance, and we shall be whole.

Thou hast brought a vine out of Egypt: thou hast cast out the heathen, and planted it.

Thou madest room for it: and when it had taken root, it filled the land.

The hills were covered with the shadow of it: and the boughs thereof were like the goodly cedar-trees.

She stretched out her branches unto the sea: and her boughs unto the river.

Why hast thou then broken down her hedge: that all they that go by pluck off her grapes?

The wild boar out of the wood doth root it up: and the wild beasts of the field devour it.

Turn thee again, thou God of hosts: look down from heaven, behold, and visit this vine.

CHAPTER VI.

THE PRIMACY AND INFALLIBILITY.

HE beginning and the ending of truth are one. As Jesus Christ, who is himself the Truth, is Alpha and Omega, the first and the last, so that truth which Christ first revealed concerning his Church is the same which the Church reasserts of herself as her crowning glory in these latter days. The foundation upon which the temple mystical was builded is made also the keystone of the topmost arch. And—let it not be deemed unbecoming if I add—the assurance upon which my own faith first rested is fitly chosen to be the conclusion and consummation of this statement of reasons of the hope that is in me.

We have been speaking, it will be remembered, of the relation of primacy to unity. I began with the proposition that the Primacy of the Holy See is the means which God has employed to secure the unity of the Church; or, as St. Augustine expresses it, St. Peter personates the Church, and represents its unity and universality. I then quoted the definition of the Council of Florence, as setting forth in general terms the modes in which the Primacy holds the universal Church together. I have said all that needs to be said upon the truth that the Head of the Church has received from our Lord Jesus Christ the plenitude of authority to rule and govern. It remains for me to say what in these days of bold denial may well be said even by a convert upon the collateral truth that the Vicar of Christ is by

Christ's appointment the doctor, or teacher, of all Christians.

Let us begin with a few words of plain, straightforward discourse. That the Church must have a visible Head has been proved. But the very mission of the Church—the Ecclesia Docens—is to teach. It follows therefore immediately that the Head of the Church must be the chief doctor of the Church. Now, the doctrine of the Church's unity requires that the dogmatical judgments of the Head of the Church should be final, or, to use a word celebrated in controversy, irreformable. The Angel of the Schools implies this, at the same time that he shows, by reasoning which is as cogent as it is condensed, that primacy is involved in the notion of unity : " For the unity of the Church it is necessary that all the faithful agree in faith. But concerning points of faith it happens that questions are raised. Now the Church would be divided by a diversity of opinions, unless it were preserved in unity by the sentence of one. So then it is demanded for the preservation of the Church's unity that there be one to preside over the whole Church."* Even, therefore, if it were possible for us to consider the question of absolute inerrancy as a speculative one, it is evident that as reasonable beings we should be compelled to admit that the chief teacher of a teaching Church must be practically infallible. This is what De Maistre means when he says : " *Infallibility* in the spiritual order of things, and *sovereignty* in the temporal order, are two words perfectly synonymous. The one and the other denote that high power which rules over all other powers—from which they all derive their authority—which governs, and is not govern-

---

* St. Thomas, *Cont. Gentiles*, l. iv. c. 76.

ed—which judges, and is not judged. When we say that *the Church is infallible*, we do not ask for her, it is quite essential to be observed, any particular privilege; we only require that she possess the right common to all possible sovereignties, which all necessarily act as if infallible. For every government is absolute; and from the moment it can be resisted, under pretext of error or injustice, it no longer exists." *

But it has been proved, with a redundancy of argument, that a Church which is divinely commissioned to teach must be divinely protected against error in its teaching. The Church is infallible. Therefore the Head of the Church is infallible; for, as St. Thomas demonstrates, *the faith of the Church must be fixed by the decisions of its Head.* An infallible Church with a fallible Head would be, not a mere monstrosity, like the famous heteroclite at which the Pisos were expected to smile, but an inconceivable absurdity.

The infallibility of the Head of the Church is, then, a logical inference from the infallibility of the Church. This, of course, is not equivalent to saying that the former term —or, more strictly, that which it represents—is, metaphysically, a consequence of the latter. It is only necessary to review the reasoning to see that the reverse is the truth. The argument is one from effect to condition (to use Whately's phrase). From the infallibility of the Church we infer the infallibility of its Head, inasmuch as the latter is an essential condition † of the former. In other words, the logical *therefore* in the enthymeme, *The Church is infallible, therefore it must have an infallible Head*, gives us the meta-

---

* *Du Pape*, l. i. c. 1.
† I do not like the word ; but *prerequisite* is no better.

physical *because* in the proposition, *The Church is infallible because it has an infallible Head.* *

It has been shown elsewhere that General Councils are neither the means by which the unity of the Church is secured nor the sovereignty by which the Church is governed. By similar reasoning it is equally demonstrable that it is not in virtue of its Councils that the Church is infallible. A Council is only the Church convened; and a Council is infallible in virtue of the infallibility of the Church.† The Church is infallible at all times and in all places. And it is always and everywhere true that the faith of the Church is determined by the faith of its Head. Accordingly, as we have seen, it is true as a matter of fact that from the fourth century to the sixteenth nothing has been "accounted valid or to be received in universal Councils but what the See of St. Peter has approved," and, on the other hand, "whatever she alone has rejected, that only is rejected."‡ There have been intervals of centuries during which no Council has been called together; and there is no reason why such intervals should not cover thousands as well as hundreds of years. Yet infallibility is neither dormant nor intermittent.

By way of caveat against possible misapprehension, it may be well to notice one or two points, which, however obvious in themselves, cannot safely be taken for granted in

---

* From the prosperity of a people we may infer the excellence of its government, but only so far as good government is a necessary condition of prosperity; and just so far we may say that the nation is prosperous because it is well governed. If good government were the sole condition of prosperity, the illustration would be more apt.

† Archbishop Manning, *The Centenary of St. Peter: A Pastoral Letter*, etc., p. 77.

‡ Pope Nicholas I. *Epist.* vii.

an essay intended for miscellaneous, and perhaps not always friendly, readers. Be it understood, then, that in speaking of the Church and of its Head I do not for an instant imply that the two are separable even in conception. It is only, therefore, from the imperfection of language that I even seem to speak of a twofold infallibility. The infallibility of the Church *is* the infallibility of its Head. Nevertheless, it is perfectly legitimate to argue that the infallibility of the Church is derived from its Head.

Again, when I speak of the Head of the Church as infallible, I mean that he is infallible *as* the Head of the Church; in other words, when he speaks by virtue of the authority of his office. Such a functional prerogative has nothing to do with any man's private character, his abilities, attainments, or discretion. The infallible Head of the Church not only may be, but must be, a fallible and peccable man. You do not comprehend this, my friend. No; it is one of those truths which are spiritually discerned. You do not think it possible that God should have put such treasure into earthen vessels. Just as, when the Church tells you that her Lord has left with her the power of forgiving and retaining sins, you do not understand how God can have given such power unto men. *N'est-ce pas?*

Let me repeat, also, what was very plainly brought out when treating of infallibility in general—that the office of infallibility is not to reveal new truth, but to protect old truth. Infallibility is one thing, and inspiration is another. When, therefore, we say that the Head of the Church must be infallible, we mean that it is an attribute of such Headship to define unerringly the faith of the Church whereinsoever that faith has been misinterpreted or misrepresented, and to decide with certainty, whenever the need of the

Church requires such a decision, whether a given doctrine —by whatever name it call itself, religious, philosophical, or political—is or is not in accordance with the original revelation. Infallibility does not go outside of the sphere of revelation. At the same time, infallibility alone is competent to determine what does or does not fall within that sphere. Because the advocates of some noxious error choose to call their heresy a social theory, or a philosophical principle, with which in their opinion the Church has nothing to do, that does not hinder the Church from asserting the supremacy of divine law over human passion, or from defending sacred truth against insidious falsehood.

Thus far we have followed reason and logic. All that has been said concerning the infallibility of the Head of the Church has been strictly developed from the simple notion of the Church itself. Let us listen now for a little while to the teaching of authority concerning its own prerogative; and then let us glance at the evidence of tradition, and finally at the testimony of history, to the truth that in the Apostolic See the faith has ever been preserved immaculate. St. Thomas Aquinas, immediately after the words which were quoted a moment ago, continues his argument as follows: "Now it is plain that Christ is not wanting in necessary things to the Church which he loved, and for which he shed his blood, since even of the synagogue it is said by the Lord, 'What more ought I to have done for my vineyard, which I have not done?' We cannot, therefore, doubt that one, *by the ordering of Christ*, presides over the whole Church." We cannot doubt, that is, *a priori*—from the reason of the case; since the unity of the Church requires that questions of faith should be determined by the sentence of one. Still less can we doubt when we know that there has always existed in the Church an authority, basing its title upon the words of Christ, by the sentence of which, as a matter of fact, questions of faith have always been determined.

The Holy See claims to be, not only infallible, but the organ of infallibility to the Church.* In proof of this assertion, which really needs no proof, I will only quote from the Letter of Pope Pius IX. to the Bishops of the Church, being his first Encyclical after his elevation to the Chair of Peter. And before giving the extract, let me, if I may, direct attention to the marvellous manner in which it sums up in the fewest possible words the entire treatise concerning the Church and concerning divine faith. "God himself," says the holy Pontiff, "has constituted a living authority to teach and establish the true and legitimate sense of his heavenly revelation, and to settle by an infallible judgment all controversies in matters of faith and morals, lest the faithful be 'carried about with every wind of doctrine by the wickedness of men, according to the contrivance of error.' This living and infallible authority is to be found in that Church only which, having been built by Christ our Lord upon Peter, the head, prince, and pastor of the whole Church, whose faith he promised should never fail, has always had its legitimate Pontiffs, deducing without interruption their origin from Peter, seated in Peter's chair, heirs and guardians of Peter's doctrine, dignity, honor, and power. And since, where Peter is, there is the Church (St. Ambros. in Psalm xl.), and Peter speaks through the Roman Pontiff (*Concil. Chalced.* Act. 2), and always in his

---

* This is the reverse of the proposition that the Pope is the organ of the Episcopate.

successors lives and exercises judgment (*Synod. Ephes.* Act. 3), and bestows on those who seek it the truth of faith (St. Petr. Chrysol. *Epist. ad Eutych.*), therefore the Divine utterances are to be taken in that precise sense which was and is held by this Roman chair of Blessed Peter, which, as the mother and mistress of all churches (*Concil. Trid.* Sess. VII. de Bapt.), has ever preserved whole and inviolate the faith delivered by Christ, and has taught it to the faithful, showing to all the way of salvation and the doctrine of uncorrupted truth."

In this wonderful passage the doctrine of the Church's unity through its Head is verbally blended, so to speak— as it is ineffably associated in reality—with that of the infallibility of the Church through the faith of him who was made its foundation. The Church, the whole Church, was built upon Peter; where Peter is, there is the Church; through Peter whose faith can never fail the promises of Christ to his Church are perpetually fulfilled.

We have no need to review again the words of these most precious promises. St. Chrysostom has already done that in our behalf; and, as if anticipating our present requirements, has shown us, not only that our Lord prayed for Peter that with an infallible faith he might be the confirmer of his brethren, but also that he declared, with an authority which attested the divinity of him who assumed it, that he would build his Church upon Peter, and, at the same time, upon Peter's confession—upon Peter, that is, as confessing the faith—in a word, upon Peter as the "ROCK OF FAITH."*

Here, then, we have found all that reason has led us to

---

* A title which St. Chrysostom applies to St. Peter more than once, in passages not quoted in the former chapter.

expect. We have discovered that 'living and infallible authority' which God himself has constituted, in that Church which Christ has built UPON PETER. This is the foundation upon which our faith shall rest henceforth immovable.

But I have promised to say something, not only upon the declarations of authority itself touching its own prerogative, but also upon the proof which sacred tradition supplies of the recognition of that prerogative by the Church. The Letter of Pius IX., by its citations and references, shows that this evidence is of essential importance; not that infallibility is grounded on the testimony of antiquity, but that the Church in all ages bears witness to infallibility as a perpetual divine fact. And here again our task is much simplified; for the Holy Father himself has quoted passages which ought to suffice even for the conviction of an Anglican; and the reader who has had the patience to follow me thus far will recall others also, scattered up and down in this book, which, unless he be not merely captious but incredulous, will furnish all that he requires in the way of attestation from the Fathers and the early Councils. It will do no harm, however, and will give an appearance of greater completeness to our present discussions, if we collect a few contributions more.

St. Irenæus, in the second century, says: "With this Church (of Rome), on account of its superior headship (propter potiorem [potentiorem] principalitatem), it is necessary that every church, that is, the faithful on every side, should agree (convenire); in which has always been preserved by those who are on every side the tradition of the Apostles."* St. Cyprian, in the third century, complaining

---

* *Adv. Hær.* l. iii. c. 3. On the meaning of *convenire* the famous

to Pope Cornelius of the proceedings of Fortunatus and Felicissimus, writes thus: "A false bishop having been ordained for them by heretics, they venture to set sail, and carry letters from schismatical and profane men to the See of Peter, and to the principal Chair, whence sacerdotal unity took its rise; nor do they reflect that they are Romans, whose faith is extolled by the Apostle, to whom false faith (perfidia) can have no access."* These passages belong to the ante-Nicene period, and of course have not that precision of statement which characterizes the language of ecclesiastical writers after the doctrine of the Church had been more thoroughly discussed.

There is a famous sentence of St. Augustine, which has already been given in a note, but to which attention may be fairly called again, since it has lately been made a pretext for the charge of fraud against some of the most learned writers as well as saintly prelates of the Catholic Church.† St. Augustine's comment upon the condemnation of Pelagianism is as follows: Jam enim de hac causa duo concilia missa sunt ad Sedem Apostolicam; inde etiam rescripta venerunt. Causa finita est. These familiar words have sometimes been abbreviated, indeed have passed into the aphor-

---

Salmasius remarks: "Necesse esse dicit omnem ecclesiam convenire ad Romanam, id est, ut Græce loquutus fuerat Irenæus, συμβαίνειν πρὸς τὴν τῶν 'Ρωμαίων ἐκκλησίαν, quod significat convenire et concordare in rebus fidei et doctrinæ cum Romana ecclesia."— *De Primatu Papæ*, c. v. Kenrick, who supplies this criticism from Saumaise, makes a neat comment of his own on the repetition of *undique:* "as it were κύκλῳ πανταχῇ. The central character of Rome, and the convergency of the local churches, as rays to a centre, or focus, is beautifully insinuated."—*Primacy*, c. viii. note.

* *Epist.* lv.
† Père Gratry, *Second Letter* to the Archbishop of Malines.

ism: Roma locuta est; causa finita est. It does not fall to me to vindicate the abbreviation; and if it did, I should scorn the task. But the atrocious imputation that the great name of Augustine has been fraudulently used to support a doctrine of which Augustine knew nothing does give me a very good occasion for quoting once more from the two letters of St. Innocent; for they are the very *Rescripta* which came from the Apostolic See, and by which the cause was finished; and what the Roman Pontiff claimed therein, the Bishop of Hippo most undoubtedly acknowledged. In the first St. Innocent says: " You have referred to our judgment, knowing what is due to the Apostolic See, since all we who are placed in this position desire to follow the Apostle himself, from whom the very Episcopate and all the authority of this title sprung. Following whom, we know as well how to condemn the evil as to approve the good. And this too, that, guarding, according to the duty of bishops, the institutions of the Fathers, ye resolve that these regulations should not be trodden under foot, which they, in pursuance of no human but a divine sentence, have decreed; namely, that whatever was being carried on, although in the most distant and remote provinces, should not be terminated before it was brought to the knowledge of this See; by the full authority of which the just sentence should be confirmed, and that thence all other churches might derive what they should order, whom they should absolve, whom, as being bemired with ineffaceable pollution, the stream that is worthy only of pure bodies should avoid; so that from their parent source all waters should flow, and through the different regions of the whole world the pure streams of the fountain well forth uncorrupted." And in the second he adds: " Especially so often as a matter of faith is under discussion, I conceive that all my brethren and fellow-bishops can only refer to Peter, that is, the source of their own name and honor, just as your affection hath now referred, for what may benefit all churches in common throughout the whole world. For the inventors of evils must necessarily become more cautious, when they see that, at the reference of a double synod, they have been severed from ecclesiastical communion by our sentence."*

St. Leo the Great, speaking as a private doctor, declares that "the solidity of that faith which was commended in the Prince of the Apostles is perpetual; and as that which Peter believed in Christ abides for ever, so does that for ever abide which Christ instituted in Peter."† And in another sermon he refers to his predecessors in the Pontificate as men "who for so many ages have been preserved by the teaching of the Holy Spirit from any encroachment of heresy."‡

---

* *Apud* Allies, *See of St. Peter*, sect. iv.
† *Serm.* ii. in die Assumptionis suæ.
‡ Quos per tot sæcula docente Spiritu Sancto nulla hæresis violavit.—*Serm.* xc. Some notable tributes to the *primitive* purity of the Roman Church might be gathered on Anglican fields. Bishop Bull, for example, arguing against the Arians, affirms that "the Church of Rome was able formerly to use, and further did use, a more succinct and shorter creed than what was required in the Churches of the East, because the latter were harassed by heretics of almost every kind, whilst in the Church of Rome there arose no heresy which taught that its shorter confession of faith [the Apostles' Creed] ought to be understood in any other way than according to the right intention (κατ' ὀρθὴν ἔννοιαν), and the genuine meaning of the Church." This proposition, he says, "is proved by the testimony of Ruffinus, who has this preface before his *Exposition of the Creed:* 'Before I begin to discourse on the excellences of the words, I think it not out of place to remark that in different Churches some additions to the words of the Creed are found. In the Church of the City of Rome, however, we do

Our next witness is one who hitherto has not appeared in these pages, and his testimony will be of even more than usual interest. There is none whose name has been more

not find that this has been done ; the reason of which, I conceive, is this, that *no heresy has ever had its origin there* [Bishop Bull himself gives the emphasis]. . . . In all other places, so far as I can understand, *on account of some heretics*, certain words appear to have been added, by which, as was believed, the sense given to the words by their novel doctrine might be excluded.'" "Indeed," he continues, "it is clear that the Simonians, the Cerinthians, the Ebionites, and the other pests of the primitive Church, did not spread their impious dogmas at Rome, but in the East, and especially in Asia. Hence Ignatius, in the epistles which he addressed to the Asiatic Churches, glances at those heretics throughout ; but when writing to the Romans, he does not reprehend any heresy as existing in their Church. So far from it, in the very salutation he expressly commends the Romans for their perfect purity of faith, calling them 'united in every commandment of Christ, filled without distinction with the grace of God, and strained off from every strange color.' And on this account principally, as I conceive, Tertullian, in his *Prescription against Heresies*, chap. 36, calls the Church of Rome *felicem ecclesiam*,—' happy and prosperous' in condition."—*Judgment of the Catholic Church*, c. v. Of course, while pressing on thus gallantly against the cohorts of M. Simon Episcopius, so correct a strategist as Dr. Bull was too prudent to leave his rear uncovered to the assault of a mightier foe. Accordingly, his long paragraph comes to a sudden *right-about* at the last, and presents this bristling termination : "Oh ! that this happiness, this purity of faith, had been perpetual in that Church ! but, alas ! we may now exclaim, in the words of the inspired prophet, 'How is the faithful city become an harlot !'" Well done, ancient trooper, well done for an Anglican ! When 'Monsieur de Meaux' thought to follow you up, he came very, very near being empaled on that spiky sentence, did he not, O valiant Dr. Bull ? (See the Letter *in answer to the Bishop of Meaux's queries*, near the beginning.) We cannot expect anything so entertaining as this from Mr. Palmer, who, in his slow manœuvring, merely exposes his flank for a moment, with his wonted calmness, and does not trouble himself about consequences. Endeavoring to account for

eagerly paraded by those who devote themselves to the work of vilifying the Catholic Church than he whom the Church, not content with enrolment in her catalogue of Saints, has honored with a grand distinction as the Last of the Fathers. The Protestant Reformers appealed to St. Bernard; would God they had followed in his footsteps, for he was a reformer indeed. Like one of the old Prophets, he cried out against the sins and apostasies of God's people. He bewailed the dangers to which the Church was exposed in her latter days, greater than those of persecution—the perils of relaxed discipline and corrupted morals. "Behold, in peace is her bitterness most bitter."* But, Christian and true Catholic that he was, he did not set himself to reform the Church, but called upon the Church to redress her own grievances and to correct the errors of her children. To the Head of the Church he betook himself, to the Chair of Peter, and there presented what was at the same time his petition and his profession: "It is right that all dangers and scandals which arise in the kingdom of God, especially such as regard faith, should be reported to your Apostleship; for I think it proper that the wounds inflicted on faith should be there healed where faith cannot fail. This is the prerogative of the See."† Think of this, Protestants! Is Saul also among the prophets?

---

the pre-eminence of the Roman Church, he mentions, among other causes, "*the purity of its faith*." "We find," he says, "that the Roman Church was zealous to maintain the true faith from the earliest period; condemning and expelling the Gnostics, Artemonites, etc. And during the Arian mania it was the bulwark of the Catholic faith."—*On the Church*, part vii. c. iii.

* Isaiah xxxviii. 17. *Serm.* xxxiii. in Cant.
† *Epist.* ad Innocent II.

And now let us go back again a few centuries, in order to take up some testimony of a more formal and public character. In arguing upon the fulfilment of our Lord's prophetical words to St. Peter, I quoted this sentence from the profession of faith of Pope Hormisdas, which was signed by the Oriental bishops early in the sixth century, and was afterwards reiterated by the Fathers of the Eighth General Council: "Hæc quæ dicta sunt rerum probantur effectibus." The completed passage will have for us now a fresh interest and a fuller meaning: "The saying of our Lord Jesus Christ cannot be passed by, who said, 'Thou art Peter,' etc. These words are proved by their actual effects; for in the Apostolic See the Catholic religion has ever been preserved immaculate and the faith taught without stain."* The same declaration affirms, further on, that "in the Apostolic See is the perfect and true solidity of the Christian religion."

Very similar are the words of Pope Agatho, which were addressed indeed to the Emperor Constantine IV., but which the Bishops of the Sixth General Council, assembled at Constantinople, made their own, receiving them with the acclamation, "Peter hath spoken by Agatho."† "Peter"— thus the letter reads—"by a triple commendation received the spiritual sheep of the Church from the Redeemer of all, to be fed by him; under whose protection this his Apostolic Church has never turned aside from the way of truth into any error whatsoever, and his authority, as that of the Prince

---

* Quia in Sede Apostolica inviolabilis semper catholica servata religio et sancte celebrata doctrina.

† It is worth remembering that the Western Empire had fallen two centuries before, and that the old political rivalry between the West and the East had been followed, politically, by bitterness on the one side and contempt on the other.

of all the Apostles, the whole Catholic Church at all times, and the universal Councils faithfully embracing, have in all things followed. . . . This is the rule of true faith, which this Apostolic Church of Christ, the spiritual Mother of your most peaceful empire, holds and defends, both in prosperity and adversity; which Church, by the grace of Almighty God, will never be shown to have strayed at any time from the path of apostolic tradition, nor to have yielded ever to the perverse novelties of heretics; but what in the beginning of the Faith she received from her Founders, the chief of the Apostles of Christ, she retains unsullied to the end, according to the divine promise of our Lord and Saviour himself, which in the Gospel he gave to the Prince of his Apostles: ' Peter, Peter, behold, Satan hath desired to sift *you* as wheat, but I have prayed for *thee* that thy faith fail not; and thou, being once converted, confirm thy brethren.' Let your serene clemency, then, consider that the Lord and Saviour of us all, whose gift faith is, and who promised that the faith of Peter should not fail, charged him to confirm his brethren; as it is well known to all that the apostolic Pontiffs, my predecessors, have always fearlessly done." Replying to this Apostolic Brief, the Council declares: "Christ, our true God, . . . hath given us a wise physician, even your Holiness, honored of God; who firmly repellest the contagious plague of heresy by the antidotes of orthodoxy, and impartest the strength of health to the members of the Church. To thee, therefore, as the first See of the Universal Church, standing upon the firm rock, we leave what is to be done, having read the letter of a true confession sent by your paternal Blessedness to our most religious Emperor, which we recognize as divinely written from the supreme Head of the Apostles."* I find it very hard to understand how any one, in the face of such evidence as this (and there is abundance besides), can maintain that the Greeks never acknowledged the Supremacy, by divine right, of the See of St. Peter. If they did not over and over again profess, not submission to Papal authority merely, but belief in Papal infallibility, then it is vain to seek for truth in history.

The Greek Schism is easily understood. Its causes and motives are very human and very patent. From the time that the first Council of Constantinople attempted to give unlawful honors to the See of the Imperial city, "because it was New Rome," to the day when a usurping Patriarch pronounced an impotent excommunication against the Successor of St. Peter, pride and its attendant passions were slowly but steadily maturing into the dire fruit of rebellion. But the Greeks were Catholic long enough to leave a glorious and indelible witness against themselves. Nor have they ever really forgotten their own record. Twice already, inspired by the memory of it, they have had the grace to abjure their treason; once at Florence, in the decree which has been made so prominent in these pages; and once before, at the Council of Lyons. The profession which they subscribed at Lyons contains these words: "The holy Roman Church holds supreme and full primacy and headship over the whole Catholic Church, which she truly and humbly acknowledges herself to have received from the Lord himself, in the person of blessed Peter, the prince and head of the Apostles, whose successor is the Roman Pon-

* Mansi, xi. 239, 683.

tiff, with the plenitude of power. And as before all others she is bound to defend the truth, so also, if any questions arise concerning the faith, they ought by her judgment to be defined. . . . By mouth and heart we confess that which the sacred and holy Roman Church truly holds, and faithfully teaches and preaches."[*] It is an interesting fact, and may yet prove, in the good providence of God, a most blessed fact, that the grandest testimonies to the infallibility of the Holy See have been given by Councils in which the Greeks have borne a conspicuous part. It seems as though they were brought to Lyons and to Florence with a divine purpose, that they might join in reaffirming the ancient truth which their forefathers confessed at Ephesus, at Chalcedon, and at Constantinople. And when they return at last to the fold from which they have so often strayed, they will have no new faith to learn, but only the old faith to repeat.

There is one point, and only one point, remaining to complete the line of argument of this chapter and this book, and to exhaust the list of topics upon which I have undertaken to speak. We have yet to consider the force of what has been called infallibility *de facto*, or, as I have expressed it, the testimony of history to the fact of inerrancy. I say inerrancy rather than infallibility, because the latter word includes the possibilities of the future, while the former, as generally used, seems to have a restricted reference to the past and the present. The phrase *infallibility de facto* is, however, the best possible; because it is a condensed argument. Inerrancy *proves* infallibility. That is, the fact of actual freedom from error cannot be accounted for except

---

[*] Mansi, xxiv. 71. The Florentine formula was subscribed in 1439; that of Lyons, in 1274.

on the supposition of a supernatural immunity from error. As De Maistre puts it : " The Chair of St. Peter, considered in the certainty of its decisions, is naturally an incomprehensible phenomenon. Replying to the whole world for eighteen centuries, how often have the Popes been found to be *incontestably* wrong ? Never. Cavils have been raised ; but never has it been found possible to allege anything decisive." *

The only possible way of fastening error upon the See of St. Peter is by proving that it has been inconsistent with itself, *i. e.*, that it has varied, or contradicted itself, *in its decisions upon the faith*. This has never been done. Everybody knows that there have been a few (a very few) wicked Popes ; there have been scandals in the Papacy ; there may have been rash Popes, and Popes who may have committed grave mistakes in matters of human judgment or policy. But remember that infallibility has nothing to do with all this. Its office is to preserve the faith inviolate. And reviewing the history of dogma through the whole period of Christianity, we find that the formal and authoritative decisions of the Holy See exhibit a system of truth whose continuity no malevolence has ever broken, and in whose perfect harmony ingenuity can discover no flaw. Are we not awe-struck by such a fact as this ? Is it not a demonstration of the presence of the Holy Ghost, reflecting in divine operation the character of the Eternal Father, " with whom is no variableness, neither shadow of turning " ?

The controversies of the past twelve months, which have attracted by their violence the attention of the whole Chris-

* *Du Pape*, l. i. c. 15. Apply again the words : Hæc quæ dicta sunt rerum probantur effectibus, quia in Sede Apostolica inviolabilis semper catholica custoditur religio.

tian world, Protestant as well as Catholic, have served to bring out this historical argument for infallibility into splendid prominence. Never before has the record of the Papacy been subjected to such a minute scrutiny. Never has learning labored more eloquently—shall we say, to make out a case against God? at least let us say—to show the weakness of the foundation upon which the Church is builded. And never have eloquence and learning so well contributed to make illustrious the truth they would have obscured. For what is it which these attacks have proved to the whole world, so that even the unlearned and the unbelieving are witnesses? That there is one only Pope, one Pope out of two hundred and fifty, upon whose orthodoxy even the shadow of a doubt can rest. What even this supposed doubt in the case of Honorius amounts to, a very few words will show.*

Pope Honorius was condemned by the Fathers of the Sixth General Council, together with Sergius, Cyrus, Pyrrhus, and other Monothelite heretics. When we have said this, we have exhausted all that history can furnish against the infallibility of St. Peter's Chair. Does it prove anything against that infallibility? Let us see. The Head of the Church is infallible when, speaking as the Head of the Church, he gives a decision upon a matter of faith. Well. Sergius, with true Greek subtlety, endeavored to entrap

---

* It is no immodesty, but rather a literary obligation to say that I have given to the charges against Honorius the best study of which I am capable, having read pretty much all that has been written on both sides, including the letters of Sergius and Honorius himself. I have not thought it necessary in the text to give even a *résumé* of the history of the case, but have contented myself with a summary proof that the Roman Pontiff did not err *in re fidei definienda*.

Honorius into a heretical definition. Honorius *declined to give any definition at all*. Here are his words: NON NOS OPORTET UNAM VEL DUAS OPERATIONES DEFINIENTES PRÆ-DICARE.* It is not necessary to urge that the letters of Honorius were of a private and, as we should say, confidential character; that they were never made public until after his death; that they show, to any one who will take the trouble of reading them, that their author was no Monothelite, but was deceived by the adroit sentences of his Eastern correspondent, supposing him to speak, not of a Divine and a human will, but of two contrary wills, of the spirit and of the flesh—all these are important considerations; but they are superfluous. It is enough that the Pope refused to exercise his Apostolic prerogative. He gave no erroneous decision, for he decided nothing. But the Council condemned him.† Certainly; and why? Utpote qui eos [Sergium, et rel.] in his [erroribus] sequutus est. Not because he defined error, but because he allowed the errors of others. But this construction of the intention of the Council might be disputed. Let it pass, then; it also is superfluous. *The Council is œcumenical only in so far as it was confirmed by the Holy See.* It is by Pope Leo's letter of confirmation, therefore, that we must judge of the character of the condemnation passed upon his predecessor. Here, then, we have the famous Papal censure upon a Pope: " We anathematize the inventors of the new dogma " (then follow the names), "and also Honorius, who did not strive with energy to maintain the purity of this Apostolic Church, by the teaching of the tradition of the Apostles,

---

* *Epist*. ii. ad Sergium.
† Forty-two years after his death, by the bye.

but who permitted that this Church without spot (immaculatam) should become stained by profane treason." * Or, as it is expressed in the letter to the Bishops of Spain: "Honorius, who, failing in the duty of his Apostolical authority, instead of extinguishing the flame of heresy, fomented it by neglect." Honorius was frightened at the bare thought of a new Eastern heresy, and instead of investigating and condemning, he strove to arrest the evil by hushing it. In a word, he erred, not in faith, but in judgment; he was condemned, not for heresy, but for negligence; non erravit definiendo, sed tacendo, et omittendo quod definiendum fuerat. †

Pope Leo condemned Pope Honorius; yes! and in the very act of condemnation he declared the Apostolic Roman Church to be immaculate. The Sixth Council condemned Honorius; yes! and it was this self-same Council which listened to the letter of a Pope who said: "This Apostolic Church of Peter has never turned aside from the way of truth into any error whatsoever"; and then exclaimed: "Peter hath spoken by Agatho." In fine, the whole history of the attempt in modern times to put a false construction upon the error of Honorius and upon his condemnation at

---

* The Archbishop of Malines, in his Second Letter to Père Gratry, has shown with cruel accuracy the blunders of the version upon which Fleury, and Bossuet, and P. Gratry himself have based their criticisms.

† Ballerini, *De Vi ac Ratione Primatus*, c. xv. § 9. The attempt of P. Gratry to make out a Papal condemnation of Honorius from the old *Libri Diurni* (Breviarii) has been demolished by Dom Gueranger, the learned Benedictine of Solesmes, in such a manner as to effectually prevent its repetition—unless, perhaps, by some American editor.

Constantinople has been a signal illustration of the words which the Fathers of Constantinople 'recognized as divinely written from the supreme Head of the Apostles': "This Apostolic Church, by the grace of Almighty God, will never be convicted of having strayed at any time from the path of apostolic tradition, nor of having ever succumbed to the perverse novelties of heretics; but what in the beginning of the Faith she received from her Founders, the chief of the Apostles of Christ, she retains unsullied to the end, according to the divine promise of our Lord and Saviour himself, which in the Gospel he gave to the Prince of his Apostles: 'Peter, Peter, behold, Satan hath desired to sift you as wheat; but I have prayed for thee, that thy faith fail not.'"

While I have been writing these pages, another great Council has been sitting, not at Constantinople, but in Rome itself. It is nearly twenty-four years since Pope Pius IX., addressing the Bishops of the Church, said: "The Divine utterances are to be taken in that precise sense which was and is held by this Roman chair of Blessed Peter, which, as the Mother and Mistress of all churches, has ever preserved whole and inviolate the faith delivered by Christ, showing to all the way of salvation and the doctrine of uncorrupted truth." And all the world is wondering and waiting to see whether the Bishops of the Catholic Church will be weak enough to answer: Peter hath spoken by Pius. *Quelle bêtise!* Does the Church of God change its faith? Nay—can it reverse the words of Jesus Christ, and remove out of its place the very Rock upon which itself is built, and built upon which the gates of hell shall not prevail against it? O flippant and forgetful generation! Ye boast of the present, and smile at the solemn lesson of the past. Ye say that wisdom was born with you, and answer the voice of God with a sneer.

I have throughout avoided all reference to the present Council, for more reasons than one; but for this among others, that it was not the Council which was the occasion of bringing me into the Church, but the invitation of him at whose call the Council came together.* The Council is an extraordinary event; it may come to naught; but the Chair of Peter abides from the beginning. I need no new definition to fix my faith; for I know already that it is Peter who confirms his brethren, and that, unless St. Peter's successor ratifies the acts of his fellow-bishops, their decrees will be worthless.

I would not have it supposed that I am capable of looking with indifference upon this great assembly of the Vatican. Heaven forbid! It may prove to be, I pray God it may be, the grandest event of modern times. By it, as Pius IX. has said, "the Catholic Church displays a fresh proof of her perfect unity and her unconquerable vitality." And who knows whether, in the times which the Father hath put in his own power, the world may not be preparing to accept the demonstration? The night is darkest towards morning. When men seem farthest from faith, they may be most ready to believe. Bitter and even supercilious as is the temper in which the claims of the Church are met, there are not wanting signs which seem to betoken a day of re-

---

* The reader has, no doubt, observed that the greater part of this work is, in one sense, only a convert's commentary upon the Letter Apostolic, which I have placed at the beginning.

pentance and return. The world is not so much moving as tossing; its commotion is the restlessness of a fever. Upon the earth there is distress of nations, with perplexity. Men's hearts are failing them for fear, and for looking after those things which are coming upon the earth. And there are multitudes who, if they can only perceive before it is too late—before their generation has died out, and their posterity have become utterly godless—if they can only see in time what must be, and what has already been, the result of their negative Christianity, will hasten back to the Church in which alone there is safety for the soul and healing for the nations. Protestantism is doomed. It is condemned already at the bar of reason. Either there is a divine revelation, or there is not; if there is a revelation, it must rest upon authority; but there is no authority outside of the Catholic Church. If men give up the Catholic Church, they must go back, slowly, it may be, and reluctantly, but inevitably, to paganism. It is this conviction which will perhaps be forced upon the minds of many by the contemplation of this wondrous spectacle of the Church in Council. Thither, to the Eternal City, all eyes are turned; and there are some who will see and believe. Eighteen hundred years have passed away, and still St. Peter's successor sits in Peter's chair; and around him are gathered those to whom the commission to teach all nations has been transmitted; they are met together at the tomb of the two Apostles and fellow-martyrs of Rome; and over the sepulchre hangs the Christian Pantheon in mid-air; and around the girdle of the dome shines the Divine sentence:

TU ES PETRUS, ET SUPER HANC PETRAM ÆDIFICABO ECCLESIAM MEAM ; ET TIBI DABO CLAVES REGNI CŒLORUM.

The Primacy and Infallibility.

And lower down on the frieze over the two pillars of the choir have been added these two lines:

> HINC SACERDOTII UNITAS EXORITUR.
> HINC UNA FIDES MUNDO REFULGET.

It is time to sum up. I will do so in the words of two distinguished men. They were contemporaries, the one an Archbishop of the Anglican Establishment, the other an Archbishop of the Catholic Church.

Listen first to Tillotson:

"This point of the Pope's Supremacy, upon which Bellarmine hath the confidence to say the whole of Christianity depends, is not only an indefensible, but an impudent cause, as ever was undertaken by learned pens. And nothing could have kept it so long from becoming ridiculous in the judgment of mankind, but its being so strongly supported by worldly interest. For there is not one tolerable argument for it; and there are a thousand invincible reasons against it. There is neither from Scripture, nor reason, nor antiquity, any evidence of it. The past and the present state of Christendom, the histories and records of all ages, are a perpetual demonstration against it. There is no other ground for it in the whole world, but that for a long time it hath been boldly asserted, and without reason stifly contended for, by the POPE'S JANIZARIES."*

And then to Fénelon:

"O Church of Rome! O Sacred City! O dear and common country of all true Christians! In Jesus Christ there is neither Greek, nor Scythian, nor Barbarian, nor

---

* From the Original Preface to the *Treatise of the Pope's Supremacy*.

Jew, nor Gentile; in thy bosom they are as ONE people, all are citizens of Rome; and every Catholic is a Roman. Behold the mighty stem which has been planted by the hand of Jesus Christ! Every branch which is separated from it fades, withers, and dies. O Mother! whoever is a child of God is also thy child; after the lapse of so many ages thou art yet fruitful. O Spouse! thou bringest forth children to thy husband in every quarter of the globe; but whence is it that so many unnatural children now contemn their Mother, arise up against her, and consider her as a cruel step-dame? Whence is it that her authority should give them such vain offence? What! shall the sacred bond of union, which should unite every one in a single flock, and make all ministers as a single pastor, shall *that* be the pretext for a fatal dissension? Shall we produce those times, which will be the last, when the Son of Man shall hardly find faith upon the earth? Let us tremble, my dearest brethren, let us tremble, lest the reign of God, which we abuse, should be taken away from us, and be given to other nations who will bear the fruits. Let us tremble, let us humble ourselves, lest Jesus Christ carry elsewhere the torch of pure faith, and leave us in that gloomy darkness which our pride has deserved. O Church, whence Peter will for ever strengthen his brethren, let my right hand forget itself, if ever I forget thee! Let my tongue cleave to my mouth and be motionless, if thou be not, to the last breath of life, the principal object of my joy and my rejoicings." *

I am both glad and sorry, O reader, to find that my work

---

* From the last Ordinance of the Archbishop of Cambrai.

is done: happy, not merely because the labor is over, but, chiefly, for the knowledge that I have done my best for your sake; sorrowful, not alone from a consciousness that my best endeavor is so imperfect, but, much more, with the heavy thought that its honest purpose may have been expended in vain. I have reasoned plainly and fairly. I have stooped to no sophistry and used no 'forged decretal.' But argument will not reach your heart. Persuasion alone will not move your will. No, nor truth itself. Even the grace of God may not avail to do that.

THE END.

www.ingramcontent.com/pod-product-compliance
Lightning Source LLC
Chambersburg PA
CBHW030007240426
43672CB00007B/856